Peril at Sea

Awaiting salvage, the German freighter **MARIECHEN** sits at a precarious angle below the snow-covered mountains of False Bay, Alaska in January 1906. Winter and Pond photo.

From surface craft to submarine is a position seemingly assumed by the wooden-hulled steamer **DELHI** wrecked in Sumner Straits, Alaska after running into an uncharted rock in January 1915. The hull remained afloat but proved to be a total loss.

High and dry on Sentinel Reef in Southeast Alaska in August 1910, the SS **PRINCESS MAY**. After evacuation of passengers the vessel was eventually refloated, ushered off for repairs and returned to service.

Peril at Sea

A Photographic Study of Shipwrecks in the Pacific

"Shipwreck Jim" Gibbs

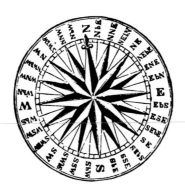

Schiffer Publishing Ltd

West Chester, Pennsylvania 19380

Printed in the United States of America.
ISBN: 0-88740-066-3
Published by Schiffer Publishing Ltd.
1469 Morstein Road, West Chester, Pennsylvania 19380

This book may be purchased from the publisher.
Please include $1.50 postage.
Try your bookstore first.

No posture for a lady of the sea. The SS **PRINCESS MAY** of Canadian Pacific, is seen astride Sentinel Reef off Sentinel Island, Alaska in August 1910. Passengers were evacuated and salvage got underway. With the help of high tides and wrecking steamers, the vessel was later refloated and escorted to port for costly bottom damage repairs.

Front cover: **CARATHAGINIAN** wreck off Lahaina. Courtesy Randy Miller.

Back cover: French bark **COL. DE VILLEBOIS MAREVIL** crossing Columbia bar.

Sad fate of the Liberian flag Liberty type freighter **SEAGATE**. In her case the sea gates were opened and she was the victim after stranding on Sonora Reef off the Washington Coast, September 9, 1956. Well off course, the vessel was inbound to Vancouver B.C. from Japan when the wreck occurred.

Dedication

"To the late Wilbur Thompson
who loved all facets of the maritime"

The Old Salt. Original pen and ink sketch by the late Charles Fitspatrick.

Tragic loss of the graceful commercial tuna seiner **BETTIE M.**, writhing in anguish, a victim of the Columbia River bar on the last day of winter in 1976. In the background, upper right stands Cape Disappointment Lighthouse. Photo by Sam Foster, Seaside photo.

Introduction

Ships that pass in the night and speak each other in passing;
Only a signal shown and a distant voice in the darkness;
So on the ocean of life we pass and speak one another,
Only a look and a voice; then darkness again and a silence.

....Longfellow

Seamen of old came to accept the fact that there was only a plank between them and eternity. They further learned that unless a man was worthy the sea would surely find him out. A ship is the largest moving creation built by men. Nothing else that he fashions takes on a personality of its own and to a man of the sea it becomes a living thing that he comes to revere. The oceans have all been charted now, and no one fears to fall off the edge of the world if he ventures too far from the shore, yet even today sometimes, old superstitions, fables and fantasies come alive.

The sea has sometimes been called a Jezebel—at times quiet, passionate and inviting and at other times showing seething anger and the primeval power of an Amazon, with intent to kill. Yet with all the anxiety, there is a feeling of exaltation, a wild and reckless sense of freedom and victory over challenging the forces of nature. When the sea is running furious the adrenaline flows and fear mixes with respect for the awesome power of the Almighty. Riding out a storm at sea is like winning a victory, but when a vessel crashes against the unrelenting, rocks, reefs, crags and shoals along the shore, the insignificance of man and his ship becomes ever apparent. Through it all, the sea itself remains unchanged and men still go down to it, each in their own peculiar way. What pulls men to the sea is something eternal, ageless. Its like a magnet. Even the landlubber who ventures no further than the water's edge feels the eternal tug. In essence, its a water world and all of us are as islanders, the sea surrounding all the continents, making them islands in one huge ocean.

Those who go to sea learn how to pray. Even the prophet Job was awe-struck by the nature of the sea when he said, "the Lord maketh the deep to boil like a pot." The sea breeds the weather. The oceans dominate the climate of the world and none of man's contrivances can alter or control it, for as Byron put it, "Man marks the earth with ruin, his control stops with the shore." He further stated, "He sinks into thy depths with bubbling groan, without a grave, unknell'd, uncoffin'd and unknown."

Herman Melville expressed his feelings when he wrote, "the sea will insult and murder man, and pulverize the stateliest, stiffest frigate he can make."

Joseph Conrad noted, "The most amazing wonder of the deep is its unfathomable cruelty." He continued by observing, "The ocean has no compassion, no law, no memory."

It is a dreadful and haunting thing for survivors of a ship disaster, be the vessel large or small, to see it vanish into the depths, in a mighty hiss and roar, upheaval of water and a giant whirlpool. Finally the sea places a covering over its dastardly deed as if the conveyance had never existed.

Sailors had an old superstition that a ship's bell rang by itself when the vessel went down, sounding its own death knell. Deepsea divers claim to have heard such sounds when diving on a wreck.

It was another time; it was the old traditional way of seafaring and now it is gone. Mariners of old would be flabbergasted at the sight of the behemoths that sail the seas today. Not even in their wildest imaginings could they have conceived a supertanker of half a million deadweight tons. The bigger they become the more business-like and less glamorous they become. It's a technical, automated age and sailors have become technicians both on the surface and beneath the surface. Safe and secure they run their ships like scientists in a laboratory. Yet with all the innovations, the peril of shipwreck, though greatly reduced, still exists and when it occurs today, involving a deepsea carrier, the cost is often astronomical. A weather eye on the dials and gauges, constant radio communication and hourly weather reports for the most part assure a safe passage. But one can never lose thought that the sea can still rise up and swamp all the dials and gauges and tear a ship to pieces. Ships keep changing but the sea, like God, is the same yesterday, today and forever.

Warning beacons along the shore stand as monuments to the eternal ambiguity of the sea. Commerce rides upon it, warships fight on and below it, fishermen reap a harvest from it, sportsmen play upon it, but the menace and the power of the sea remain.

Around the shores of the Pacific lie the rotting hulks of legions of vessels of every description and every flag. Some lie buried in the deeps where they may never be found. Others lie as twisted remains along the beaches or entombed down in the sands. Others have been completely eradicated by the forces of nature. A few carried treasure; some of it has been discovered; most will never be. There are both recorded and unrecorded wrecks found here and there only by bits of treasure impervious to the destructive forces. Some have left behind only some brass or copper and maybe even an old anchor or cannon to mark the spot. Great treasures have been found in recent years with highly sophisticated instruments and improved diving equipment. The greatest treasure has been discovered along the Caribbean and eastern seaboards as most of it was originally lost there while much of the Pacific lay undiscovered. The Pacific rim may yet yield some unrecorded finds of fabulous value. The known wrecks that carried treasure in the Pacific have been pretty well probed, some with disappointing yield, but if instruments can find the locale of such difficult targets as the ironclad *Monitor* and the luxury liner *Titanic* who can say the limits of seeking treasure at the bottom of the sea.

Certainly, the legendary Davy Jones Locker is stocked with enough treasure to pay off the debts of every nation on the face of the earth. This however, is not a book on sea treasure, it is a work on peril at sea and the continuing battle of man against the elements, those who go down to sea in ships and do business in great waters, as stated in Psalms. Their lot has improved in modern times but the danger is always there and units like the American and Canadian Coast Guards, as well as rescue units of other Pacific countries stand ever ready to aid those in distress, often risking their own lives in their endeavor.

The great writers of another day told it so well: Said Bryon,
Then rose from sea to sky the wild farewell,
Then shriek'd the timid, and stood still the brave,
Then some leap'd overboard with fearful yell,
As eager to anticipate their grave.
And Falconer in his *Shipwreck*, penned:
Again she plunges! hark! a second shock
Bilges the splitting vessel on the rock;
Down on the vale of death, with dismal cries,
The fated victims shuddering cast their eyes
In wild dispair; while yet another stroke
With strong convulsion rends the solid oak:
Ah Heaven!—behold her crashing ribs divide!
She loosens, parts, and spreads in ruin o'er the tide.

Running the gauntlet of breaking surf near ominous Cape Disappointment Coast Guard motor lifeboats go where other craft dare not venture. U.S. Coast Guard photo.

A great innovation in the saving of lives for those in peril on the sea is the helicopter. Here, zooming over her area of surveillance, is the Astoria-based HH3 helicopter **1489** which has taken part in several sea rescues, patrol and allied service missions. U.S. Coast Guard photo.

Table of Contents

9

Norwegian freighter **EVANGER**, owned by Westfal-Larsen interests of Bergen, Norway, shoulders a terrific erupting wave while aground at Newport Beach, California in 1929. A credit to her builders, the vessel withstood the punishment and was eventually pulled free and sent to a Los Angeles drydock for repairs. *Courtesy Joe Williamson.*

Surgery needed on superstructure of the log ship **SILVER SHELTON**. She is in drydock here. On September 21, 1967 she and the container ship **FAIRLAND** collided in fog off Point Wells, on Puget Sound. She suffered a gaping hole in her hull and housing damage. The vessel was beached to prevent her sinking. The **FAIRLAND** had a badly crumpled bow. Cost of repairing the **SHELTON** came to $2.5 million. Pilot Dewey Soriano had the **SHELTON** and Pilot D. J. Kelly the **FAIRLAND**. Capt. A.M. Troyan was master of the **SHELTON** and Capt. George Loder skippered the container ship. A lengthy Coast Guard hearing followed the collision.

CHAPTER ONE

Breakers Dead Ahead

At no period in maritime history was the term, "Breakers Dead Ahead!" used as much as during the heyday of coastwise shipping along Pacific coastal shores. The exclamation was accompanied with alarm and terror for little succor was offered in adverse weather and sea conditions. It was a battle of wooden ships peopled by iron men versus the awesome powers of nature. Each vessel was an entity unto itself, small floating islands, once out of port without communication with the shore. When in distress the alternative was inverting Old Glory from a flagstaff or masthead, burning a bucket or drum of tar, or, after abandonment, to challenge the sea in frail lifeboats, hoping for rescue.

Old salts could often sense impending doom when fierce winds whistled through the rigging as great acclivities rose mountain high and then dropped a helpless vessel into a seemingly bottomless liquid pit. Heathen or saint were at the mercy of the Almighty, for He alone commanded the elements, and will to the end of the age.

In those early years there were no direction finders, no radio communication or radar and only primitive lead lines determined the depth of water beneath the keel of a vessel hugging the coast. Many shipmasters were forced to depend on instinct during clamy weather. Standard equipment was a wheel, a compass and a sixth sense. Sextants, dividers, protractors, parallel rules and nautical almanacs were foreign to many units of the fleet. Pipe smokin' skippers accepted their roles and the accompanying dangers with complacency. In the middle of the past century aids to navigation were non-existent along most sections of the Pacific rim and the mortality rate was legion. Sail was the common means of transport which might well have been described as a wing and a prayer.

The birth of regular coastal shipping was spawned by the discovery, in 1848, of gold in California. The basic cargo northbound included anything from a kitchen sink to a squealing pig. While southbound it was basically fir, hemlock, cedar or spruce lumber and logs from the Pacific Northwest, or giant Sequoias from northern California's redwood coast, most of which was shipped to San Francisco.

Coastwise shipping goes back to the time of British explorer and trader, Captain John Meares, who built the schooner *Northwest America* at Nootka on

A sad end to the wooden ship-building industry speaks for itself in the wake of World War I. Some of the wooden vessels built under the emergency program are seen waiting out their days in Seattle's Lake Union. From Joe Williamson collection.

Captain James J. Winant, pioneer shipmaster of schooners, both sail and steam, was instrumental in starting oyster harvesting and transport of the bivalves on the Pacific Coast. Below, the steam schooner **MISCHIEF**, one of Winant's fleet is pictured July 23, 1889 docked in Yaquina Bay on a special occasion. Lincoln County Historical Society photos.

Vancouver Island's west coast. Launched September 20, 1788, she was designed for trade along the island's shores. Spain in 1790 laid claim to the area, pilfered the *Northwest America* among other British craft, and renamed her *Gertrudis*. Britain got her back after a treaty was signed at Nootka, narrowly averting a possible war between the two maritime powers.

Captain Robert Gray, discoverer of both the Columbia River and Grays Harbor built the second trading vessel on Northwest shores when he wintered at Meares Island on Clayoquot Sound. The sloop *Adventure*, a 44 ton craft with fine sailing qualities, was launched in February 1792. Later Gray sold the vessel to the Spaniard, Juan Francisco Quadra.

Not till a half century later was the pattern of coastal trading vessels followed when on the banks of

Oregon's Willamette River in 1841, local pioneer farmers built the 53 ton schooner *Star of Oregon.* Tenacious in their effort, they not only built the schooner but sailed her to Yerba Buena Island on San Francisco Bay and sold her for use as a coaster at a good profit. In fact, it allowed them to return to the Willamette Valley the following spring, 42 strong, driving a herd of 1,000 cattle, 600 horses and mules and 3,000 sheep.

A few years later, one of the greatest armadas of ships ever to converge on a port of entry headed for San Francisco in the wake of the discovery of gold. The west would never be the same again. Crowds stormed up on Point Lobos daily to watch the grand parade of sailing vessels of many rigs, hulking side wheelers, sleek steamers and a few nondescripts. The Golden Gate, so prophetically named, was wide open and swarthy men of the sea along with thousands of passengers of all colors, and creeds hoping to strike it rich at the diggings, came en masse.

The arrival of the mail steamer *California* on February 28, 1849, was welcomed by throngs of newcomers anxious to get word from home. The steamer was even given a salute by the 120 gun naval ship *Ohio*, but that did not deter its passengers and crew from practically knocking each other down in a mad rush to get to the gold fields. "How far to the mines?" was the most often asked question as neophytes crowded the smoke-filled whiskey dens, hotels and restaurants along the waterfront.

As of April 1848, San Francisco had a population of 1,000 who had managed to erect 200 buildings fronting the waterfront and steep hills. The saloons dominated along with brothels, flanked by shanties, warehouses, two hotels and a single church where the clergy found Satan's competition kept many pews empty on the Lord's day. A dozen mercantile houses challenged each other for business as more and more people arrived both by sea and covered wagon to seek their fortunes near the Coloma and American rivers.

As gold dust and nuggets began pouring into the settlement, even the more level-headed merchants jumped on the bandwagon, forsook their enterprises and joined the treasure hunt. Of the multi-thousands that sought their fortunes only a small percentage ever gained wealth. Some gambled their gold away, became alcoholics, lost their health or their very lives.

By July of 1849 more than 200 vessels were amassed on the harbor mudflats, deserted by their crews, many with cargo rotting in their holds, feasted on by packs of ravenous rats. Some of the abandoned fleet listed to port or starboard, tides ebbing and flowing against their rotting timbers as swelling cargo forced the oakum from their hull planking causing them to sink. Rigging hung like a thousand broken spider webs, blocks swung free, and creaking, haunting noises wafted over the waterfront. Among the ghosty armada was the century old Chinese junk *Whang Ho* that had lumbered across the Pacific, plus two aging lorchas designed for celestials for operation in the South China Sea many years before. Legend said they were former pirate craft, but nobody really seemed concerned. Even the Mediterranean was represented by a few feluccas and a galliot.

Of the 700 craft that entered the bay in 1849-50 season, few ever again returned to sea. No port ever hosted such a fleet of deserted tonnage. By the summer of 1850, an estimated 526 ships were afloat or partially afloat in that vast collection of maritime miscellany. They could have been purchased for a pittance but they might just as well have been white elephants. Though some were purchased dirt cheap for storage, housing and even a jail, most settled into the mud. One, the *Euphemia* is still remembered in the history books as San Francisco's first jail.

Some shipmasters and owners tried to save their ships by mooring them up the San Joaquin and Sacramento rivers. More than 100 strained at their moorings at Stockton, Sacramento and Benicia but even they were eventually abandoned or left to the elements.

As San Francisco grew, it became obvious the bay would become the center of shipping on the west coast. Essential was lumber to construct permanent buildings, houses, docks and ships. Virgin trees, tall, thick stands were waiting the cutter's axe northward on the Mendocino coast and in the Pacific Northwest. Though it didn't have the glitter of gold it was to put considerable wealth in the pockets of those willing to accept the challenge to set up and equip sawmills, or to

be members of a fraternity of hardy woodsmen that would tackle any tree, no matter how large.

The gunk holes and dogholes of the northern California coast and the fickle bar entrances and intricate passages in the Pacific Northwest demanded rugged, adventurous individuals to plot and man the little coastal sailing vessels and later the steam schooners that would become the backbone of the fleet. The initial vessels mostly had come around the Horn from New England. There were a few aged clippers, brigs and brigantines past their prime, some little better than floating coffins. In the five decades following the goldrush, large numbers of vessels were turned out at yards along the Pacific Coast, specially designed to carry lumber and logs. Mill towns popped up all along the redwood coast of Mendocino and Sonoma counties while Oregon and Washington territories offered a sprinkling of coastal lumber portals from Brookings to Puget Sound, including the Columbia River. The earliest vessels were basically stout, wooden-hulled two-masted schooners, compact, maneuverable and seaworthy sailing craft without any frills. Very few even carried a figurehead, a tradition of the sea for centuries. Above all, they had to be able to endure the punishment doled out by the hostile forces of nature along the north Pacific rim. The redwood coast had the largest number of loading ports, more than 100, many of which were little more than holes in the rocks. Labeled as dogholes by the seafarers in the trade, the only unrestricted ports of call were at Crescent City, Humboldt Harbor, Noyo, and Mendocino. Oregon had bar crossings at the Chetco, Coquille, Coos Bay, Umpqua, Suislaw, Yaquina, Siletz, Nestucca, Nehalem and Columbia rivers, and a half sheltered bay at Port Orford. North of the Columbia were bar entrances at Willapa, Grays

Deserted ships in San Francisco Bay, 1849 or 1850. Courtesy of Edward Strong Clark.

Harbor and the desired Strait of Juan de Fuca which led to the many lumber ports that blossomed on Puget Sound in the early years. There were also great strands of timber along Vancouver Island's intricate waterways and mainland coast and along the complexity of channels and waterways in southeastern Alaska. Most of the bar crossings were totally unpredictable, for in the pioneer years no jetties existed to control the depths, and sands shifted constantly, forming dangerous shoals. Charts when available were often erroneous and seldom was a coastal voyage undertaken without the danger of shipwreck.

Storms in the late fall and winter seasons were the bane of the coasters. Through the murk and mist, the great headlands loomed somber appearing for all the world like gigantic tombstones brooding over watery crypts waiting to be filled.

Working before the mast on the coasters was a demanding occupation. Seamen were sometimes victims of runners, pimps or bar tenders who slipped a mickey in their grog, dropped them through a trapdoor and collected blood money. Victims awakened from stupors as buckets of cold sea water were splashed across their hungover bodies. Deckhands were sometimes illiterate, targets for tough bucko mates. For the main part, however, seamen were far better off aboard the coasters than on transocean square-riggers on voyages requiring many months, often beset with cruelty. Coasters by comparison made short passages and afforded better food inasmuch as ports were never far away. They did, however, face greater danger of shipwreck by hugging the hostile shoreline and sometimes having to load in perilous arenas with little or no protection from the sudden tantrums of the ocean. The majority of wrecks occured along the coast and not on the open ocean. Often jostled about like corks the coasters were in constant combat with

Typical of the colorful fleet of wooden steam schooners, which for several years were the backbone of the coastwise fleet, is the **SANTA ANA** seen here loading at Bryant's Mill. The 1,203 ton vessel was built Marshfield, Oregon in 1900.

deadly cross rips, contrary currents, mammoth inshore swells and hidden rocks and reefs. Nor was there any solace when they anchored beneath loading chutes cradled high on the rocks above, open to the whims of the ocean on three sides.

Quarters on the coasters were extremely cramped, always damp and on most of the schooners there was no warmth except from the galley stove. The smaller vessels carried as few as four men while the larger units, of around 100 tons, had crews of six or seven. Every hand had to carry his own weight and owners and shipmasters demanded an all out effort from paltry pay. When business was slack for the lumber fleet some of the schooners ranged as far away from the coast as the Okhotsk and Bering seas, into the Arctic ice, to Mexico, Central and South America or the South Seas. For the main part however, their courses were along the Pacific Coast, and up until 1880 most of the remote coast settlements were totally dependent on the little droughers for their survival.

Through evolution, the coastal sailing schooner developed into a steam schooner, a type of vessel which attracted mostly those of Norwegian and Swedish extraction resulting in the coined title of the "Scandanavian Navy." Colorful skippers with amusing nicknames and reputations commanded many of the craft, exceptional seafarers and navigators, fearless, courageous, sometimes reckless, but seldom "wreckless." Few skippers ended their careers without having lost at least one command to the elements, and all had left the paint and splinters from ships' bellies on one or more bar shoal or doghole outcrop.

The Olson steam schooner **DAVENPORT**, in trouble on Puget Sound after her deckload of lumber shifted. The wrong was righted and the vessel resumed her voyage. She was built in 1912 and was afloat till 1943.

Venerable Coast Guard cutter **CAMPBELL** which took part in many sea rescues and special missions. U.S. Coast Guard photo.

In the eyes of the coaster men, on a deepwater ship a man before the mast was considered nothing more than an animal, while on a coastal schooner, he was a man. Bluewater sailors however, often chided the coasters as inferiors though secretly they respected the shipmasters for their ability to operate their charges under the most unpredictable sea and weather conditions.

More than 400 coasters up to 100 tons were built and operated along the Pacific coastal shores between 1850-1900. Nearly 750 commercial sailing vessels of more than 100 tons were constructed on the Pacific Coast between 1850 and 1905. Better than three-quarters of the smaller breed met with tragedy along the Pacific slopes, mostly while engaged in the lumber trade, an exceptionally high percentage. There were also more than 225 wooden steam schooners constructed at various yards on the west coast in the 1880's, 1890's and the early 1900's, many of which left their bones to bleach on the breaker-swept sands or in the vice-like grip of the iron-bound rock barriers.

Then there were the ugly wooden sailing craft known as scow schooners. They originated on San Francisco Bay and operated in the bays and tributaries of that water system and occasionally braved the open seas in trading from Eureka to San Diego. Such vessels were flat-bottomed, blunt bow, two-masted, averaging 60 feet in length with a 20 foot beam. The smallest could be operated by a single hand, the larger by two, and though they were able to carry tremendous amounts of cargo sometimes reducing their freeboards to a minimum, they were not designed for the open seas and could easily be swamped in angry ocean conditions. The largest of the fleet was the *Mono*, 100 tons, and for the most part she carried wine from Winehaven on the shores of San Pablo Bay to San Francisco for transshipment to the Orient.

Many of the doghole schooners declared obsolete in the era of the steam schooner shifted to the pelagic sealing fleet that once boasted more than 260 commercial vessels. The west coasters joined many of the east coast constructed sailers and several schooners built in British Columbia especially for the sealing industry. The rookeries were so divested of seal and otter by 1895 that the wanton killing was outlawed. The basic fleet had homeported at Victoria B.C. and it became a highly lucrative business from 1875 until its closure. Some of the sealing fleet was based on San Francisco Bay and the era was immortalized by Jack London in his best selling novel, *The Sea Wolf*, based on factual happenings. That fleet too, afforded Davy Jones several occupants for his locker.

Typical of the early Pacific coasters was the schooner *Amethyst* built at Benicia, California in 1883.

On her second voyage to sea she collided with the scow schooner *Mayflower,* but escaped serious damage. Later she made a voyage to Mexico with a full load of explosives, a rare case where the seamen profited double pay from the safe arrival of a hazardous cargo. In 1902, lumber-laden, the 72 foot *Amethyst* sailed from Coos Bay for San Francisco with a crew of seven and vanished from the face of the sea.

In the case of the 104 foot schooner *Wing and Wing*, built at San Francisco in 1881, rough going becomes an understatement. She set a long voyage record in 1883 in a battle against gale force winds and contrary seas. It took the *Wing and Wing* 40 days to sail a few hundred miles from Santa Cruz, California to Coos Bay, Oregon, much to the chagrin of her frustrated skipper and nearly starved crew.

Then there was the schooner *Uncle Sam*, built on the Mendocino River in 1873. She capsized off Cape Foulweather, Oregon, and her battered hull washed up on the beach on March 4, 1876. There was no trace of her six man crew, it being presumed that they all perished in an attempt to abandon ship somewhere off the Oregon coast several days earlier.

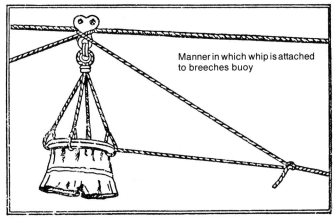

Manner in which whip is attached to breeches buoy

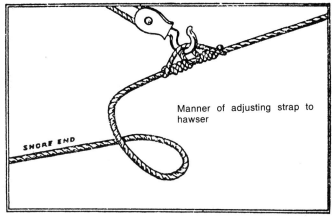

Manner of adjusting strap to hawser

SHORE END

The breeches buoy, an age old conveyance instrumental in the saving of thousands of shipwreck victims when rigged between a stranded vessel and the beach.

An unusual entry in the logbook of the schooner *J.G. Wall,* constructed in Eureka in 1875 for Hobbs, Wall & Co., is worthy of mention. Five years later the vessel while approaching Crescent City Harbor at night, had an unusual thing happen. A flash storm sent a bolt of lightning that streaked downward from an ominous sky and struck the vessel's foremast, ran down the port side and ripped a hole eight feet long and a foot wide just above the waterline. With each roll, seawater slopped in at an alarming rate and all the crew except the shipmaster were certain that they were doomed. Captain Stockfleth, however, had other ideas. With a line secured about his waist he was lowered over the side bearing a sheet of canvas, a hammer and nails. While the pumps were operating continuously, in what appeared to be a losing battle, he affixed the canvas over the hole, hanging on like a barnacle as the vessel rolled up to 30 degrees. Part of the time he was above the frigid water and part of the time below. Determined not to lose his ship, he tenaciously completed the task. The influx of seawater was controlled to a degree that the *Wall* was able to stay afloat for 20 days, a nightmarish eternity that saw Stockfleth repeating his risky maneuver whenever the canvas began to work loose. Such determination was well beyond the call of duty, but he was finally able to pilot his command across the bar and onto the beach where the gaping hole could be repaired.

Unfortunately, just three years later in December, the *Wall* capsized on the Crescent City bar and this time had no reprieve. An Indian and two white men attempting to reach the wreck in a skiff were thrown from their craft and only the Indian survived.

A grizzly episode took place off the Oregon coast in 1907 involving the little gas schooner *Bessie K..* Built for the lumber trade at Alameda in 1893, she had taken her share of hard knocks. In February 1907, the vessel took on a full cargo of cedar lumber at Port Orford, Oregon. Despite the outright objections of the crew, the mate ordered the light dry lumber stowed in the hold and the heavy dimension timber for the deckload, a practice considered extremely dangerous in the era of the coaster.

It so happened that during the loading, Captain Lazarevitch was up town and on his return the lashings had already been placed on the deckload, the vessel ready to sail. Four days later the *Bessie K.* was reported bottom up off the Coquille River entrance with no trace of her crew. A grim reminder of the regrettable tragedy was the ship's nameboard that washed up on a nearby Oregon beach. Though no bodies were ever recovered there was a strange twist to the story. The derelict which had become a menace to navigation refused to sink. The inverted hull was sighted from time to time by passing vessels and then suddenly seemed to vanish as had her crew. Ironically, like the proverbial flying Dutchman she was caught up in the ocean currents and mysteriously drifted across the Pacific, grounding months later on Oriental shores near Swatow, China.

Beachcomers swarmed over the wreckage only to find that everything above deck was gone except 20 feet of the foremast. The lumber in the hold had remained in tact but the ten by 14 foot engine had dropped out sometime during the long drift. In the aftermath, several homes popped up along that coastal section of China, all made of Port Orford cedar.

Prior to the final voyage of the *Bessie K.,* Captain Lazarevitch was heard to say on the Port Orford waterfront that he was planning to terminate his seagoing career following the fateful departure of the schooner.

An interesting situation confronted the three-masted schooner *J.C. Ford.* The following report appeared in the *Honolulu Press* on January 12, 1886.

"On the 12th of Jan. 1886, the schooner *J.C. Ford,* while about 300 miles east of Honolulu was struck by a falling meteor and the mainmast and staysail were set afire. Larges pieces of scoria, or burning metal, fell to the deck setting fires to sails and deck coverings. For a few moments great excitement prevailed on board, but Captain Brown and his crew quickly went to work to put out the fires on the mast and sails, the latter of which were thrown overboard. Water was hauled up to the masthead and the fire extinguished. Pieces of the meteor which fell on the deck were red hot and resembled burning lava. The captain preserved pieces which were now in a cool state."

Fate was not so kind on February 2, 1893 when the *Ford* foundered off Grays Harbor laden with machinery and lime. While crossing the bar she stranded in shoal water. By kedging off, she was freed and drifted toward the sea, pumps going constantly, but in the process the cargo of lime caught on fire. Leaping fingers of orange flame enveloped the vessel and all efforts to save her failed, the sealing schooner *Brenda* arriving just in the nick of time to rescue the crew.

On the night of November 10, 1865, ten coastal schooners were driven aground along the redwood coast due to ill-tempered gale conditions creating giant seas. Shakespeare once wrote that "Ships are but boards, sailors but men." Samuel Johnson added his feelings by writing that "Being in a ship is being in a jail, with the chance of being drowned."

Wreck charts reveal scores of marine disasters along the Mendicino Coast mostly those in the lumber trade in the bygones. Shouts of drowning seafarers and passengers were often inaudible above the roar of the surf, and along the fringes of that shoreline many are at rest, asleep in the deep. During one storm in the winter of 1882, five schooners went ashore between Navarro and Westport in a single day. Point Arena has been the area of many wrecks, for in former times the point was pivitol for vessels voyaging north or south. Today vessels traversing the coast remain well offshore.

In the yesteryears when gales or squalls erupted suddenly the dogholes often proved to be traps when schooners were loading under the chutes. Ill-fated craft were swept rudely onto the ravenous manacles, enveloped in the curl of the mighty breakers. The results, more often than not, were negative.

Some of the chutes extended 80 to 100 feet down and out over the rocks, spidery in appearance supported by an A-frame and a trestle. An apron on the extreme lower section was suspended by cable from the A-frame and swung back and forth in the wind, like a horizontal pendulum. By such means the sling loads of lumber were lowered. Cables from high landings were secured to the schooners rigging and a carriage block lowered the lumber by gravity, the ride controlled by winch. It was a risky business at both ends especially on a vessel tightly moored among the rocks, open to the wrath of the sea.

Probably no period in the history of Pacific coastal shipping was more colorful than that of the steam schooner. About 1880 an imaginative individual conceived the idea of installing a small steam engine on one of the smaller Mendocino schooners. Some claim it was the *Beda,* while others desiring their respective schooners to be accredited with that honor claimed it was the *Alex Duncan, Laguna, Newport* or *Surprise.* But regardless of what vessel had that distinction the steam schooner was an irrevocable innovation much to the joy of coastal mariners and passengers. The vessels depending on sail alone were often beset by contrary winds and limited maneuvering capabilities. Passengers had long depended solely on the sailing coasters to get from one port to another, and often faced long delays. At first the steam schooners maintained their sails, for the early steam engines were often cranky and undependable. On occasion, canvas proved a necessary asset. The later breed of wooden steam schooners no longer needed sails in their lockers. The evolution was not an overnight situation. In fact, it was almost three decades after the first engined schooner that coastal sail became a thing of the past. The latter day steam schooner could carry beams up to 75 feet in length which cut labor at the loading berth, plus improved deck winches operated by a single driver. Some of the double-enders were equipped with loading gear fore and aft and runways under the midship housing to facilitate lengthy timbers.

Prior to the steam schooner, powered vessels were not entirely foreign to the north Pacific. The *Beaver*, built in England in 1834-35, came around the Horn as a brig and had paddlewheels connected at Fort Vancouver on the Columbia River before going to British Columbia waters for nearly five decades of valuable service for the Hudson's Bay Co. She was wrecked while serving as a tug at Vancouver B.C.'s front door in 1888.

No longer at the mercy of contrary winds, no longer bar-bound, the steam schooner lumber fleet flourished. Further, the previously inaccessible small rivers and shallow harbors were no longer prohibitive. The traditional way of hauling lumber didn't go down easy with hard core windjammer men, and some of the old skippers quit the trade rather than become masters of "teakettles." Like in all modes of progress the protests died out with the passing of time and the steam schooner ran its course. It was an even sadder day when the gallant wooden steam schooners gave way to the steel steam schooners, and even moreso the steel steam schooners to coastwise barges and truck transportation.

The innovative steam schooner was a type of vessel that belonged exclusively to the west coast. Though usage of engines speeded up transport, gave greater reliability and generally streamlined a risky operation, it by no means eliminated shipwreck. The cry "Breakers Dead Ahead!" was still heard on frequent occasion and Davy Jones never seemed to lack new occupants.

Compound engines for the most part were around 100 horsepower, driving a single screw. The principal manufacturer was the Fulton Iron Works in San Francisco. Engined schooners had a top speed of about eight knots, wide open. The later steam schooners, built from the keel up, were fitted with triple expansion engines which upped the speed to ten knots. None of the more than 225 specially designed steam schooners were ever accused of being speed queens, but they seemed to "lumber" through foul weather or fair, flat sea or hurricane. Though the percentage of losses from the hostile acts of nature was high, it was better than their forerunners. About half of the steam schooner fleet eventually became casualties. Even the luckier units of the fleet scraped over more than one reef during their active years, in fact those that came through unscathed after a quarter century of service were extremely few.

One of the units of the wooden fleet that went through the gauntlet of adventures was the little steam schooner *Mischief*. Built at Oneatta, Oregon in 1886, she was the pride of James J. Winant, a pioneer in the coastal oyster business. Willapa(Shoalwater)Bay and Yaquina Bay were the two most productive areas for harvesting oysters, and from the 1860's a group of small schooners were engaged in exporting the tasty bivalves to San Francisco to tickle the palates of gourmet diners. If a vessel dependent on sail was held back by contrary winds and cantankerous seas, the

Like a game of seagoing Russian roulette, two Coast Guard 44 foot lifesaving craft undergo practice runs under surf and bar swell conditions. U.S. Coast Guard photo.

18

Bucking bronco, sea variety. A Coast Guard 44 footer leaps over a bar swell at the Columbia River entrance. U.S. Coast Guard photo.

entire cargo could be destroyed before the destination was reached. Fast passages were essential.

Captain Winant saw the necessity of a steam schooner as a safeguard, and thus the birth of the *Mischief,* which was to become the first steamer in regular trade to and from Yaquina Bay. Winant first saw the value of shipping oysters when America was involved in the Civil War. He and Captain Freeman Dodge became competitors, the latter operating out of Yaquina Bay in the schooner *Elnorah.* Winant, however, won out establishing a harvesting area which he named Oysterville, ironically the same name given to a similar oyster harvesting center on Willapa Bay where both captains had also operated their respective commands. Yaquina's Oysterville has vanished, but Oysterville in Pacific County, Washington, once the county seat, still survives, though the oyster industry is handled at places elsewhere on the bay.

In Oregon, there was a court battle in the early years concerning a treaty with the local Indians as to whether the white traders had a right to extract oysters from Yaquina Bay without compensation to the natives. The court ruled that since the government had the right to establish a reservation it also had a right to dictate how the tidelands could be utilized, which left the market wide open for Winant. He continued to operate his oyster operation out of Yaquina Bay running vessels north to Portland and south to San Francisco.

Born in New York in 1838, Captain Winant had an exciting maritime career. He operated in the South Pacific trading and hunting for pearls, made several voyages as far north as Icy Cape, Alaska, the Aleutians and Siberia hunting walrus and whale. He was master of vessels on the Pacific Coast for a third of a century having commanded the schooner *Anna G. Doyle* out of both Willapa and Yaquina Bays to San Francisco in the early 1860's. He further made a wrecking trip to Mexico and explored the sunken wreck of the SS *City of San Francisco*, recovering $22,000 of her lost treasure. He was master of the *Mischief* for several years as well as skippering the steam schooner *Bandorille,* also built at Oneatta in 1889 for the coasting trade. Winant continued to operate his oyster business out of Yaquina Bay until his death in 1895 at age 52.

As master of the *Bandorille,* he attempted to cross the Umpqua bar November 21, 1895 en route to the Siuslaw River. He had just left the pilot house when the steamer was struck by a towering wave. In an awesome explosion it cascaded over in a geyser of water pinning the vessel in a chasm, tearing the shipmaster from his grip on the railing and throwing him into the vortex. As the ship shuddered from the impact seemingly shaking itself like a wet dog, the startled crew, humbled by the sneaker wave, threw liferings and lines over the side where Winant was sighted struggling for his life. He had almost reached a lifering when his strength gave out and he slipped beneath the surface. The vessel was thrown into the uncontrollable surf, its engines having ceased to operate, water having poured down the stack. Thumping hard against the sandy obstruction a mile south of the bar, 800 feet offshore, rescue units rushed to the wreck scene, managed to set up a breeches buoy and bring the ten survivors ashore. In the interim, the captain's body was sighted in the surf. He was pulled to the beach but died 20 minutes later.

His tragic death brought an end to the oyster business. The native beds had been virtually depleted by over harvesting. The native rock oyster, a small delicious species found only on Yaquina Bay, was no more. Eastern and Oriental oysters had to be planted on the bay in later years.

Though the *Bandorille* was pounded to pieces on the Umpqua shoals, Winant's *Mischief* continued to operate. She was chartered by 25 Canadians in the 1890's to engage with other sealing schooners in transporting the spring catch of skins from Sand Point, Alaska to Victoria. After departing the Canadian port on June 14, 1890, she reached Sand Point on July 4 and loaded 13,000 pelts for the return voyage.

Over on her beam ends this Coast Guard motor lifeboat from the Cape Disappointment station is close to doing a 360 degree roll. The vessels are self-righting, but the experiencing of a complete roll causes the heart to palpitate and one must hang on despite the watery immersion. Official U.S. Coast Guard photo.

In 1892 her steam engine was removed, the British flag raised, and under command of Captain William Petit, took 661 skins from the northern climes. After a stint at halibut fishing the 80 foot vessel took home 334 more seal skins.

With the end of the sealing industry the *Mischief* was up for grabs. Eventually she was placed in a shipyard, cut in half, lengthened, re-engined and renamed *Alaskan*. Placed in the service of the B.C. Coast Freight Co. Ltd. of Vancouver, B.C., she was nearing the end of the line. While en route from Victoria to Kildonan on Barkley Sound, January 2, 1923 carrying a cargo of box shooks, the vessel was sighted off Pachena Point in a southeast gale clawing her way toward Cape Beale. As the bitter night came on, shore dwellers reported sighting distress flares. She must have sunk like a rock with the loss of her entire crew of 11. Three bodies later washed ashore and pieces of wreckage littered nearby beaches.

Front page headlines screamed of the dramatic shipwreck of the 600 ton wooden steam schooner *Hanalei*. In her 13th year of service on a murky fall morning in November 1914 she was southbound out of Eureka with a full deckload of lumber, several head of cattle, plus hogs and sheep. Her passenger accommodations were full, booked by 34 passengers. The *Hanalei* carried 26 officers and crew, and to say the least was fully packed with a valuable payload.

Amid periods of rain, fog filtered down over the troubled waters five miles offshore, and speed was reduced in the vicinity of Point Reyes. Captain J.J. Carey squinted through the rain-smeared windows of the wheelhouse confident that all was well. He then elected to go below leaving instructions with the mate on watch. In the interim, the fog settled in with a vengeance reducing vision to almost zero. The helmsman pulled the whistle cord at frequent intervals to warn any other fogbound vessels in the vicinity.

Suddenly came the dreaded call that all seafarers fear. The lookout shouted, "Breakers ahead!"

As the ship's telegraph signalled the engine room for full astern, Captain Carey scurried back to the bridge with the gait of a racehorse. Foamy brine appeared astern as the screw reversed its arc. Backing off into deeper water the vessel was entirely enveloped in the white wraith leaving her exact position open to speculation somewhere off the Golden Gate. As a precaution, the skipper ordered the wheel hard over until the steamer was turning in wide circles to avoid menacing shoals lurking in the vicinity. Passengers popped their heads from stateroom doors pondering the peculiar course of the vessel. Those moments of uneasiness passed slowly. Finally the engines were rung up to stop, the ship drifting, eyes peering into the scud hoping to hear a fog signal other than their own and dreading the reality of hearing crashing breakers once again. It was an eerie operation, and in the confusion no order was issued to take soundings. Lost in a sea of fog, disaster awaited.

She struck hard on razor-like Duxbury Reef, a dreaded ship killer, and was hung up by the stern, her bow pointing seaward 300 yards offshore. The whistle sounded repeatedly, the distress signal at last reaching the ears of the employees at the Marconi Wireless Station on Duxbury Point. San Francisco was only nine miles away, and the message alerted two powerful steam tugs, the *Defiance* and *Hercules* which moved out of the bay at top speed, despite the fog. Two commercial fishboats, the Navy transport *Rainbow* and the steamer *Richmond* also responded. Unfortunately there was no ship to shore communication apparatus aboard the *Hanalei*. The lifesaving crews from both Fort Point and the Golden Gate stations put to sea with lifesaving gear, for whenever the word of a vessel in the Duxbury trap was received there was no hesitation on the part of would-be rescuers.

The situation was desperate. Captain Carey knew his command was in deep trouble and he immediately ordered passengers to don lifejackets and to stand by the boats. A Lyle gun aboard ship was broken out of the locker and rigged to shoot a line ashore. There was only enough gear for a single shot effort and if the line

failed to reach its mark the gun would be useless. As it turned out, the line fell well short of the mark. Two swarthy seamen then offered to swim ashore with a line, but the surf around the reef was a seething caldron of white-lipped breakers. Nonetheless, both made the attempt and both paid with their lives being sucked to their deaths in the undertoe.

The tugs were unable to locate the wreck in the fog and were forced to return to port. A plane hired by a local newspaper to cover the story was likewise unable to spot the wreck scene in the pea soup mantle. The lifesaving craft tried again and again to run the surf but were repeatedly swamped. Getting closest to the *Hanalei* were the two commercial fishboats but they had to withdraw after almost stranding.

For the next 16 hours the steam schooner shouldered one breaker after another. Terror was in the hearts of the victims as the deck began to buckle. Loose gear floated free, the masts canted precariously. Terrified livestock was washed overboard in the mishmash of brine. Soaked to the skin, passengers were hoping, praying and hanging on to anything that appeared solid. Breaking up fast, the vessel was in her death agonies. Cargo booms swung free like weapons of death and the deckload ripped through the lashings scattering lumber like ten pins.

Night came on with violence. Fires were built on the beach so the victims would know rescue efforts were continuing. A truck was dispatched from San Francisco

Close up view of the Coast Guard motor lifeboat **44336.** Self-righting and virtually unsinkable such craft work in the most rugged of surf conditions but require Coast Guard personnel with excellent seamanship qualities. U.S. Coast Guard photo.

Cape Disappointment Coast Guard Station in the lee of the historic monolith is the headquarters of one of the busiest search and rescue and lifesaving units in the Pacific. A Coast Guard training school is affiliated with the station to train recruits in the rigorous pursuit of lifesaving under the most severe conditions of sea and surf. For more than a century the government has maintained rescue craft at the same location. U.S. Coast Guard 13th District photo.

with a high powered Lyle gun, 2,000 pounds of gear and nine additional men to bolster the rescue team.

It was pitch dark aboard the wreck and the lives of all aboard hung in the balance. Captain Carey with tears in his salt stung eyes felt the heavy weight of responsibility, helpless as he watched the wretched passengers, women and infants among them, screaming, whimpering and struggling for survival. One by one they were swept into the watery waste.

Several lines were fired from the shoreside cliff but in the black maw it was impossible to see if the ropes were retrieved. Floodlights danced about on the tempestuous surf searching for survivors, or for bodies. At last a line was made fast and rafts were utilized to get the remaining survivors away from the wreckage. The lifesaving crews showed great courage risking their lives in the surf to save victims. Rescue craft searched the vasty deep but it was like operating in a basin of ink and foamy detergent. Still the work went on around the clock, the beaches littered with broken timbers, oil slicks and a vast collection of wreckage. Rescuers shuddered at finding bodies among the debris, both human and animal. One child was discovered dead, its little hands still clutching a doll.

With the pale dawn a dismal scene presented itself. Where a fully loaded steam schooner had been a few hours earlier was a mess of devastation. The *Hanalei* was a total wreck. The survivors received by sympathetic arms were rushed to San Francisco hospitals some with injuries and depression. The death toll stood at 23, among them 18 passengers.

Captain Carey, broken in spirit had been last to leave his ship and though burdened by the circumstances bore up with dignity at the board of inquiry. Blame for the loss fell to the shipmaster, and his license was suspended, but an understanding board, including men who well knew the rigors of the sea, showed mercy. After considerable testimony from the survivors attesting to the valiant efforts made by the captain to save those aboard, leniency was shown and his seagoing career was not terminated.

Out of the grievous calamity came a concerted effort to pass laws that all coastal vessels carrying passengers be equipped with ship-to-shore communication equipment.

Typical of the steam schooners that vanished at sea was the 301 ton *South Coast*, a stout, little lumber carrier built at Seattle in 1887. After a relatively charmed life spanning over four decades, well over the average age of her counterparts, she came to a tragic end in September 1930. The nation was in the midst of the depression when numerous coastal vessels were rotting away in backwater moorages.

Under Captain Stanley Sorenson, a seasoned steam schooner skipper, and 19 crewmen, the vessel departed Crescent City with 100,000 board feet of cedar logs destined for Coos Bay mills. A few days later the tanker *Tejon* owned by Standard Transportation Co., reported sighting a floating deckhouse offshore from Port Orford. The SS *Lake Benbow* reported steaming into a sea of cedar logs and recovered an empty lifeboat from the *South Coast*. Other wreckage believed from the ill-fated vessel came ashore in the vicinity of Cape Blanco, but no trace of Captain Sorenson nor his 19 man crew was ever found, the events of those final hours left only to speculation.

Equally tragic was the loss of the steam schooner *Brooklyn*. Just slightly larger than the *South Coast*, she was a product of the Lindstrom yard at Aberdeen on Grays Harbor, circa 1901.

Putting out to sea from Eureka on November 8, 1931, the *Brooklyn* moved toward Humboldt Bay bar, her destination San Francisco. Slightly off course, the vessel scraped over the bar and hit a shoal area which held her fast, shackled under the load of timber. Heavy seas were running and the vessel teeter-tottered on the barrier, the strain becoming so great that it broke her back, leaving her at the mercy of the bar breakers. Captain T.J. Tufvesson and his crew faced peril. The 450 horsepower engine ceased to operate and the steam pipes burst. Word of the stranding was quick to reach her owners, S.L. Whipple of San Francisco, and the insurance company, but there was little to do but wait out the results.

Seething surf offered no chance of getting a boat lowered although the crew was desperate enough to try. Meanwhile Coast Guard lookouts that had earlier spotted the wreck had alerted the motor lifeboat contingent. The bar, however, was so rough that they were unable to get anywhere near the wreck. Meanwhile, nearby Samoa Beach was being littered with wreckage. A Coast Guard plane tried to make contact but was repelled by fog and rain squalls. It became a desperate battle of men against the sea, and with each passing hour it became apparent that the sea was winning the battle. After the tempest calmed sufficiently for rescue crews to get near the wreck scene there was no sign of survivors. The death toll was 18, not one left to tell the tormenting tale, or was there? Three days after the wreck, a miracle occurred. First officer Jorgan Greve, gaunt and numbed from exposure was sighted clinging to a hatch cover, five miles at sea, 20 miles northwest of where the *Brooklyn* had gone to her grave. Rescued and rushed to a hospital, he fully recovered from his ordeal, the ship's lone survivor. Somewhat of a hero, he eventually returned to sea to pursue his chosen occupation, accepting the risks associated with it.

Mrs. Rappmoudt did everything in her power to convince her husband to quit the sea. He was master of the schooner *San Buenaventura*, (built at Fairhaven, California by Hans Bendixsen in 1876). She had a vested interest, for on many occasions she had sailed with her husband on coastwise trips. On the threatening day of January 12, 1910 the schooner departed Arcata with 170,000 board feet of lumber. Total complement was Captain Rappmoudt, his wife, 16 years old son, and infant daughter and a crew of five. Shortly after reaching the open sea, sail was reduced as the vessel ran head on into mounting seas aroused by strong winds. Despite constant work at the pumps, water began seeping into the hold at a faster rate than it could be pumped out. Fearing he might be drowned, one of

the crew went beserk and had to be restrained and locked in his cabin.

In order to afford greater buoyancy the captain ordered the deckload of lumber cut loose but during the effort the mate got his leg trapped between the timbers and suffered a painful break. All the while boarding seas flooded the deck, trapped by debris clogging the scuppers. For two days the vessel settled deeper, but refused to sink. When the next dawn broke cold and cheerless, the wretched individuals at last found something to cheer about. Sighting the wallowing vessel near St. George Reef was the steam schooner *Fairhaven*. She came to the rescue and managed to pluck the victims from the battered floating prison. Comfort in the form of warm blankets, hot coffee and spirits made life worth living again.

Captain Rappmoudt watched his partially sunken charge drift away in solitary, a menace to navigation. Two weeks later the derelict washed up on the rocks near the Rogue River in southern Oregon and quickly went to pieces. The captain considered his wife's suggestion of retiring to a farm, counting his blessings that he and his family were saved from what might have been a watery grave for all hands.

One of the last of the traditional wooden steam schooners as well as one of the largest to be built, was the *C.A. Smith*, constructed at the Kruse and Banks yard in North Bend, Oregon in 1921. The curtain was falling on the once flourishing wooden shipbuilding industry, it having reached an apex during the emergency program of World War I when numerous sailing ships, steamships and motorships were turned out en masse at west coast yards.

Edward S. Hough was commissioned in 1917 to design a wooden vessel of large carrying capacity to be completed in a minimum amount of time. Several Hough class hulls were built, among them the *C.A. Smith* and the slightly larger *Johanna Smith*. On completion, the twins, due to war shortages, remained engineless and initially were operated as barges by the Smith Lumber Co. Eventually they went back to the builders and in 1921, became the first and last of the standard steam schooner fleet and the only ones fitted with steam turbines and twin screws.

On December 16, 1923, the 1,878 ton *C.A. Smith* became an obituary after barely two years of service as a steamer. Under a full load of 1.5 million board feet of lumber, she struck the Coos Bay jetty. As the crew attempted to escape the stricken vessel by lifeboat, it capsized in the heavy surf and ten crewmen lost their lives. Fourteen others were rescued from the ill-fated vessel which was pulverized by the elements in short order, strewing its lumber cargo for miles along the southern Oregon shores.

23

Bow section of the tanker **Emidio** which drifted ashore near Crescent City, California after being torpedoed by a Japanese submarine 20 miles offshore December 17, 1941.

Wreck of the SS **Bear** which stranded in the fog near Sugar Loaf Rock south of Cape Mendocino, June 13, 1916. The passengers evacuated by lifeboat found refuge at the Blunts Reef Lightship. Captain Nopander had his license suspended for six months. The ship was a total loss.

CHAPTER TWO

Tombstone Coast

A wreck for every mile was the way mariners of old described the pristine shores of Vancouver Island's ragged west coast. There are sectors of that shoreline which even in our present day are extremely isolated and difficult to reach. It is a place of giant headlands, dense forests, jagged rocks, reefs, sea caves and sea stacks. In some areas rain exceeds 200 inches a year. Offshore some of the most feared seas in the Pacific are generated. Frequent storm warnings are posted. Most of the little settlements that have popped up through the years were a result of the bountiful fishing waters and tall timber, factors that attracted Indians to the land many centuries ago. A person could easily get lost from the world among the nooks and crannies of the nonconformable coastline, and one can find the remains of ghost towns where big dreams turned into nightmares. Many of the coastal ramparts seem unaltered from the time the great flood receded from mother earth.

There is no way of knowing how many ships have come to grief on the Vancouver Island shores from Port San Juan to the northwesterly tip at Cape Scott and the smattering of lonely islands along the route. The 282 miles of shoreline are broken by inlets, sounds, river bars and a collection of menaces to navigation to numerous to mention. One of the largest islands in North America, it is also one of the least populated in comparison to its size.

Approximately 300 seagoing vessels have been officially placed in the disaster log. In addition there are countless numbers of commercial fishboats and unknown wrecks, plus legions of Indian war and trading canoes. Among the unidentified wrecks are the remains of one believed to be well over 200 years old. It is buried in the sand and debris of Long Beach, well out of the recollection of the earliest Indians encountered by the pioneer settlers. The remains smack of a trading schooner and lie just above normal high water near what used to be known as the Old Lovekin residence. Evidence suggests that natives may have plundered the vessel and then set it afire. During the World War I era a group of American college students took on the project of investigating its origin.

Moving into the drift logs with picks and shovels they managed to expose the upper section of the hull but heavy seas and shifting sands were quick to bury the ghostly carcass again. Working against the elements soon proved a losing battle and the group was unable to shed further light on the possible identification of the vessel.

Numerous other unidentified and somewhat mysterious bits of ship wreckage are found in many places along those shores. The highest percentage of shipwrecks involved commercial sailing vessels entering or departing the Strait of Juan de Fuca. Contrary winds and troublesome seas plus complex current systems often placed navigators in jeopardy. When driven toward the lee shore, frantic efforts were made to beat away from the dangerous and menacing outcrops that lurked like the teeth of hungry sharks. There is a strong prevailing north setting current and frequently ships overran the entrance in dirty weather. Sometimes the lighthouses at Cape Flattery (Tatoosh Island), Carmanah, Pachena Point and Cape Beale were mistakenly identified in the din of an inclement nightfall. On other occasions faulty compasses, navigational errors, especially in the fog, or an over indulgence in liquor were responsible for the wrecks. Dismasted sailing vessels caught in the current and swept toward the dreaded coast were sometimes abandoned, the crew taking their chances in the open boats rather than risking the inhospitable obstructions along the shore, from which hopes of escape were slim at best.

Before the turn of the century there was such a rash of wrecks and the locations were so isolated that humanitarian dwellers hacked out crude trails leading to the lighthouses and to survival shacks stocked with imperishable goods to aid would-be castaways. Several survivors of shipwrecks owed their lives to the aids provided. Later, a telephone wire was strung from tree to tree so contact could be made with the nearest government facility. The severe storms in the area frequently knocked down the wire, in fact it was useless almost as much as operational.

Battle of the giants. The American flag cargoliner **C.E. DANT**, with her bow rammed into the forward section of the Somalian flag freighter **AEGEAN SEA** in September 1972 at the entrance to the Strait of Juan de Fuca. The vessels were pulled apart and both rushed to drydock for urgent repairs. Ed Delanty photo.

Many perished along the shipwreck trails. Through the years lifeboats and surfboats of the government stations at Bamfield and Tofino made several daring rescues resulting in saving many who might otherwise have perished.

Before the days of miracle radio-oriented aids to navigation and helicopters, the most notorious ship-wreck zones on the entire Pacific Coast were at the entrance to the Columbia River, the lower west coast of Vancouver Island and the entrance to the Strait of Juan de Fuca. Reminders of those hectic years of the past are sometimes revived when a ghostly shipwreck is unearthed from the beach sands for a brief period only to be covered over again by the dunes piling up in the wake of a storm.

From Port San Juan (Port Renfrew) to Barkley Sound little shelter is available for vessels in trouble. Makeshift shelters are frequently open to the onslaught during gale force winds. The only settlement between the two points is at Clo-oose, a locale inhabited by natives for centuries before the white men came. In later years a cannery was erected at nearby Nitinat Lake. It flourished for a time but with its closure most of the two hundred residents packed up and left leaving only a small number of fisherman and Indians behind. The lake is joined to the ocean by a treacherous tidal channel a mile west of Clo-oose, once the home of a powerful tribe of Nitinat Indians who built fortifications there to protect them from their arch enemies, the Makahs.

Nitinat bar has claimed many lives through the years when vessels have risked the crossing. In the autumn of 1918 the fishpacker *Renfrew*, with twenty six cannery employees aboard capsized in transit at the irascible entrance. In a mad scramble for survival in the cantankerous breakers it was every man for himself. The beach was littered with the bodies of thirteen who drowned in a fruitless effort.

On October 26, 1906 when the barkentine *Skagit*, out of Port Gamble tried to seek shelter from the storm she was driven shore on Clo-oose Point. Captain Rose was swept overboard and the ship's cook, attempting to rescue him, was also drowned. The scene of the wreck was only 12 miles from the entombed steamer *Valencia* which a few months earlier, was wrecked with the loss of 117 lives. The steam schooner *Santa Rita* stranded at Clo-oose Beach on February 14, 1923 but her crew all reached shore safely.

Not only was the lonely west coast known for its shipwrecks, but contentious natives were responsible for the plundering of several early trading ships and the murder of their crews. Among the unfortunate was the trading ship *Boston*, at Friendly Cove, where the Nootkas annihilated all but two of the ship's company after Captain Salter got into an argument with Chief Maquinna over possession of a gun. The shipmaster insulted the celebrated tribal leader who had previously been treated with honor by both Spanish and British factors. Revenge was swift with a sneak attack, his warriors killing the captain and the entire crew with the exception of John R. Jewitt, the armourer, and sailmaker John Thompson whose skills proved useful to the tribe. They were held in captivity for two years

Canadian salvage tug **SALVOR** aiding the stranded freighter **SIBERIAN PRINCE** aground in British Columbia waters July 29, 1923. The British cargo ship was hung up for 14 days.

Like a panting monster, the **C.E. DANT** tied up at a Seattle dock in 1972 after her encounter with the MS **AEGEAN SEA**.

before gaining their freedom with the arrival of the brig *Lydia* in the summer of 1805. In the interim, the *Boston* was burned and sunk in Friendly Cove after being plundered of its wares, the first of several known trading vessels to meet a similar fate. The Nootkas at times prone to savage tendencies were never taken lightly, and in all fairness many of their hostile acts were undoubtedly attributed to the lack of diplomacy on the part of the intruders.

In 1805, the ship *Atahualpa* was lying in Sturgis Cove, Milbanke Sound when it was attacked by the natives. Captain Oliver Porter and ten of his crew were butchered, but the vessel was able to make sail and escape destruction with a skeleton crew.

Near Village Island on Clayoquot Sound in June 1811, the Astor trading ship *Tonquin* out of New York via Astoria, was attacked after Captain Jonathan Thorn, allegedly displeased with the chief's hard bargaining, threw him overboard. The following day the tribesmen masquerading as traders murdered the entire crew. The last survivor, badly wounded, touched off the powder magazine a day later and killed more than 100 natives. In recent years a wide search has been made for the remnants of the vessel which thus far has eluded detection.

The Victoria sloop *Trader*, skippered by Captain Barney, was plundered and burned by the Kyuquot Indians in Kyuquot Sound in 1854. His Indian shipmate was also killed to prevent word of the atrosity from reaching the outside.

In 1864, the trading vessel *Kingfisher* met with tragedy while anchored in Matilda Inlet, Flores Island when a group of Ahousat Indians led by Chief Capshap attacked and plundered the vessel killing Captain Joseph Stevenson and his three man crew. Rocks were tied about the deceased and they were dumped into the waters of the inlet. Eleven prisoners were later brought to Victoria to stand trial. However, due to lack of evidence they were acquitted. The old chief was never captured, alluding the law till the day he died.

There was much consternation among the white settlers when in February 1859, the brig *Swiss Boy*, bound for San Francisco from Port Orchard with lumber, was forced into Barkley Sound leaking badly. Great numbers of belligerent Indians boarded the vessel while it lay at anchor, held the captain and crew at bay and continued to plunder all the gear before setting her afire. The lives of Captain Weldon and his five man crew were spared only by the intervention of the Indian chief who for some unknown reason decided against killing them despite the insistence of his subordinates. The schooner *Morning Star* finally rescued the castaways after which the HMS *Satellite* was dispatched to the area to arrest the guilty. Several were rounded up, taken to Victoria, jailed for six months and then set free.

Some of the provocative acts of treachery on behalf of the natives involved traffic in liquor which they received in trade for animal skins. Drunken savages were not totally responsible for their villianous acts and it was the white man that introduced the "fire water" to the natives.

One of the first shipwrecks from natural causes along the rugged western shores of Vancouver Island was that of the brig *William* on New Years Day 1854. En route to Victoria from San Francisco she was driven onto a reef five miles east of Pachena Point. As breakers cascaded into the wreck the captain and cook were drowned. Fourteen others made it to the beach with the assistance of the local Indians. Fed and housed by their hosts they were later transported to Sooke in the native canoes. One of their number, William Thomson decided to give up the sea and settle down on Vancouver Island to till the land.

That same year, the British bark *Lord Weston* also became a casualty. She was the initial vessel wrecked on Flores Island near Rafael Point. Loaded with timber from Sooke, she was outbound for England when overcome by gale-force winds. Driven ashore unceremoniously, the Ahousat Indians came to the rescue of the ship's crew and all survived.

Cannery tender **ALASCO** afire in the Strait of Juan de Fuca in 1931, as photographed from the deck of the SS **OLYMPIA**.

November and December of 1860 proved to be one of the stormiest periods ever recorded along the island's western shores. Several sailing vessels came to grief. On November 10, the schooners *Dance* and *D.L. Clinch* were wrecked on either side of Sombrio Point, which the Spaniard, Lt. Manuel Quimper had earlier named for its "dark and shady appearance." The point and the river of the same name are about 12 miles east of Port San Juan.

During the same time period, the brig *Consort* was wrecked in mid-November 1860. Historians appear to differ as to the place of her demise. The first account alleges that while in the command of Captain McLellan, inbound to Port Discovery from Honolulu, she was dismasted in a late October hurricane. A jury rig had to be installed off Cape Flattery, but protracted bad weather drove the vessel into Nootka Sound in early November where she dragged her anchors and ran aground. The 13 whites and nine Hawaiians (Kanakas) comprising the crew, all reached shore safely.

The conflicting account insists the *Consort* was wrecked in San Josef Bay, near Cape Scott at the northerly end of Vancouver Island on November 15, 1860. The passengers and crew numbering 22 in all survived and were picked up at a later date by the HMS gunboat *Forward* which transported them to Victoria.

Stuck fast on the out-crops of Austin Island near the entrance to Barclay Sound, the Panamanian flag freighter **VANLENE** succumbs to the elements. She was wrecked March 19, 1972, but Captain Lo Chung-hung and his 37 Chinese crewmen were all rescued. The wreck was blamed on defective navigational instruments, the vessel being off course. Photo by E.A. Ed Delanty.

Also wrecked in early November 1860 was the 320 ton ship *John Marshall*, San Francisco for Port Discovery. She was victim of a storm off Cape Flattery on November 10. Riding high in ballast, raucous seas opened her seams and water built up in the bilges at an alarming rate. Evidently, the shipmaster must have decided his ship would go down for he took to the boats with his crew of ten and in turn vanished from the sea forever. The derelict, badly pummeled by the elements, was carried ashore near Bonilla Point at Camper Bay and soon broke up.

The earlier mentioned schooner *Morning Star* was also wrecked in November 1860, near Bonilla Point.

On December 8, 1860, the Peruvian brig *Florencia*, Utsalady for Callao, was struck by a raging gale off Cape Flattery. Decks stacked high with lumber she was forced onto her beam ends for three hours, riding a deep trough and leaking badly. In an almost suicidal battle against a devil sea, the captain, cook, supercargo and a doctor passenger were swept overboard and drowned. Half submerged, the vessel was catapulted into Nootka Sound going hard aground on a small island. Fortunately the remainder of the crew were able to reach shore safely. Via the Indian grapevine, word of the wreck reached the HMS *Forward* which altered course for Nootka Sound and attempted to pull the wreck free and tow it to Victoria. Unfortunately the gunboat experienced boiler trouble when the tow got underway and the brig was set adrift going aground on an unnamed islet, which thereafter and still is, known as Florencia Island. There the wreck broke up, at a spot about five miles west of Amphitrite Point.

In command of Captain Mitchell, the brig *Cyrus*, Maine built in 1832, sailed from Steilacoom December 11, 1860 with lumber for San Francisco. Departing

Stately three-stacker, the SS **EMPRESS OF CANADA** in the trans-pacific passenger trade ran aground on Albert Head, near Victoria B.C. in the fog October 13, 1929. It was a costly undertaking getting the 26,000 ton Canadian Pacific liner afloat again. She once held the transpacific speed record-Yokohama to Race Rocks B.C.-eight days, ten hours and 52 minutes under Captain A.J. Hailey RNR. Average speed was 20.6 knots.

Port Townsend Bay on December 15, she was six days beating out of the Strait of Juan de Fuca and no sooner entered the open ocean than a gale struck raising seas of voluminous proportions. Cargo shifted both in the hold and on deck causing the vessel to ship tons of water. Mitchell had no alternative but to run for the safety of San Juan Harbor where anchors were dropped. After minor repairs, sail was made and an effort undertaken to move out of the harbor against head winds. To no avail, the anchors were again dropped. Once again the weather soured as another front as fierce as the first lashed the vessel and her exhausted crew. As the hooks dragged over sea bottom the 213 ton *Cyrus* was driven ashore at the head of the bay never to sail the seas again. The survivors, all hands accounted for, retrieved considerable spoils from the wreck and set up temporary shelter near the Gordon River where they remained until help came.

Needless to say, the year 1860 was a maritime nightmare for shipping on Vancouver Island's west coast.

Though there were many tragic shipwrecks along that coast in the decades that followed, some are still spoken of today because of the drama and/or loss of life accompanying the episodes. As already mentioned, the most tragic was that of the passenger liner *Valencia* in 1906 (see British Columbia section). One of the more dramatic was that of the four-masted iron bark *Janet Cowan,* a beautifully appointed British flag vessel hailing from Greenock, Scotland and built at Glasgow in 1889. At 2,497 tons she was one of the

The Alaska passenger steamer **HUMBOLDT** crunched up on the rocks at Pender Island at Mouat Point, British Columbia, September 29, 1908. Passengers and crew were safely evacuated and in a major salvage undertaking using the salvage ship **SANTA CRUZ**, the steamer was eventually refloated and after extensive repairs returned to service.

Scale model of the steamer **BEAVER** as she originally appeared on her arrival in the Pacific Northwest. She was the first steam-powered vessel to operate in the North Pacific arriving at Fort Vancouver from England by way of Cape Horn, Juan Fernandez and the Sandwich Islands in 1836. Her paddlewheels were attached on the Columbia River. The vessel was built by Green, Wigrams & Green, Blackwall-on-the-Thames in 1834-1835. The model was built by master model maker Ralph Hitchcock of Lopez Island, Washington. The vessel was wrecked July 15, 1888 near Prospect Point, Vancouver, B.C. while serving as a tug.

larger square-riggers calling regularly at Pacific ports near the end of the last century.

Inbound for Royal Roads, 108 days out of Cape-town, South Africa in ballast, the tall ship was on the docket for a berth at bustling Hastings Mill to load lumber. Off Cape Flattery on December 28, 1895 a storm of near hurricane proportions was raging, and for two days the vessel tacked off the entrance to the strait awaiting the right wind conditions. Blowing its lungs out, the sou'easter forced the bark to seek temporary shelter in Barkley Sound, after earlier almost getting abreast of Neah Bay on the American side of the strait. As the fierce winds veered between southeast and southwest the vessel came about, was caught in a strong inshore current and carried north-ward. Barkley Sound was the only alternative for temporary respite, but in the bleakness lay coastal barriers like a portcullis, closing off that destination.

Like an assassin, dangerous Pachena Point seemed to pull the big iron vessel toward its rockbound ramparts like a magnet. Only four years earlier the point had claimed the bark *Sarah* and the schooner

Laura Pike and now appeared hungry for its biggest prize yet.

Out of the ominous gloom came the horrifying sound of iron grating against obstructions of undersea rock. The *Janet Cowan* crunched against the unrelent-ing reef receiving punishing blows from walls of water inundating the reef and leaping across her deck. So rough was the surf that there was no thought of lowering a boat. Amidst that numbing December storm, a seaman stepped forth and volunteered to swim ashore with a line tied about his person. Strong and muscular, he was the only one among the crew who was an excellent swimmer. Even so, his chances of survival in the white-lipped breakers were considered minimal at best. But he would not be deterred, and cheered by his shipmates, he was put over the lee side. In a herculean effort not unlike Captain Ahab's attempt to kill the white whale, he fought and struggled, miraculously managing to gain the beach riding the crest of a mighty breaker which dumped him in a heap on a stretch of sand. Like a fighter getting up off the mat at count nine he secured the line and before

Devasted by fire, the wooden motorship **BOOBYALLA** at Esquimalt, B.C. after the flames were put out in May 1929. The engines from the wooden hulled vessel were salvaged but little else.

Two victims of the Inside Passage. Upper photo, shows the wreck of the barge **CHARGER**, a former Downeast sailing vessel built in 1874 on the east coast. In service of James Griffiths & Company, she broke loose from the tug **TYEE** and went hard aground at Karta Bay, Alaska, becoming a total loss in an October storm in 1909. Lower photo shows the death of another former sailing vessel, the Downeaster **JAMES DRUMMOND**. Last serving as a barge, she was fully laden with 2000 tons of gypsum from Gypsum, Alaska, bound for Tacoma, and additionally had a locomotive aboard. She broke away from the tug **TATOOSH** in heavy seas and crashed ashore at Dall Patch Shoal, Milbanke Sound, B.C. becoming a total loss October 22, 1914.

Wreck of the British freighter **TUSCAN PRINCE** on Village Island, B.C. The crew of 43 was rescued by the U.S. Coast Guard cutter **SNOHOMISH** which during the same time frame rescued the crews of the MS **NIKA** and the steam schooner **SANTA RITA,** while ranging between the Umatilla lightship and the west coast of Vancouver Island, February 15, 1923.

long a crude breeches buoy was rigged between the wreck and the beach. The entire crew of 29, the last to leave being Captain Thompson, made it to shore, but the worst was yet to come. The weather was biting cold and no shelter was available. As they watched the vessel being hammered hour by hour their bodies were blue with the cold and damp and it became a case of survival. In a daring attempt to re-board the wreck to recover badly needed blankets, provisions and the ship's medicine chest, two apprentices were drowned and the second mate broke his leg. It was a scene of utter despair.

Realizing that they all might perish, seven crewmen went exploring the bleak coastline and found a downed telephone wire that had been strung from tree to tree but broken in several places. They followed it, and a mile and a half distance to the west came to a crude shelter placed there for just such an emergency. Providentially it was stocked with a few provisions

and dry wood. Writing on the wall told the castaways to help themselves. There was a telephone there also but the storm had broken the line all along the route of the shipwreck trail from Cape Beale to Carmanah.

In time, rescue was bound to come reasoned the seven and they accordingly set up housekeeping and devised a survival plan between the shelter and the wretched souls huddled under a tarpaulin against a bluff near the wreck scene. Sharing what food was available, they tried to encourage the weak and injured to hang on a little longer. On the fifth day, Captain Thompson died of exposure. On the seventh day the ship's cook and two able seamen succumbed. Still another member of the miserable contingent went berserk and died from exposure.

When everything seemed hopeless, prayers were answered. The ocean tug *Tyee*, Captain William Gove, spotted the wreck of the *Janet Cowan* in the distance and altered course standing in as near the

31

treacherous shoreline as possible. A boat was launched to run the surf and after several hours 15 miserable castaways were rescued and transported to Port Townsend. Those remaining at the shelter decided to await the arrival of a Canadian vessel which in turn was dispatched to take them to Victoria. Many weeks later a government vessel was sent to recover the partially decomposed bodies of the deceased including those that had drowned trying to recover goods from the wreck.

One of the survivors, first officer Charles Legalle, was outspoken in his criticism of the lack of communication and the slow assistance in the wake of the tragic wreck.

Another calamity that is still talked about along the shipwreck trail is that of the Chilean bark *Carelmapu.* That tragedy was to cost the lives of 19 on the fateful day of November 23, 1915. Only five members of the 24 man crew lived to tell the tale, plus the ship's mascot, a dog which could only tell his part of the saga by a sharp whine and a wagging tale.

The Canadian Pacific passenger vessel *Princess Maquinna*, Captain E. Gillam, departed Tofino on its run down the coast and encountered some of the heaviest seas in the skipper's recollection. The passengers were suffering from mal de mer and the wind howled like a banchee. As the weather worsened Gillam decided to come about and run for shelter when the lookout shouted, "Shipwreck off the port bow!"

Two sets of distress flags were flying from the troubled vessel's mizzen mast, the canvas on her yardarms had been torn to ribbons and she was almost in the breakers off Gowland Rocks at the western extremity of Long Beach.

Not unfamiliar in Pacific Northwest waters, the *Carelmapu* was the former British square-rigger *Kinross* built at Liverpool in 1877, an iron hulled vessel of 1,447 tons.

Risking his ship, its passengers and cargo in true grit fashion, Gillam with little hesitation went to the rescue of those in peril on the sea.

Captain Fernando Desolmes, master of the *Carelmapu* had only 20 fathoms under the ship's keel at dawn on that fateful day, and the anchors were dragging only a few cable lengths from the rocks. Inbound for Puget Sound from Caleta Buena, Chile via Honolulu, the square-rigger had been unable to secure the services of a tug off the strait and was at the same time being hammered by near hurricane winds. That was her plight when Captain Gillam courageously maneuvered his command to within 150 yards of the wallowing bark, and dropped anchor to hold his position. What was left of the stricken ship's sails were

torn bits of canvas appearing like pieces of laundry waving in the wind. Terrified seamen could be seen running about the deck, but voice communication between the respective vessels was totally inaudible over the howling blasts. An attempt was made to drift a line down wind with its end attached to a water breaker, but it failed. Suddenly an erupting sea of mammoth proportions struck the *Maquinna* lifting her bow like a lobtailing leviathan. The strain was so mighty that the anchor winch was actually ripped from its fittings splitting the shafts and supports, necessitating the cutting loose of the anchor and 60 fathoms of chain. The situation was such that the *Princess Maquinna* could end up in the same precarious situation as the vessel it was trying to save. In the face of grave danger members of the steamer's crew volunteered to man a lifeboat. Wisely, Captain Gillam pondering their chances of survival in the mountainous seas, refused their offer. Out of desperation those on the *Carelmapu* attempted to lower two boats into the seething tempest. One was smashed against the ship's side and its passengers thrown into the sea. The other with seven aboard cleared the wreck but was then capsized and its occupants all sent to a watery grave. There now appeared only six remaining aboard. In a flash, another giant sea carried the vessel right over the rocks into a pin-cushioned marine graveyard. Nothing was left that Gillam could do. He put about for Ucluelet and immediately alerted the Tofino lifesaving crew with the terse words that the *Carelmupa* was a total loss with no survivors. The wreck had broken in two, the stern holding fast on the rocks, the forward section sinking.

At that juncture, the hand of God intervened. From the battered wreckage of the after section, Captain Desholmes, and four of the ship's company, some badly cut, and all bruised, staggered out like eels from underseas caverns. Struggling ashore in the gathering dusk the wretched individuals roamed the area and found an abandoned Indian shack. One of their number, in a daze, wondered off into the woods. With no matches and soaked to the skin the survivors experienced a night that seemed an eternity. When at last the pale light of morning appeared against a threatening sky, the errant one came out of the forest raving like a maniac and had to be restrained from drowning himself. In addition to Captain Desolmes, three seamen, a 19 year old Chilean student and a dog were the only survivors.

Darkness and raging seas had prevented the surfmen of the Tofino Lifesaving Station, from putting to sea the previous night, but instead they set out on foot to reach the wreck scene as did two other independent groups, one headed by the constable from Clayoquot,

Like a battle between two sea monsters, the cargoliner **C.E. DANT** of States Line takes a big bite out of the Liberian tramp ship **AEGEAN SEA** off the entrance to the Strait of Juan de Fuca in 1972. Both vessels were taken to port for costly damage repair.

and another from Tofino. The former, after an exhaustive search, found the miserable members of the ship's company and escorted them to Long Beach where a settler and his wife cared for them and lovingly adopted the canine mascot. Later, when the Tofino lifeboat arrived to take the five survivors to the Clayoquot hotel to rest until the return of the *Princess Maquinna*, the dog, fond of its new warm home, remained behind.

Later still, six bodies were recovered and given proper burial near the scene of the wreck. With the moderating weather, the Tofino lifeboat crew revisited the site and recovered some personal belongings, ship's papers and other items from the wreck, the after section still resting on its perch, high and dry at minus tide. Located at Shelter Bay less than a half mile east of

Portland Point, some of the wreckage was visible for years thereafter. Iron frames may still be seen as a grim reminder despite the fact that a salvage company recovered a quantity of her metal for the war effort during World War I.

Though unable to rescue any survivors from the *Carelmapu*, Captain Gillam was nevertheless hailed as a hero for his courageous effort. A passenger aboard his ship, H.H. Tanner, a mining man by profession, had presence of mind to snap some photos of the *Carelmapu* just before she was swept over the rocks to her final grave. Those photos made the front pages of many newspapers revealing a dramatic battle in a death struggle for survival. Those pictures as the old adage tells, were worth a thousand words.

CHAPTER THREE

Washington Shipwrecks

One can stand at the edge of the timeless bastion known as Cape Flattery and daydream back through history. Beyond lies the crossroads of the Pacific, split in half by an international boundary separating two great nations—the United States and Canada. These waters hide a deceptive cemetery of lost ships. The shore is a hallmark of nature where sea and land come together in constant turmoil, a sort of no man's land with rocky ramparts in ragged array standing sentinel against the encroaching ocean. To the south lies the rugged Washington coast—138 nautical miles to the Columbia River.

From the standpoint of nature, the view from Cape Flattery northward to Vancouver Island's Pachena Point has been little altered since the earliest explorers cast their misty eyes upon it in their frustrating efforts to find the fabled Northwest Passage.

Yes, upon Cape Flattery, one not only finds himself on the absolute northwest end of continental United States, but he looks beyond to the "stolen" former Indian Island of Tatoosh, and into the path of a steady parade of seagoing ships passing in and out of the Strait. The onlooker can well imagine the ships of yesteryear with billowing canvas, manned by Spaniards, British and Russians—searching, searching, searching—and of the stout ships and brave men asleep in the cradle of the deep.

The changeable coastline from Cape Flattery to Cape Disappointment is controlled immediately north of the Columbia River by the river and ocean currents creating, via the northerly drift, great sand beaches. From Cape Disappointment, the coast extends northward for 22 miles to Willapa Bay as one low sandy beach, with sandy ridges about 20 feet high parallel with the shore. Willapa Bay entrance is 24 miles northward of the Columbia. Next comes Grays Harbor, another important seaport entry, located 40 miles northward of the Columbia. From Grays Harbor to the entrance of the Strait of Juan de Fuca, there are no deepwater harbors, and much of the shoreline is craggy and in its natural state. The rocks, reefs and islets and much of the shoreline is as it was before the coming of the white man.

The Puget Sound basin lies between the Olympic and Cascade Mountains in the form of a broad trough, extending from Juan de Fuca Strait which connects Puget Sound with the Pacific. Puget Sound is 80 miles long, eight miles in width at the broadest point, and has depths of up to 900 feet, a body of water flanked by forested bluffs and low dikelands, with extensive bays, inlets, and passages between the 300 islands that lie within. Of these, the 172 islands of the San Juan group and Whidbey Island, second largest in continental United States, are most widely known. Under these waters lie the hulks of more than 600 vessels, large and small, that have fallen victim to some type of calamity through the years.

With a water area of 1,721 square miles, there are avenues for every type of vessel activity, and per capita, Puget Sound is the boating capital of the world in mostly protected waters.

On the other hand, the rugged coastline south from Cape Flattery (and Tatoosh Island), is open to all weather and its waters have claimed scores of ocean going ships many of which have been lost without trace. The phrase, "Lost off Cape Flattery without trace," was virtually a household word just before and around the turn of the century.

Pacific Disaster

Of all the dramatic and tragic shipwrecks off the Washington Coast none has been so great in loss of lives and in futility as the foundering of the steamer *Pacific*. She sank after a collision with the ship *Orpheus* just south of Cape Flattery in the fall of 1875. A total of 277 persons were aboard that ill-fated passenger vessel, and only two survived, one of which later died. Had the *Pacific* been carrying twice that number of persons, in all probability they too would have perished.

The repair bill came to more than $80,000 after the Norwegian MS **OREGON EXPRESS** stranded in the fog at Bush Point, on Whidbey Island, Puget Sound, December 29, 1940. The vessel was brought to Seattle for repairs at the Todd yard. The **OREGON EXPRESS** of the Fruit Express Line, was built in 1933, and finally lost during World War II.

The wooden-hulled sidewheeler departed Victoria, B. C. on the morning of November 4, 1875, with skipper J. D. Howell in command. She had taken on passengers and cargo at both Puget Sound and British Columbia ports and was San Francisco-bound.

Rounding Cape Flattery well into the afternoon, she ran into a fresh southwest wind which created small greybeards. Speed was slowed as night came on like a damp, wet blanket. The kerosene lamps flickered in the lounge which was emptied early, many of the passengers feeling the pangs of seasickness. Even in steerage, where the occupants usually whooped it up, it was quiet. It was very dark on the bridge. Standing on the hurricane deck in his oilskins—the wind and rain beating in his face, Captain Howell searched in the murk for a dim outline of the harsh shore. He knew the coast well and had a healthy respect for it; and that was why he always kept his ship well out to sea once rounding the cape. He knew well that he was sailing through a proverbial graveyard of ships. Finally satisfied that all was well, he entered the pilothouse, checked with the helmsman and left word with the officer on duty to wake him if he deemed a change in course to be necessary. The skipper then made one round of the deserted decks, passed through the galley to warm himself with a hot cup of coffee and then retired to his cabin.

The *Pacific* might have been just another ship that passed in the night but the haunting shadow of death seemed to hang over her. Just shortly after 10 p.m. her whistle blew followed by a crash. The *Pacific* had collided with another vessel striking it a relatively light blow on the starboard side. It didn't seem possible that such a mishap could cause any major damage to a liner

the likes of the *Pacific* but within a matter of seconds the steamer was drinking gallons of ocean water and the decks were a total mass of confusion. Her bow was slowly dropping. Passengers rushed from their staterooms, clad only in night clothes. The ship heaved violently, the decks began to twist and live steam rose in a great cloud after reaching the boilers. Women began screaming. A wave raced along the *Pacific's* side, its edges splashing aboard. The passengers and crew began struggling with each other for space; fear masked their pale faces. The vessel careened portside and the captain and officers tried frantically to get to the lifeboats to cut the davit ropes and get them afloat. But the human stampede created only mayhem. The *Pacific* was dead weight; she was in her death agonies and going down fast.

Finally one of the lifeboats was cut free, but its plug was not affixed and as 15 women and six men piled into the craft, a lunging sea caused it to crash against the side of the steamer; it filled and sank throwing all its occupants into the dark vortex. Within minutes the *Pacific* made her final plunge and those not trapped within her confines were swept into the irascible waters to fend for themselves. The sea was filled with struggling humans and an assortment of flotsam and jetsam.

Off in the distance faded the *Orpheus* which the *Pacific* had struck. Captain Charles Sawyer, her master, had seen the *Pacific's* lights and heard her whistle just before the crash. The steamer bounded off and again struck the *Orpheus* at the main topmast backstays breaking the chain plates. The *Pacific* rose on the next swell and plunged again striking the mizzen topmast chain plates carrying away the backstays and bumpkin, main and main topsail braces, leaving the *Orpheus* in a wrecked condition on her starboard side. Captain Sawyer's wife who had come up on deck was so infuriated by what she felt erroneous navigation on the part of the *Pacific* that she attempted to jump aboard the steamer immediately after the crash. Captain Sawyer prevented her effort and the *Orpheus* sailed on into the night toward the Strait of Juan de Fuca, her crew occupied with trying to unscramble the welter of damaged rigging.

Unaware that such a light crash could possibly have caused the foundering of the *Pacific*, the *Orpheus* made no attempt to come about or to lower her boats to look for survivors. This was to bring Sawyer misery for as long as he lived. Corpses drifted up on coastal beaches for weeks after the tragedy with the constant abuse of the public and press only adding to his torment.

Technically Sawyer was never proven guilty but in every disaster one must bear the brunt of indignation and Captain Sawyer was the man. Nor was his cause aided by the fact that the *Orpheus*, after striking the *Pacific*, overran the entrance to the Strait and piled up on Vancouver Island's Cape Beale. The *Orpheus* became a total loss. All hands escaped, but Captain Sawyer was immediately charged with purposely wrecking his ship. Until after they reached civilization, none of the *Orpheus'* company had any inkling the *Pacific* had foundered.

Nor was Captain Sawyer's position aided any through his reputation as a hard master, his commands on occasion having been labeled as "hell ships."

The terrible plight of the survivors of the *Pacific* facing a watery grave, is one of the most terrifying dramas in Pacific Coast maritime annals. A handful escaped on pieces of wreckage, but only two survived the acid test of man against the open sea. One was named Henry Jelley (Jelly), who some time after his rescue died from the results of long exposure; the other was quartermaster Neil Henley. For 80 hours of hell at sea, in an unprecedented human effort, Henley tenaciously clung to a piece of wreckage until finally the searching revenue cutter *Oliver Wolcott* plucked him from the frigid waters, more dead than alive.

It was his testimony at the later court of inquiry that has remained as a living chronicle of that night of terror when the *Pacific* went down with those who now sleep in an unmarked sepulcher of the sea.

Beecher once wrote: *"Oh, what a burial was here! Not as when one is borne from his home among weeping throngs and gently carried to the green fields, and laid peacefully beneath the turf and flowers. No priest stood to perform a burial service. It was an ocean grave. The mists alone shrouded the burial place. No spade prepared the grave, no sexton filled up the hollowed earth. Down, down they sank, and the quick returning waters smoothed out every ripple and left the sea as though it had not been!"*

Such words might well apply to those lost on the steamer *Pacific*. Quartermaster Henley's account remains as grim testimony.

"I was off watch and about 10 p.m. was awakened by a crash and getting out of my bunk found the water rushing into the hold at a furious rate. On reaching the deck all was confusion. I looked on the starboard beam and saw a large vessel under sail, which they said had struck the steamer. When I first distinguished her she was showing a green light. The captain and officers of the steamer were trying to lower the boats but the passengers crowded in against their commands, making their efforts useless. None of the lifeboats had plugs in them. There were 15 women and six men in the boat with me, but she struck the ship and filled instantly, and when I

Going down, down in the sands at Copalis Beach, Washington. This photo was taken September 9, 1928, nine months after the Japanese SS **TENPAISAN MARU** went aground. The freighter struck December 1, 1927 and her crew had to be brought ashore by breeches buoy as a huge crowd gathered on the beach to watch the Coast Guard in action. The 5,019 ton vessel, owned by Mitsui Bussan Kaisha, Ltd., was in transpacific service and registered at Kobe. She was built at Sunderland, England in 1911.

Wreck of the tug **MARTHA FOSS** of the Foss Launch & Tug Company, after being rammed by the steamer **IROQUOIS** in a heavy fog off Port Angeles, Washington, May 20, 1946. One member of her crew was lost, and the veteran tug, built in 1886 as the **DOLPHIN**, finally went to the bottom. The 96 ton diesel powered craft was of wood construction.

came up I caught hold of the skylight which soon capsized. I then swam to a part of the hurricane deck which had eight persons clinging to it. When I looked around, the steamer had disappeared leaving a floating mass of human beings, whose cries and screams were awful to hear and the sight of which can never be effaced from my memory.

"In a little while it was all over; the cries had ceased, and we were alone on the raft, the part of the deck on which was the wheelhouse. Besides myself the raft supported the captain, second mate, cook and four passengers, one of them a young lady. At 1 a.m. the sea was making a clean breach over the raft. At 4 a.m. a heavy sea washed over us, carrying away the captain, second mate, the lady, and another passenger, leaving four of us on the raft. At 9 a.m. the cook died and rolled off into the sea. At 4 p.m. the mist cleared away and we saw land about 15 miles off. We also saw a piece of wreckage with two men on it.

"At 5 p.m. another man expired and early the next morning the other one died, leaving me alone. Soon after the death of the last man I caught a floating box and dragged it on the raft. It kept the wind off, and during the day I slept considerable. Early on the morning of the eighth I was rescued by the revenue cutter *Wolcott...*"

Henley's account was plain and factual, but any man who has gone down to the sea in ships can easily read between the lines and can well imagine the torment.

The other survivor, passenger Henry Jelley (Jelly), along with four others, seized hold of an overturned lifeboat after the *Pacific* went to her grave. One after another the occupants were swept off until only Jelley remained. For 48 hours he clung until the blood all but froze in his veins. Finally the steamer *Messenger* located him. A few more hours and he would have been dead. He never fully recovered from his ordeal and eventually died.

In all, 17 persons had managed places on life rafts after the *Pacific* sank but only Henley and Jelley lived to tell the tale.

The rest of the story was in the courts of inquiry at churches and funeral homes.

Toll for the brave!
The brave that are no more!
All sunk beneath the wave
Fast by their native shore!
    —Cowper

There have been many other chilling shipwrecks on or near coastal Washington waters and others in the inland seas that have taken a heavy toll in lives. Among the most regrettable from the standpoint of loss of life are the following:

The British warship *Condor* vanished somewhere off Cape Flattery en route to Honolulu from Esquimalt, B. C., in December 1901, with the total loss of lives given in some accounts as 104, in some 130 and in others 140 lives, there being some disagreement as to how many were actually aboard. The vessel was lost without trace except for a few bits of wreckage that drifted up on the British Columbia coast.

The Black Ball steamer *Clallam,* foundered at the eastern end of the Strait of Juan de Fuca, midway between Dungeness and Smith Island, January 9, 1904 with the loss of 54, some accounts claiming 51. She went down in stormy seas just six months after being placed on the Seattle-Victoria run.

As a result of a collision with the steamer *Jeanie,* the passenger steamer *Dix* foundered off Alki Point on the Seattle-Port Blakely run with the loss of 39 lives on November 18, 1906.

Another tragedy was the loss of the entire crew of the freighter *Iowa* which ran aground and broke up on dreaded Peacock Spit at the north entrance to the Columbia River, January 12, 1936 in a full gale. Thirty-four men lost their lives.

Only three survivors escaped the stranding of the tanker *Rosecrans* lost on Peacock Spit January 7, 1913. A total of 33 men were taken to a watery grave in that incident.

There was a rash of ships that were totally lost or which vanished with all hands off Cape Flattery, most probably due to overloading and storm-tossed seas. Such losses where a heavy toll of life occurred, included the ship *Ivanhoe*, September 1894; the SS *Keweenah* and SS *Montserrat*, December 1894; sealer *Active*, April 1887; SS *Matteawan*, December 1901; British freighter *Haida* in October 1937, all of which went down with their entire crews, ranging from 23 to 33 men per ship.

Other tragic wrecks in Washington State waters from the standpoint of loss of life included the Norwegian bark *Prince Arthur*, south of Cape Alava, January 2, 1903; the British bark *Andrada*, lost supposedly somewhere off the Washington coast December 1900; the SS *Admiral Sampson* which went down off Point No Point in Puget Sound, August 26, 1914 after a collision with the CPR liner *Princess Victoria*. A group of sailing vessels which were either totally wrecked or lost with all hands off Cape Flattery or along the Washington Coast included the *Lord Raglan*, a British bark in 1852; the ship *John Marshall*, November 10, 1860; the British ship *Hartfield* in January 1908; ship *Florence* in December 1902, the ship *Sierra Nevada* in September 1886; British bark *Abercorn*, January 12, 1888 and the bark *Cowlitz* in January 1893, to name but a few. In all of the latter mentioned wrecks the death tolls ran from 15 to 21 lives per ship.

The Faithful "Sparks" of The Sampson

The publication, Port O' Call, the sounding board of the Society of Wireless Pioneers tells of a man named W. E. "Sparks" Reker who is on the list of Marconi men who died as heroes. He was senior wireless operator of the SS *Admiral Sampson*, which sank off Point No Point near Hansville, Washington after a collision with the Canadian steamer *Princess Victoria*. The tragedy resulted in the deaths of 16 persons, in that foggy setting August 26, 1914.

The *Sampson*, commanded by Captain Zimro Moore and owned by the Pacific Alaska Navigation Co. was feeling her way carefully along her course shortly before 5 a.m. The majority of the 57 passengers were asleep in their berths, but some, aroused by the siren, had come on deck. The *Princess Victoria*, skippered by Captain P. J. Hickey and owned by Canadian Pacific, was also making her way through the fog in much the same cautious manner.

The fog whistles on both vessels were blasting continuously, but the thick pall blocked out all visibility. Neither ship was steaming faster than three knots when the crash occurred. The *Victoria* rammed the *Sampson* directly on a line with the after hatch, cutting three-fourths of the way through her, opening a wide jagged gash. The hatch cover of the *Sampson* was still jammed into the Canadian Pacific liner on her later arrival at Seattle.

Immediately after the impact the *Sampson* began to fill, and the master of the *Victoria* realizing the danger to the doomed ship, rang for slow speed ahead and kept the bow of the *Victoria* tight into the gaping wound. The vessels

In December of 1891, the SS **EASTERN OREGON** was destroyed by fire on the ship gridiron at Olympia, Wash., where she had been placed for cleaning and painting. The fire-gutted vessel had been operating on the Seattle Vancouver, B.C. run opposite the **SS PREMIER**, in command of Captain Leander Green. Later the charred craft was towed to San Francisco. The iron-hulled vessel was originally built at Chester, Pa., in 1883 as the **CITY OF PALATKA** for the St. Johns, N. B. run.

With the Seattle fireboat **ALKI** hugging her and the tug **DELLWOOD** towing her to open water, the fine old Alaska Steamship Company passenger liner **ALAMEDA**, speed queen of the fleet, burns furiously after catching fire at Pier 2, Seattle, Nov. 28, 1931. The fire broke out in the early morning hours and gained headway so rapidly that it was necessary to tow her from pierside to prevent a major waterfront fire. The liner was beached near the East Waterway and burned for many hours. Last serving as master of the ship was Captain C. A Glasscock. The vessel was never rebuilt and her hull was scrapped a few years later by Neider & Marcus of Seattle. The **ALAMEDA** was built at Philadelphia in 1883 and was of 3,158 tons.

were so close together that the majority of the *Sampson's* passengers were able to climb on board the other ship. The *Sampson* was hit at a point where a considerable quantity of fuel oil was stored. The impact crushed several large containers which were set ablaze and in an instant both vessels were enveloped in flames. For a time it seemed as if they would be destroyed by fire. The *Victoria,* however, soon backed away and stood by to pick up the passengers that were being lowered to the water in lifeboats. The gap in the *Sampson's* side was left uncovered and the liner began to settle. The entire drama was enacted in four minutes from the time of the crash until the liner filled and foundered in a wild flush of water. The hissing and gurgling was over quickly leaving behind only bits of wreckage covering a massive hole in the sea which momentarily covered over all traces of the grave.

During this final drama, the ship's wireless operator aboard the *Victoria* had not been idle. He sent out an SOS call which was picked up at the Marconi station at Seattle by A. E. Wolf, who immediately established communication with the SS *Admiral Watson.* The first information that came by wireless was to the effect that the *Sampson* and the *Victoria* had collided followed by a Marconigram saying that the *Sampson* had gone down. The alerted revenue cutter *Unalga* departed Port Townsend and immediately began searching for survivors. Among the victims of the accident was Z. M. Moore, master of the *Sampson.* Fortunately only two passengers out of a total of 57 lost their lives.

Assistant wireless operator Wiehr, who was on duty on the ill-fated *Sampson* when the collision occurred, immediately awakened Reker. The latter had every opportunity of finding a way to safety with the remainder of the survivors but would not. Wiehr said he saw the senior operator a minute before the *Sampson* sank, leaving the social hall. He was next seen on the bridge with Captain Moore. Reker did not possess a life preserver and was unable to swim.

The Marconi Wireless Telegraph Company of America sent the following letter to Theodore Reker, father of the operator:

"Dear Mr. Reker: Now that the first shock of your bereavement has passed, this company ventures to extend to you some measure of its appreciation of the noble devotion to duty shown by your son, the senior Marconi operator on the *Admiral Sampson*, who calmly and heroically went down with the ship he had served so well.

"Our official reports show that as the vessel was sinking he made his way to the bridge to report to his captain, deliberately ignoring opportunities of securing safety with the passengers and thinking only of his duties as a ship's officer. It is evident that had he so chosen he might have saved his own life, for he was off duty and asleep at the time of collision, and the wireless appeal for aid to the sinking vessel had already been answered. That he further upheld the Marconi tradition and sought instead his post by the side of the commanding officer makes his record an immortal one with those who have courageously gone to death in the simple discharge of duty."

Demise of The Governor

Ernest E. Wolcott, a wireless operator, tells of the last moments of the SS *Governor*, which foundered after a collision with the SS *West*

Candidate for surgery—The British SS **STRATHALBYN** after she collided with the SS **VIRGINIAN** between Robinson and Pulley Points on Puget Sound, January 12, 1912. The **STRATHALBYN** is seen here at Tacoma following the crash, that would have sunk the average freighter. Literally torn open from her stem to number 2 hold, repairs were long and costly to both ships, especially on the **STRATHALBYN**. The collision occurred at 8 p.m. at night, but the weather was clear. *Aldrich photo.*

More than 14,000 tons of disabled passenger liner on her side at the Todd Shipyard in Seattle presented a major salvage problem. The 535 foot American Mail Liner capsized and sank March 23, 1933. She was the SS **PRESIDENT MADISON,** one of the fine fleet of transpacific passenger ships operating out of Seattle to the Orient. The accident happened after four shell plates had been removed from the vessel's side, opening up a hole 90 by six feet, only four feet above the waterline. The pull of a scow loading lumber alongside is believed to have rolled the ship just enough to allow the inflow of water. The bulk of the ship soon heeled over trapping and drowning one man in the engine room, and imprisoning others inside the hull. Shipyard workers scurried to safety on the dock as the ship heeled over in a stark moment of drama. Those trapped inside were eventually rescued through portholes by the Coast Guard. Described as the greatest salvage operation, to that date, at an American port, the **MADISON** was refloated in just three weeks, but was to lay idle and in disrepair for six years. During that time, while tied up at Pier 41 in Seattle, in the big gale of October 21, 1934, she parted her moorings, drifting away, crashing into sternwheeler **HARVESTER,** totally wrecking and flipping her over, and then crashed into the SS **NORTH HAVEN.** *Joe Williamson photo.*

Hartland, off Point Wilson while en route to Seattle from Victoria in the coastwise passenger run. Eight lives were lost on the *Governor,* five passengers, (two of which were children) and three crewmen.

In Wolcott's own words; "It was a few minutes before midnight, March 31, 1921. I had left the radio room and gone below to the pantry on the starboard side, forward of the dining room, for a 'bowl' of coffee before being relieved. I had poured the coffee and the pantryman went into the chill room for some cold cuts, when I heard three short blasts of the ship's whistle.

"There had been no indication of any trouble, but I knew enough about the sea to recognize an emergency signal, so I abandoned the coffee and ran through the dining room heading for the radio room, on the top deck aft, next to the dance floor. Some passengers (in the dining room) were at the table, and I remember thinking that I was probably frightening them, being on a dead run.

"There were several decks and ladders between me and the radio room, so it was probably a minute or two before I reached it. Just as I stepped over the sill, there was a terrific crash, and the lights went out.

"I immediately hooked up the emergency batteries and as I recall, cut in a couple of sections of the quenched gap. Then I sat down to the receiver, and the SS *West Hartland's* apparatus nearly tore my ears off with a full power 'SOS SOS SOS, Any Ship. Struck some ship off Port Townsend!'

"I did not open up until Victoria, about ten miles away, came on and asked, 'What Ship'? I replied, 'It's (Governor) WGR.' We chit-chatted a moment, then KPH gave a call for details.

"The SS *West Hartland* KEGS, kept banging in and in between times was in touch with KPH, VAK and Operator Greenway at the Seattle Harbor Station KPE.

"It was very quiet after the first shock. Ralph Butler, my assistant, showed up at the radio room in a few minutes in his skivvies. I remember telling him to go below and get dressed, as he would scare the passengers; then to report to the bridge. He replied that our room was full of steam (we were right off the engine room on the port side below). After a few minutes, someone came by and asked how I was doing, then disappeared.

"I did not actually send an SOS. KEGS was doing a good job with a 2 kw transmitter and I saw no reason for cluttering up the air. I never did see Butler again until we met shoreside. There was no commotion and the ship was settling evenly, although I didn't know it. After a few moments more I rang the bridge for instructions, but received no answer. I tried two or three times, when I felt the ship give a little tremor and began listing.

"Thinking I better find out what was going on, I took off my phones and stepped over the sill into the dance floor. I saw no one.

"Just about then, the SS *West Hartland's* searchlight came on from about a quarter-mile away, and I could see the water almost at my feet, although I was on the next to the hurricane deck. It seemed like a good time to adopt an old Navy slogan, so I decided to . . . 'get the --- out of there.'

"I returned to the radio room, put on my cap, buttoned my coat, picked up my watch, took my licenses off the wall, picked up some cash from the desk drawer and the top sheet from my log, grabbed a life preserver and went to the rail. There was evidently a boat or two out there somewhere, because as I stood there, still not sure she was going down, the searchlight on me, someone yelled, 'Jump, you --- fool!', so I jumped over the rail into the water.

"I threw away the life preserver, because I couldn't swim with it on, and I'm a good swimmer, even in the water at a temperature of about 45 degrees. However, I was less than 50 feet from the *Governor* when she slid down by the stern until her bow was pointing straight up beside me. In the searchlight she looked like the Empire State Building, and then I got scared!

"Just about then, her stern hit the bottom at 240 feet and her pilot house jarred loose. I heard later that it drifted ashore near Port Townsend but I was doing a good Australian crawl for the Point Wilson light, leaving a rooster tail in my wake. I thought the old gal would topple over on me, and I didn't want any part of that!

"I had gone about a hundred yards or so, when a lifeboat picked me up. I heard later that it was the skipper's boat. As far as I know I was the last to leave the ship. I wasn't trying to be a hero—just didn't know she was going under.

"Butler later told me that he went below, and fighting steam and wreckage completely dressed, including peacoat, and went to the bridge where he was told to get in a lifeboat immediately. I guess he forgot to tell me.

"I'll say again that when I looked over my shoulder and saw some 250 feet of *Governor* looming over my head, I upped my swimming speed by several knots."

The *Governor,* a stately passenger ship of 5,474 tons, measured 392 feet in length; she carried 540 passengers and a crew of 120. Her service speed was 15.4 knots. On her final voyage she was commanded by Captain E. P. Bartlett, who handled the evacuation of the passengers and crew with commendable tact. The *West Hartland* was skippered by Captain John Alwen, who three years earlier was master of the SS *Umatilla* when it sank off the coast of Japan. Owned by the Pacific Coast Steamship Co., the *Governor* broke all existing records on the run from San Francisco to Seattle in 1913 by covering the distance in only 49 hours, dock to dock. A near sister to the SS *President,* the *Governor* was a favorite with passengers. She was built at Camden, N. J. in 1907.

The *West Hartland* had just left Seattle and Port Townsend bound for Bombay (under the U.S. Shipping Board) and after the wreck, limped back to Seattle with a badly bashed snout. The *Governor* was about six miles south of Victoria, where she had let off some northbound passengers. She was steaming slowly toward Seattle when the ships locked horns in an awful grinding of steel. Fortunately, only

A stern view of the capsized SS **PRESIDENT MADISON** at the Todd yard in March, 1933, with salvage work underway. After six years of idleness, the **PRESIDENT MADISON** was sold to Philippine interests headed by Jose Cojuangco, Manila sugar magnate. It is reported that $350,000 in cash was brought to Seattle in a suitcase in exchange for the liner. Skippered by Captain C. J. Onrubia, the vessel was given minor repairs and the name **PRESIDENT QUEZON.** She sailed for the Orient, via Long Beach, Calif. with a 10,500 ton cargo, but while going to the aid of a vessel in distress, she herself ran hard aground off the island of Tanegashima, Japan January 16, 1940 and became a total loss. One of her crew perished. *Joe Williamson photo.*

The crumpled bow of the SS **WEST HARTLAND** pictured here, was the weapon that pierced the sleek coastwise passenger liner SS **GOVERNOR** April 1, 1921, and sent her to the bottom one mile off Point Wilson. The two ships struck at 12:04 a.m. Several minutes later, the **GOVERNOR**, went down in 200 feet (wreck still marked on USC&GS charts), claiming five passengers and three crew members. The failure of Pilot Marsden of the **GOVERNOR** to change course in time to avoid the collision, after he confused shore lights with those of the ship, was perhaps the main reason for the crash. The **GOVERNOR** was moving at 15 knots, the **HARTLAND** at six. Both Captain John Alwen of the freighter and the **GOVERNOR'S** Captain E. P. Bartlett, were exonerated of blame. The **GOVERNOR** was operating as a unit of the Admiral Line, and the **WEST HARTLAND** was a U. S. Shipping Board freighter.

eight persons lost their lives despite the quickness with which the liner plunged to the bottom.

Major blame for the accident fell on the shoulders of the *Governor's* pilot, Captain Thomas Marsden who failed to change course in time, apparently because the lights of the *West Hartland* became confused with those at Fort Flagler on Marrowstone Island.

The simplicity of Wolcott's description of the *Governor's* loss made it seem like a light-hearted affair but actually the drama ran high when the two ships struck each other nigh on to midnight.

Passengers streamed out of their staterooms. The lights remained on for a few minutes and then everything was in total darkness, so noted William Lane, the quartermaster at the wheel on the *West Hartland*. It was the searchlight from the freighter that was the only means of lighting up the ill-fated liner in those last final moments.

"I was at the wheel of the *West Hartland* and was steering according to orders," Lane recalled. "The captain was on the bridge and the first I knew of impending approaching danger was when he came into the pilot house and said, more to himself than to me, 'I wonder where that fellow *(Governor)* is going?' With that he walked out and 30 seconds later he blew one blast on the whistle. Immediately the *Governor* answered with three blasts of her whistle.

"Immediately the *West Hartland* signaled for full speed astern. We were at that time about five lengths, or 2,000 feet away from the *Governor*. It seemed about 30 seconds before the propeller stopped and then another 30 seconds before they started astern. In that minute we plunged ahead a considerable distance toward the *Governor*. I focused my eyes on the *Governor*, realizing that we were about to collide and knowing we were in grave danger. I saw the prow of the *West Hartland* when she was 20 feet away from the side of the *Governor*. Then I braced myself for the shock, at the same time keeping my eyes on the *Governor*. I watched the prow of the *West Hartland* bury her nose into the very heart of the *Governor*."

"After we struck, the captain of the *West Hartland* ordered 'full speed ahead' to keep the hole in the *Governor* plugged up. When our bow began sliding out of the hole in the *Governor*, the order of the captain of the *West Hartland* was 'hard aport wheel' this, I believe, to keep the vessel close by. It was then 12:04 a.m."

The *West Hartland* had the right of way, findings later revealed. The *Governor* went down in deep water off Point Wilson, irretrievably lost.

Explosion on Bunker Hill

At approximately 0402 on March 6, 1964, while the SS *Bunker Hill* was en route from Tacoma, Washington to Anacortes in waters of Puget Sound, (in 48 degrees 23 minutes North 122 degrees 45 minutes West), there occurred an ear-rending explosion.

The 10,590 ton T-2 tanker *Bunker Hill* was ripped apart by a blast, originating in No. 9 cargo tanks. In less than an hour, the 504 foot tanker went down and of the 31 persons on board only the master, Captain M. J. Abraham and four crew members who were in the midship house, perished.

It was still dark when the violent explosion occurred. The vessel broke in two along a diagonal line between the after end of the No. 9 starboard wing tank. The forward portion of the vessel veered to port and immediately started settling by the after end. As soon as the first explosion was over, the lookout who was on the bow went into the rope locker below and obtained a life preserver. By the time he started back up the ladder to the foc's'cle head, the after portion of the bow section had settled in the water sufficiently that the deck was at an angle of about 45 degrees. As he completed fastening his life jacket, a second violent explosion occurred in the No. 4 center tank and he was engulfed in fire. After that, everything went blank and he could not remember anything else until safely aboard a rescue craft.

Following the explosion, the night engineer on watch in the engine room slowed the main propulsion turbine, and left. The emergency lights had come on. The 440 volt, 400 kw generator circuit breaker having been tripped, stopped most of the electric motors, including the main and auxiliary circulating pumps. Following the engineer out of the recesses were the firemen and water tender. The chief engineer then ordered the oiler out of the engine room and after a quick inspection to see that nobody was left behind, he abandoned the engine room also.

On the after portion of the ship, crew members attempted to launch the starboard lifeboat. In the darkness someone inadvertently released the inboard gripes first. The increasing starboard list created a hazardous situation for anyone attempting to release the outboard gripes, and instead, the port lifeboat was lowered. While going down the falls, however, the boat was flooded by gushes of water coming out of the overboard discharge from the main condenser. The boat was in a swamped condition when it left the side of the tanker. Seven crewmen stayed on the after portion of the ship, and the remainder abandoned ship either by jumping into the water or in the lifeboat.

In the interim, the scene of devastation was observed by lookouts in the Naval Air Station control tower at Ault field on Whidbey Island, five miles away. They spread the word of the explosion and rescue operations were immedia-

tely initiated. Within 45 minutes all of the survivors were picked up by Coast Guard helicopter and the remaining 22 men by a Navy crash boat.

The disaster pointed out the ever present danger of ships engaged in petroleum transportation. The source of ignition was believed due to a magnesium anode or a piece of the chemical wash pipe falling in the tank; and that the application of the gas exhauster lowered the petroleum vapor air concentration to the critical range for explosion.

The board of inquiry which met after the sinking ruled that magnesium anodes should be removed from all tank vessels reducing danger of an incendive spark.

Had the explosion occurred on the high seas or in rough weather the hasty abandonment could have resulted in more deaths.

In the pre-explosion hours it had been shipboard life as usual on the tanker. The main propulsion unit was purring at 7,000 hp. On the bridge, Captain Abraham and the junior third mate were on duty. On deck the chief pumpman and two seamen under supervision of the chief mate were cleaning cargo tanks and associated piping.

In calm waters, the ship was proceeding at about 15 knots on a northerly course in Rosario Strait and was to have arrived at Anacortes at 0600. Due to the vessel's light load condition and her speed, she experienced severe vibration. All operating equipment and machinery, however, was functioning normally when the explosion occurred.

The *Bunker Hill* went down in deep water beyond profitable salvage and became the cript of five unfortunate seafarers.

Aground at Apple Tree Cove, Puget Sound, August 24, 1911, the Union Oil tanker **SANTA RITA.** Several hours later, the vessel was refloated but had sustained $20,000 in bottom damages. The 430 foot vessel, built in 1901, was unique as one of the early tankers, featuring twin stacks with a large U suspended on brackets.

Awkward posture—the steam tug **WALLOWA** aground at Ben Ure Bay, Washington in 1902. She was eventually refloated just as in 1898 when she struck an uncharted rock off Mary Island, Alaska. The **WALLOWA** had her brighter moments also. She played a major role in the movie, Tugboat Annie in the 1930's. Later named the **ARTHUR FOSS**, and converted to diesel power, the wooden-hulled vessel was still afloat at this writing as the **THEODORE FOSS**. Her owners, Foss Launch and Tug Company have since presented her to Save Our Ships, a non-profit ship preservation society and restored her name, **ARTHUR FOSS**. She was built at Portland, Oregon before the turn of the century. (1889).

Rammed by the freighter **PARAISO** in the fog at her Seattle pier, the SS **ADMIRAL WATSON** went down in 15 minutes. Captain M. M. Jenson, master of the **WATSON**, ordered the mooring lines cut and let his vessel go down in shallow water. The incident occurred on August 29, 1915. The **PARAISO** was only slightly damaged. A major salvage job was undertaken to raise the 2,009 ton Pacific Steamship Company coastal liner. During her career, the **WATSON** also suffered major strandings at Ivory Island, Milbanke Sound, B.C. in 1927 and at Waada Island in 1910. Both times she was salvaged. *From Joe Williamson files.*

Stranded on Waada Island off Neah Bay, September 1, 1910, the SS **WATSON** was a victim of the fog. The ship's bottom plates were extensively damaged but there were no injuries among the passengers and crew. A major salvage job freed the ship which in later years was rebuilt as the SS **ADMIRAL WATSON**. In the above photo, the damages incurred came to $23,000. Some $30,000 in cargo was removed while the vessel was still aground. U.S. Lifesaving crew at Neah Bay came to the aid of the stranded ship, and this was one of their official photos.

Crashing into the dock at Tacoma, Washington December 28, 1921, the steamer **VIRGINIA IV** of the West Pass Transportation Company, probably came out second best. She was refloated, pumped out and towed away for repairs.

Grim moment! The 192 ton Island Transportation Company steamer **CALISTA** is shown after being rammed and sunk by the Japanese SS **HAWAII MARU** in the fog, July 27, 1922 off Meadow Point, on Puget Sound. All hands were removed from the **CALISTA** before she went to the bottom. Captain Bart Lovejoy was her master.

45

On July 9, 1909 in broad daylight, the veteran sidewheel steamer **YOSEMITE** went hard aground in Port Orchard Narrows at full speed. The mysterious grounding happened when the vessel suddenly swerved from her course just two miles from Bremerton on her regular run from Seattle. Breaking her back on the rocks, Captain Mike Edwards, master, said that he was avoiding the current, but it was generally believed the vessel was wrecked for her insurance, her owner, promoter C. D. Hillman, being of questionable reputation, and later going to prison on another count. The famous old Sacramento River sidewheeler dated from 1862.

River stay away from my door! No more bends of the river for the abandoned Skagit River sternwheeler **GLEANER** which ran afoul of a sandspit at the north fork of the Skagit River on December 6, 1940. Lying upstream from the North Fork Bridge, the river steamer, owned by Skagit River Trading and Navigation Company, had her machinery and fittings removed. Operating between Seattle and Mt. Vernon, the 422 ton vessel was built in 1907.

In September, 1923, the new motor vessel **RUBAIYAT** of the Puget Sound Freight Lines capsized and sank in Tacoma Harbor shortly after loading a cargo of gypsum for Seattle. The vessel began listing to port when Captain G. F. Ryan turned the wheel in the opposite direction. The vessel did not recover. She rolled over and went down with four of her crewmen. Captain Ryan and seven others were picked up by the steamer **FULTON**. The vessel, built only a few months earlier, was the target of a major recovery job. In a novel salvage experiment, the 88 ton craft was raised with slings from 380 feet of water, in March 1924 and eventually beached, as seen above. The wreck was rebuilt as the motor ferry **CITY OF KINGSTON** and later as the **LAKE CONSTANCE**.

Like a ship out of Dante's inferno, the steamer **URANIA** was a charred mess after burning at Houghton, Washington, on Lake Washington, February 12, 1914. Built at Seattle, seven years earlier, the steamer was owned by Captain J. L. Anderson. The bow section of the 93 ton vessel was rebuilt into a 65 foot passenger steamer and used many years thereafter.

46

Running water in every room. The Puget Sound passenger steamer **DODE**, which started her life as the schooner **WILLIAM J. BRYANT** at Hoquiam in 1896, was wrecked at Marrowstone Point, July 20, 1910 at 6:45 a.m., bound for Seattle, in command of Captain Charles Stanley. Salvage efforts got underway but the **DODE** was too far gone to be retrieved. Her 300 hp engine was removed and placed in the tug **FOREST CROSBY**. Note mattresses piled in lifeboat. *Torku's Studio photo.*

Dense clouds of smoke pour from the furiously burning Japanese freighter **TOKUYO MARU**, afire 60 miles southwest of the Columbia River May 3, 1921. The fire had eaten into the $200,000 cargo of sodium nitrates that had been loaded in Chile. The furiously burning vessel drifted northward and finally went down with the loss of eight of her crew. The others were rescued by the SS **SANTA ALICIA**. The ship was outbound from the Columbia River for Japan when the fire broke out.

Canadian Pacific's steamer **PREMIER** was almost cut in half after being struck by the steam collier **WILLAMETTE** 1½ miles southeast of Marrowstone Point at 2 a.m. October 8, 1892. Four persons were killed on the **PREMIER** by the impact. The vessels were solidly locked for 24 hours, the **WILLAMETTE** pushing the **PREMIER** aground on Bush Point to keep her from sinking. Twenty others on the **PREMIER** were injured. The **WILLAMETTE** was able to proceed under her own power after the separation, and went to Seattle for repairs. The **PREMIER** was raised by Commodore John Irving and taken to Victoria, repaired and placed under the British flag as the SS **CHARMER** for the Vancouver and Victoria run.

Photograph of the Seattle-Port Blakely steamer **DIX** taken a few months before her tragic collision with the steam schooner **JEANIE** off Alki Point, November 18, 1906. There were 77 persons aboard the **DIX**. Captain Percy Lermond of the **DIX** was below collecting tickets, when mate Dennison, at the wheel, got his signals mixed up and ran right across the path of the much more ruggedly built **JEANIE**. It was over in a matter of minutes, 39 dead or missing on the **DIX**. The virtually undamaged **JEANIE** picked up 38 survivors, including Captain Lermond. Captain P. H. Mason was master of the **JEANIE**.

Some of the survivors of the steamer **DIX** disaster photographed following the tragic episode. The only female saved was a Miss Alice Simpson, 17. She lived in Bremerton for many years thereafter (Mrs. J. E. Bassett). Most of those pictured here were employed by the Port Blakely Mill Company.

Aerial view (official Coast Guard), of the motor vessel **ALASKA REEFER,** owned by Alaska Reefer Fisheries, afire off Point Partridge, Whidbey Island, Puget Sound, August 29, 1961. The 174 foot reefer ship, returning from Bristol Bay with frozen salmon, carried a crew of 12, all of whom were safely removed by the Coast Guard and commercial craft. The stubborn fire continued and the vessel was finally towed to a beach at Whalen Point on Indian Island in Port Townsend Bay where she rolled over and sank in 20 feet of water. The wreck is marked on C&GS charts and has been visited by many skin divers. Most of the useable gear has been stripped off. The **ALASKA REEFER** was built in 1944.

Like a plunging whale, the Greek freighter **HELLENIC SKIPPER** raises her snout in the air on her final plunge 125 miles off Grays Harbor following a mysterious explosion on July 10, 1940. Only a short time earlier, the ship had been sold in Seattle to Greek interests by the Alaska Steamship Company, with whom she had operated as the SS **CURACAO**. Miraculously no lives were lost, though the crew was badly shaken up as they took to the boats. The vessel had last loaded lumber at Grays Harbor. Less than a day out, she caught on fire and 20 minutes later, exploded. The 17 crewmen drifted in the boats for two days before being picked up by a fish-boat and transferred to a Coast Guard vessel from Astoria. The 257 foot Greek vessel was built as a passenger liner at Philadelphia in 1895.

Mountain high swell erupts almost burying the stranded wooden steam schooner **TRINIDAD**, driven ashore in a 60 mile gale between buoys 6 and 7 at the entrance to Willapa Bay, May 7, 1937. She was en route to San Francisco from Raymond with lumber. The daring work of H. J. Perssons and his Coast Guard motor lifeboat saved the skipper and 21 crewmen, only one life being lost. The vessel drove up on the north spit when Captain I. Hellestone, trying to put about, got into trouble, not far from the Willapa Light. Distress flares were sighted by the Coast Guard and the rescue undertaken.

You are standing on the forecastle of the SS **FENN VICTORY**. You have just knifed into the side of the MS **DIAMOND KNOT** giving her a fatal blow. The date is August 13, 1947; the place six miles from Port Angeles in the Strait of Juan de Fuca. What would you do? The **DIAMOND KNOT** was returning from Alaska with a $3½ million cargo of canned salmon. The two vessels were tightly locked together, the impact occurring at 1:15 a.m. Both vessels drifted westward and soon a fleet of rescue ships were on the scene. The **FOSS NO. 12** and the **SALVAGE CHIEFTAIN**, helped by the Coast Guard, pulled the two ships apart. The **MATHILDA FOSS** and **FOSS NO. 21** attempted to pull the mortally wounded **DIAMOND KNOT** to shallow water where she could be beached. Her crew was removed; the **DIAMOND KNOT** could not hold back the torrent pouring into her inwards. She went down in 17 fathoms off Crescent Bay, northwest of Port Angeles. Here, she became the target of a novel salvage operation to recover her valuable cargo. Walter Martignoni of Pillsbury & Martignoni, (San Francisco salvage engineers), and Captain Loring Hyde with Walter McCray and Fred Devine, the best collection of salvage experts and divers available, teamed up to recover more than $2.1 million of the cargo by use of a giant compressed air vacuum sweeper. The **FENN VICTORY** went to Seattle for repairs.

Broken in half on Peacock Spit, at the entrance to the Columbia River, the SS **LAUREL**, an inter-coastal freighter of the Quaker Line, was a total loss. She was wrecked June 16, 1929, when she suffered steering gear trouble outbound with a full cargo of lumber for New York and Philadelphia. The ship was driven aground and almost immediately began to show signs of breaking up. The mad array of lumber, spread all over the water, prevented the CG cutter **REDWING** from perfecting a rescue, and one of the **LAUREL'S** crewmen was killed. The next day, the ship parted, just forward of the bridge. Finally the Coast Guard rescued all but Captain Louis Johnson, who refused to leave his ship. He kept a vigil for 54 hours before finally surrendering, figuring there was no longer hope of salvaging the after part of the ship. Hailed as a hero by the press, the inspectors later reprimanded him for failing to make use of emergency steering gear and suspended his license for 90 days. The **LAUREL** was a World War I vintage vessel of 5,759 gross tons.

Caught in a sea of driftwood, the 72 foot cannery tender **SUSAN**, was totally wrecked in the area known as Peacock Spit, near the Columbia River north jetty. The **SUSAN** was driven ashore in a blinding snow storm, the Coast Guard lifeboat rescuing Tom Delahunt and Jack Sheridan, the only two aboard. The vessel was built at Seattle 1920. The incident occurred January 21, 1952. *Arnold Hariju photo.*

Something's missing on this vessel. Pummelled by the Pacific surf, the steam schooner **CAOBA**, (ex **COASTER**), lies a wreck on the beach five miles north of Ocean Park, Washington. She was outbound with lumber from Willapa Harbor for San Francisco on February 5, 1925, when she encountered a gale which opened her seams and disabled her engine, causing her to drive ashore. At the height of the storm the crew abandoned in the boats. One boat was picked up by the Grays Harbor tug **JOHN CUDAHY** and the other by the rum-runner **PESCAWHA**, which after landing the survivors in Astoria was seized, her crew jailed and the ship confiscated. Though the government was roasted by the public over the incident, Captain Robert Pamphlet went to prison, despite his humane act. The **CAOBA**, operated by Sudden & Christenson, was skippered by Captain Alfred Sandvig. The vessel was a total loss.

Beauty and the shipwreck! Bathing belles of 1927 gather on the North Beach Penninsula in the summer sun to have their pictures taken with the wreck of the **CAOBA** in the background. The vessel was wrecked two years earlier. Only her old boiler marks the grave at this writing.

The next thing to a total wreck—the Norwegian freighter **CHILDAR** under tow of the Coast Guard tug **REDWING** after running aground on the southwest end of Peacock Spit, at the entrance to the Columbia River, in a severe gale May 3, 1934. Within a short while her masts were ripped out, her deckload of lumber splintered to pieces and four crewmen killed. Down to her marks with lumber, the ship was outbound when cascading seas drove her off course and into the breakers. Lt. A. W. Davis, pulled a remarkable feat of seamanship when he maneuvered the **REDWING** in and got a line on the **CHILDAR**. Fearing to take the ship back across the bar he began a nerve straining 58 hour tow up the coast toward Puget Sound. En route, the remainder of the **CHILDAR'S** crew was removed by the motor lifeboats from Grays Harbor. Partially flooded and highly unwieldly, the tow continued. Finally taken into Esquimalt, B. C., the 4,138 ton ship was almost completely rebuilt and later renamed **AAKRE**. She was owned by Weil & Amundsen of Halden, Norway and originally built in 1926. *Official Coast Guard photo.*

One of the most bizarre tragedies to occur at the entrance to the Columbia River was the loss of the SS **IOWA**, driven onto Peacock Spit, January 12, 1936 with the loss of her entire crew of 34. A Coast Guard motor lifeboat stands by here, overlooking the grim scene. **IOWA** was totally raked by savage breakers, formed by 76 mile-an-hour winds. It was never known why the **IOWA**, operating for the Quaker Line (States Line subsidiary), crossed out over the bar into such a terrible gale at 4 a.m., instead of waiting more favorable conditions—but Captain Edgar L. Yates, an experienced master, and his crew all perished, and dead men tell no tales. Only one faint distress message was heard and only six bodies were recovered. The Coast Guard cutter **ONONDAGA** went out to assist, but it was too late. The 5,724 gross ton **IOWA**, was built at South San Francisco in 1920 as the **WEST CADRON**. *Photo by Sherman Ellis.*

Man's control stops at the shore! Destructive breakers rip into the Russian SS **VASLAV VOROVSKY**, hopelessly aground on Peacock Spit at the entrance to the Columbia River. The freighter ran aground April 3, 1941, packed with a full cargo of machinery and general cargo for Vladivostok. The 374 foot vessel, after clearing Astoria at midnight, encountered a 40 mile southerly gale while crossing the bar. In an attempt to come about, the steering mechanism jammed and the anchors were dropped to keep her from grounding. They failed to hold and the vessel went on the spit. Three Coast Guard vessels took off the 37 man crew, including two women. Captain T. Tokareff, aware of the penalty for losing a ship under the harsh law of Joseph Stalin, elected to remain with the wreck, but 24 hours later the vessel developed serious cracks fore and aft, and he yielded and was taken off by the Coast Guard. The old freighter, built in England in 1912, was of 4,793 gross tons. Both she and her $1.7 million cargo were a total loss. In the photo, Cape Disappointment Lighthouse can be seen in the background.

The forward section of the MS **DIAMOND KNOT,** (owned by the government and operated by Alaska Steamship Co.), partially awash a short time before she plunged to her watery grave in the summer of 1947. The wreck was abandoned after her cargo was salvaged but several skin divers have visited it since, one succeeding in removing the ship's huge bronze propeller.

The destructive teamwork of sea and sand can be seen here as the Russian SS **VASLAV VOROVSKY** breaks up. Note how seas have torn away the starboard bridge wing and worked the hull on the spit until it split into three sections. When the mishap occurred, the freighter was outbound from Portland for Siberia in April, 1941. *Joe Williamson photo.*

The old four-masted schooner **KING CYRUS** works on the beach after grounding at Point Chehalis, at the entrance to Grays Harbor, July 17, 1922. The 717 ton vessel, built at Port Blakely in 1890, was inbound from Honolulu under tow, when she went aground. The crew of the lumber schooner was rescued by the local lifesaving surfmen but the schooner eventually broke up and became a total loss.

Unwieldly tow—the nearly submerged coastal freighter **C-TRADER**, a 256 foot long vessel laden with 2.4 million board feet of lumber, lost steerageway early on the morning of December 6, 1963, five miles off Willapa Bay, en route from Raymond to Los Angeles. The W. R. Chamberlin & Co. vessel began taking on water, and despite the 1,000 gallons per minute pump, the ship could not hold back the inflow. Captain F. Leary sent out an SOS, and chief engineer G. F. Steiner and his black gang were forced up out of the flooded engine room. The **SALVAGE CHIEF** rushed out of Astoria to take the foundering vessel in tow and managed to get her safely inside the Columbia River, as seen in the above photo, when the stern sank and the entire vessel filled. The **SALVAGE CHIEF** beached her inshore from the main ship channel where there was hope of salvaging the vessel. The breakers however, soon did considerable structural damage to the **C-TRADER** and eventually she had to be dismantled as a menace to navigation. The 2,392 ton vessel was built at Camden, N. J., in 1944, as the **LAUCHIAN McKAY**.

Future voyages cancelled for an indefinite period. The veteran Pacific Coast Company passenger steamer **CITY OF TOPEKA** found herself at the bottom of Elliott Bay alongside Seattle's Pier A after mysteriously sinking in 1904. Built at Chester, Pa. in 1884 for the Atchison, Topeka and Santa Fe Railway, she came west in 1886 and operated many years thereafter. She was raised from this watery position and repaired. Two years later she played a major role in the **VALENCIA** disaster off Vancouver Island.

A nasty place to be. The 3,321 ton lumber barge **GEORGE OLSON** (ex steamer), broke loose from the veteran tug **MIKIMIKI** while crossing the Columbia River bar with a full load of lumber at 1:20 a.m. January 30, 1964. Coast Guard vessels went to the aid of the runaway barge and got lines on it, and began the tricky tow toward Astoria in rough waters. But the 321 foot jumbo barge had been damaged in crossing the bar and was sinking fast. To prevent her from sinking in the channel, they drove her aground on the seaward side of Jetty A, 1,350 yards off Cape Disappointment Light. When the Coast Guard cutter **YOCONA** arrived on the scene she reported a third of the barge had broken off at the stern and the lumber was all breaking loose. The vessel carried 3.5 million board feet of lumber. Owned by Oliver Olson & Co., the barge, a short time earlier had been converted from a steel steam schooner, built originally in 1919, as the **CASTLE TOWN.**

The big French "bounty" bark **ERNEST REYER** stranded at the entrance to the Quinault River, Washington, December 4, 1901. The crew managed to get safely to the beach but the surf made short work of the ship which was virtually new. She was built just a year earlier in France. A great gale was blowing when the bark grounded. A new **ERNEST REYER** was launched in France, 18 months later and she was sunk by a German U-boat in 1916. *Courtesy Harold Huycke.*

The huge German bark **ALSTER-NIXE**, 3,059 tons had a miraculous escape from dreaded Peacock Spit, where few ships have ever been freed. In command of Captain Richard Auhagen, the Hamburg-registered vessel stranded 1½ miles southwest of Cape Disappointment Light when she got out of the marked channel in heavy weather at dusk, February 9, 1903. The lifesaving crew was on the scene quickly to remove the ship's complement. After several weeks of intensive salvage work the big ship made her escape and was taken to Esquimalt, B. C. for repairs. She returned to Portland in time to hold onto her lumber charter. *Supplied by Charles Fitzpatrick.*

A combine of a full gale and contrary currents put the British ship **KILBRANNAN** hard aground near Point Wilson, Washington on the morning of February 5, 1896. The 1,573 ton iron-hulled ship commanded by Captain N. McCallum, found five of Puget Sound's most powerful tugs at her side at daylight. Despite their full combined thrust they could not move her. She lay on the beach for several months, her fate being in doubt. Finally a new channel was dredged about her and the battered vessel was refloated and taken to Esquimalt. There she was abandoned to the underwriters and sold to Captain Richard Chilcott, Seattle shipping agent. At Quartermaster Harbor drydock on Puget Sound, the ship had 44 new plates installed, five frames and a rebuilt keel, emerging as the **MARION CHILCOTT**, for operation with Barneson & Chilcott.

British ship **POLTALLOCH**, en route to Puget Sound to load grain for the United Kingdom, got ashore near Cape Shoalwater, at the entrance to Willapa Bay, November 26, 1900. The vessel spent several months on the sands, many believing she would be a total loss. Her master, Captain Young, stayed by his ship for more than a year, conducting salvage operations which eventually paid off for the 2,250 ton vessel, owned by Potter Brothers of London. The **POLTALLOCH** eventually went under the American flag. *Courtesy Chas. Fitzpatrick.*

Being sucked down into the sands, to be buried in her own cargo of cement, the French ship **ALICE**, was doomed immediately after being wrecked January 15, 1909, in a gale, at the end of a 176 day passage. She was seeking a pilot to enter the Columbia River after arriving from London, via Hobart, Australia. The 2,509 ton vessel finally ground ashore, and the barking of a dog, alerted a boy who in turn alerted the Klipsan lifesaving station; the horses were soon pulling the surfboat down the beach approach on the North Beach Penninsula of Washington. By the time they arrived, most of crew had gained the beach. The 3,000 tons of cement in the holds, consigned to Hind, Rolph & Co. at Portland, solidified holding the masts up for several years, the last one tumbling in the 1930s.

Wrong port. The SS **LAKE GEBHART** ran aground in the fog at Toleak Point, south of Hoh Head, May 9, 1923 while carrying a cargo of salt. She slipped from the reef four days later and went to her grave in the Giants Graveyard, six miles south of the Quillayute River. The crew of the vessel had earlier abandoned without incident. The 2,810 ton vessel, owned by the U. S. Shipping Board, had just a short while earlier been purchased by the Alaska Steamship Company. Part of her cargo was removed before she sank; only the tip of her mast broke the surface.

Outbound from Aberdeen with a full cargo of lumber and pulp, the SS **TEXMAR**, a Liberty type freighter of the Calmar Line, ran aground on a mud bar just off the main channel near Moon Island in Grays Harbor, December 30, 1960. Headed for East Coast ports, the **TEXMAR** grounded while attempting to cross from the upper range into the cross-over channel leading to the bar. Two tugs attempted to remove her, but the heavy load the ship was carrying caused her back to break as some of the sand and mud was washed out from under her keel. The Army Corps of Engineers took over, soliciting for bids for her removal. The cargo was retreived, and Quigg, McDonald, of Hoquiam was low bidder for removal of the vessel at $233,800. The ship was dismantled piece by piece until it was no longer a menace to navigation. The vessel, built in 1945 was the ex **HAROLD WILSON**, ex **NORTH BEACON**. *Official U.S. Army Engineer District photo.*

Death of a ship. Broken in half, the SS **SEAGATE** opens the floodgates to the hostile Pacific. The Greek-owned, Liberian flag, ex American Liberty ship was the victim of mysterious circumstances when she stranded on Sonora Reef, off the Washington coast on September 9, 1956 inbound from Japan to Vancouver, B. C., and 100 miles off course. The ship's master blamed fog and faulty gyro compasses. Three tugs worked for the better part of a week to free the ship, then after removal of the **SEAGATE'S** crew, abandoned the vigil; the freighter slipped off the reef, totally abandoned, and drifted ashore just south of the Quinault River, 30 miles north of Grays Harbor. The CG cutter **WACHUSETT** located the wreck and two Canadian and one American tug rushed to the scene. But the little Grays Harbor tug **A. G. HUBBLE** was there first, and put three men aboard, claiming salvage rights on the abandoned ship. Allman–Hubble and Foss teamed up on a salvage effort, but the ship had already broken in two. In the above photo, note would-be salvager on the starboard bridge wing, brought out to the wreck by helicopter.

Another view of the two halves of the SS **SEAGATE**. Note the water-filled holds. In later minor salvage efforts much of the steel was removed from the wreck before the Pacific made its final assault.

Another view of the wounded SS **TEXMAR** abandoned after running aground in the Grays Harbor channel, outbound in the intercoastal trade, in 1960. *U.S. Army Engineers photo.*

When Captain Cairny, mistook Grays Harbor Light for the one at North Head the night of January 22, 1919, the five-masted schooner **JANET CARRUTHERS,** (Canadian flag), of the Canadian West Coast Navigation Company, ended up beach four miles north of Grays Harbor jetty. While trying to escape the wreck, six crew members were drowned when their boat upset in the surf. At low tide the following day the others were able to virtually walk ashore. The 240 foot wooden-hulled vessel, built at the Wallace yards in Vancouver, B. C. two years earlier, was outbound from Tacoma to Astoria to finish loading lumber for Shanghai when the accident occurred. Salvage efforts got underway, but were halted when claims of polluting the clam beach were lodged by the state fisheries department. The vessel soon broke up.

She escaped! The stranded Liberty type freighter **LIPARI** on the beach near Grayland, seven miles south of Grays Harbor, Washington. She went aground October 23, 1959 and was stranded for eight days before being freed by Fred Devine's **SALVAGE CHIEF,** out of Astoria. The **SALVAGE CHIEF** was aided by Wes Lematta and his Portland helicopter, which flew messenger lines back and forth, until its blade hit a davit on the wreck, and crashed. Lematta survived. As the CG cutter **YOCONA** stood by, the rest of the work came off as planned and the ship was taken to Portland after being freed. There, the survey showed it would cost $300,000 to properly repair the ship, far more than its value. She was in turn towed to Japan and scrapped. The **LIPARI** was owned by the Aoelian Steamship Corp. The stranding occurred in the fog and was blamed on faulty navigation equipment.

One of the most dramatic episodes in the North Pacific was when Coast Guard personnel helped rescue 54 crew members, including eight women from the Russian freighter **LAMUT** trapped inside the inescapable Quillayute Needles off the Washington Coast. One of the rescued women was injured and another woman killed when a cable snapped dropping the bow of a lifeboat into the sea. The ship was driven aground in a storm, after losing her bearings, March 31, 1943. Rolling over on her beam ends, the vessel could not be reached from the sea. Coast Guardsmen had to scale the towering Needles and from a ledge, using their shoestrings tied together, drop them to the wreck in order to pull up a line. The line made fast, the Russians had to get to the ledge hand over hand. All made it. The vessel, built in 1919 as the **LAKE ELPUEBLO**, had been en route to Vladivostok from Puget Sound when wrecked. *Coast Guard aerial photo.*

Coastguardsmen hover on a ledge of the Quillayute Needles in April, 1943 from where they rescued the 54 members of the crew of the Russian SS **LAMUT**. This CG air photo shows the dramatic scene. It was only a miracle that the crew was saved. Americans intervened on behalf of the ship's skipper so that Joseph Stalin would not put him to death over the loss of his ship.

Beachcombers delight—wreck of the big German bark POT-RIMPOS, lying on the broad sand beach north of Long Beach, Washington. This is what happened as the result of a salvage operation that failed. The wreck occurred December 19, 1896, when the ship, in command of Captain Hellewegge, en route to Portland from Hamburg, via Manzanillo, drifted on the beach seven miles north of the Ilwaco lifesaving station, in heavy fog, at 9:30 a.m. The peninsula railroad (Ilwaco RR and Navigation Co.) was dispatched to carry lifesaving gear to the wreck after the horses balked. Four of the crew had already gained the shore, but the lifesaving craft removed 14 others safely. Several months later, after intensive salvage efforts, the tug RELIEF and a series of well placed donkey engines were pulling the lightened bark back into the surf, with the salvage crew aboard, when suddenly the tall ship heeled over, the men narrowly escaping with their lives. The above photo shows the end result. *Courtesy Charles Fitzpatrick.*

Calmar Line's intercoastal freighter YORKMAR, commanded by Captain Oscar Kullbom, arrived off Grays Harbor in ballast in heavy weather in December of 1952. Bar conditions prevented a pilot boat from crossing the bar so the YORKMAR rode out the storm for two days. On December 8, Captain Kullbom was advised to bring his ship in to escape further punishment in the rough seas. During a lull, he started in but while near the jetty was thrown off course in a cross sea and high wind, and at the crest of the flood tide was cast high up on the sands just north of the jetty. The salvage vessel SALVAGE CHIEF, owned by Fred Devine, was called in to refloat the vessel from an area where only one known large ship had escaped, once being trapped. Wagers were heavy that the YORKMAR would be a total loss. But in just 12 days the SALVAGE CHIEF, using the Devine-method of lines from the freighter to the salvage ship, and lines from the salvage ship to heavy anchors, finally freed her, a feat hailed as one of the greatest recovery jobs of that decade. The vessel is seen aground in seething surf, from the air. On the beach is the wreck of the fishboat MURRE.

Anchors out, and pulling from a dangerous spot in the surf, the **SALVAGE CHIEF** inches the 7,200 ton **YORKMAR** off the beach in the epic marine salvage job of 1952. The **YORKMAR** was ushered off to a shipyard for repairs, which, strange to say, were not of a serious nature. *Ackroyd Photo.*

Ship of death. The sidewheeler **PACIFIC** which plunged to the bottom of the Pacific, southwest of Tatoosh Island after being struck by the ship **ORPHEUS**, November 4, 1875. Some 275 persons perished and only two survived, one of whom later died. The **ORPHEUS**, several hours later, crashed up on the West Coast of Vancouver Island, her crew escaping.

Trapped in the surf near the north entrance to Grays Harbor, the wooden steam schooner **HALCO**, stranded November 30, 1925. The Hammond Lumber Company vessel, of 970 tons, built in 1917, at Fairhaven, California become a total loss. She had long been operating in the coastwise lumber trades. *Anderson Studio photo.*

Skeleton of the four-masted schooner **SOLANO**, after it was accidentally set afire by clam diggers in 1910. The vessel ran aground February 5, 1907 in a fog, but being little damaged, immediate salvage endeavors were undertaken. They might have been successful too, if a tug had showed up to tow the vessel away. In turn, the schooner was driven even higher on the beach and became a total wreck. *Photo supplied by Art Appleton.*

Stern view of the Japanese SS **CANADA MARU** aground near Cape Flattery, victim of fog. The passenger vessel, of 5,700 tons, was inbound for Puget Sound from Japan with 176 passengers. The passengers and crew were removed from the OSK Line vessel, and a major salvage job undertaken. Badly damaged, the ship was refloated in August of 1918 seven months after stranding.

Remarkable photo of the 40,000 ton Japanese bulk carrier **CHITOSE MARU**, ripped open after being struck by the Danish MS **MARIE SKOU**, in the center of the Strait of Juan de Fuca entrance, north of Neah Bay, September 20, 1967. Inbound in ballast the new vessel, is seen here with some of the deck gear from the Danish ship lodged in her hull. The **CHITOSE**, was taken to a Canadian shipyard for repairs. *Jim Ryan photo.*

When the **MARIE SKOU** arrived at Victoria, B. C. after striking the Japanese bulk carrier **CHITOSE MARU** at the entrance to the Strait of Juan de Fuca, she looked like this. She had to be fitted with an entirely new bow section. The collision occurred in September, 1967. *Jim Ryan photo.*

Let's take five. The Kern salvage crew of Portland and their team of horses take a rest during their salvage job on the barge **COLUMBIA CONTRACT CO. NO. 38.**, which went aground in 1916, five miles south of Copalis Beach, Washington, with the loss of four men. *Courtesy Grace Kern.*

This was the final resting place of the schooner **CHARLES E. FALK** which went ashore 12 miles north of Grays Harbor, near Copalis Rocks, March 31, 1909. Her crew of eight reached shore safely. Built for N. H. Falk of Eureka, the 298 ton vessel created by H. D. Bendixsen in 1889, operated in the coastal lumber trade.

Extreme minus tide found the passenger liner **ADMIRAL BENSON** of the Pacific Steamship Company in this condition several weeks after stranding on Peacock Spit. In command of Captain C. C. Graham, February 15, 1930, the ship was inbound with 39 passengers and 65 crewmen, when she was enveloped in fog. The motor lifeboats from Point Adams and Cape Disappointment came to her aid and removed the passengers and part of the crew. Later the remaining crewmen came ashore by breeches buoy, leaving only Captain Graham aboard. He gave up on February 24. At the hearing, he pleaded guilty to negligence and had his license removed for six months. Underwriters meanwhile salvaged most of the cargo in the ship. The wreck is still marked on the USC & GC charts.

Broken in half, the Panamanian freighter **ANDALUSIA**, 7,700 tons, ran aground four miles east of Neah Bay, November 4, 1949, after fire broke out at sea. Commanded by Captain George Lemos, the vessel was outbound from Canadian ports with 5 million board feet of lumber. The fire was extinguished in 90 minutes, but before the vessel could be refloated it broke in two under the heavy cargo and became a total loss. Some of the lumber was pilfered and some legally salvaged.

Bottoms up. The motor vessel **OSHKOSH**, 145 tons, struck bottom off the south jetty of the Columbia River bar, on February 13, 1911, enroute to the Umpqua from Tillamook. She ran before a severe S. W. gale after sea water filled the fresh water tanks. Trying to enter the river, Captain Latham, found himself in dire straits when the vessel was tossed ashore and flipped over carrying six of her seven man crew to a watery grave. The one survivor struggled up on the jetty rocks and was later rescued. The **OSHKOSH** was owned by the Elmore Navigation Company. *Woodfield photo.*

American schooner **ZAMPA**, 385 tons, stranded on Point Leadbetter just south of the Willapa Harbor entrance July 17, 1904. Captain Kellenberger, his wife and crew of nine were all rescued. The schooner grounded because of losing her rudder. For several months she was a prisoner on the beach but was finally refloated, one of the only sailing vessels salvaged from that area.

It cost $210,000 to repair the SS **H. F. ALEXANDER** at the Todd drydock in Seattle after she struck Cake Rock off the Washington Coast at a high rate of speed. She crumpled her bow clear back to the foremast from the impact, August 7, 1922. Nobody was killed, but the passengers were badly shaken up. Only the collision bulkheads kept the vessel from sinking. The Pacific Steamship Company (Admiral Line) ship, one of the fastest under the American flag, earlier distinguished herself as the Army transport **GREAT NORTHERN.** After the above crash, the **ADMIRAL SCHLEY** removed 317 passengers and 135 crewmen just in case the vessel sank. Only a skeleton crew remained aboard.

The steam schooner **FRED BAXTER** rolled over on her beam ends in Port Townsend Harbor in 1920. The vessel had loaded piling at Everett for San Francisco and while outbound, her cargo shifted off Marrowstone Point, when the vessel was caught in a rip tide. Heeling over 40 degrees, a tug tried to get her to Port Townsend. But slowly, over she went on her side 100 feet off the Union Dock. The crew got safely away. Later, when W. J. Moloney inspected the hull, she turned turtle and he narrowly escaped. Washington Tug & Barge Company and a salvage crew eventually righted her at the head of the bay. She was owned by J. H. Baxter and built in 1917. 1,294 tons.

The former Great Lakes freighter **TAMPICO** of the Pacific Coast SS Company went to the bottom of Elliott Bay, Seattle while berthed at the Pacific Coast Coal Company pier, May 18, 1911. The tug **LUMBERMAN** and the fireboat **SNOQUALMIE** tried to keep her afloat, but the 2,133 ton vessel resisted their efforts. Salvage and repairs cost $50,000, after the vessel was raised in late June. The exact cause was never determined, claims against the ship's engineers being dismissed.

This photo was taken a few weeks before the Black Ball passenger steamer **CLALLAM** foundered in the Strait of Juan de Fuca, east of Point Wilson, January 9, 1904 with the loss of 54 lives. Tugs picked up 36 survivors, but most of those who perished were women and children. The **CLALLAM**, a new vessel was on her regular run to B.C. ports. Three boats were lowered and all swamped. At the subsequent hearing, Captain George Roberts had his license suspended and Chief Engineer De Launey had his revoked.

71

Study in contrasts—the lady and the shipwreck. At low tide the tramp freighter **LIPARI** is pictured aground seven miles south of Grays Harbor. The ship ground up on the sands on October 23, 1959 and was eventually refloated by the **SALVAGE CHIEF.** She was later declared too costly to repair due to damage suffered in the mishap.

Her remains now scattered on the bottom of Rosario Strait, after a sharp explosion in the early morning hours of March 6, 1964, the T-2 tanker **BUNKER HILL** is now only a memory. She is pictured here under tow of the tug **HERCULES** several months before the disaster. The 504 foot tanker built at Chester, Pa., in 1942 was in command of Captain M. J. Abraham, with R. H. Blake as first officer, when she was blown apart en route from Tacoma to Anacortes. The ship's master was one of five who lost their lives. The others were rescued by Navy and Coast Guard craft. Owned by Keystone Tankship Corp., the vessel had hauled Shell products coastwise for several years. *Photo by Joe Williamson.*

Like a toy in a basin, the trooper **GENERAL M.C. MEIGS** wrapped her carcass around a pinnacle rock and split in half in the winter of 1972—a typical example of a man-made creation testing the powers of nature. Photo by E.A. Delanty.

Storied vessel, the **BELLINGHAM** purposely set afire for Seattle's Seafare celebration in 1951. Earlier she was raised after sinking at Deer Harbor in the San Juans. She was the initial passenger ship of the Black Ball Line, Alaska Steamship Company and Northland Transportation Company, ending her days as a cargo carrier.

German ship **FLOTTBEK** in trouble near White Rock, south of Cape Flattery, Washington January, 1901. All hands were removed and the ship was eventually towed to safety by an ocean tug.

73

One of the most controversial incidents in Puget Sound piloting came about as a result of the striking of a submerged rock off Smith Island by the MS **ISLAND MAIL** of American Mail Line, May 29, 1961. Pilot Dewey Soriano elected to take a route seldom used by Puget Sound pilots. As a result of striking the rock, a 134 foot gash ten feet wide was torn in the starboard side. The vessel had to be beached in 25 feet of water off Fidalgo Island to prevent her sinking. There was heavy damage to cargo and ship, and long litigation followed. Master of the ship was H. D. Smith. The **ISLAND MAIL** is seen here after lengthy repairs at Todd Shipyard in Seattle.

Rough sailing in a sea of sand. Wreck of the ex Union Steamship Co. steamer **CATALA**, blown ashore in a storm at Shore Acres at the north entrance to Grays Harbor while serving as a sports fishermen's hotel. Photo taken by the late Wilbur Thompson in 1972.

74

Twisted wreckage of the troop transport **GENERAL M.C. MEIGS**. The vessel ran aground near Portage Head, south of Cape Flattery, January 28, 1972 after breaking loose from the tug **GEAR** towing her from Bremerton to California. Built in 1944 in New Jersey, the 622 foot vessel ended her career with a true sailor's death. Ed Delanty photo.

The former clipper ship **AMERICA** cut down to a barge went aground while under tow of the tug **LORNE** August 31, 1914. Though the **LORNE** which went aground with the **AMERICA** was eventually salvaged the **AMERICA** became a total loss.

CHAPTER FOUR

Oregon Shipwrecks

Like contrasting the beauty with the beast, so it is with the Oregon Coast, alluring, compelling grandeur fraught with an abundance of treacherous rocks, reefs, and shoals which have menaced shipping since the first native dipped his paddle in the ocean, eons ago. No shoreline in the continental United States is such a magnate for tourists due to its relatively easy access, but down through the years navigators have been constantly aware of its hazards. Before the days of bar jetties, dredging, and sophisticated navigation aids, shipwreck was legion. The sailing vessel was very susceptible especially in bar crossings, where the

Wreck of the commercial fishing vessel **KIM B**. in a pin cushion of rocks near Ten Mile Creek, six miles south of Yachats, Oregon August 31, 1982. The crew was rescued but salvage efforts failed. The vessel, out of Eureka was wrecked under mysterious circumstances

channels were unpredictable and the chance of the wind failing while in transit was an ever present concern. When the canvas fell limp and the currents were contrary with no tugboat available, it was frequently curtains for the ship and sometimes her crew as well.

Intriguing tales of shipwreck and treasure have been prevalent on the Oregon Coast since white man first came to its shores. In past centuries numerous Japanese, Taiwanese and Chinese junks, disabled at sea, were swept to Pacific Northwest shores by the Kuroshio, known to the Orientals as the 'Black Stream' due to the dark color of its waters, but better known to Americans as the Japanese Current. It is one of the world's greatest current systems starting its circuit at the northern branch of the west flowing equatorial current, traveling along the coast of Japan where it mingles with the colder northern waters of the Oyashio Current. It then sweeps like a river within an ocean eastward across the North Pacific, widening and slowing as it flows out in the Gulf of Alaska where it turns southward depositing a great variety of flotsam along the coasts of S.E. Alaska, British Columbia, Washington and Oregon before reversing its course and heading toward Hawaii and finally westward back to Oriental shores.

The Spanish learned to use the Japanese Current in their eastward voyages from the Indies which always made the passages of the galleons more acceptable than the more southerly routes. Vessels made their landfalls on both the Oregon and northern California coast before sailing southward to New Spain (Mexico). Sometimes they were wrecked en route and frequently their chronicle went unrecorded when survivors were murdered by savages or taken as slaves never again to see the so-called civilized world. If the wreck survived, it was plundered and burned by the natives. Thus living legends were handed down from tribe to tribe about such incidences and were told to the first white men who came to the Northwest shores. Follow up of such stories often uncovered mute evidence that indeed those legends were truth.

Wreck of the Japanese freighter **BLUE MAGPIE** just outside the north jetty of the Yaquina Bay entrance. Going aground at night November 19, 1983, the Coast Guard performed a dramatic rescue of the crew of 19 by helicopter. U.S. Coast Guard poto.

Harry E. Rieseberg, internationally known diver and treasure hunter, tells of a man's intriguing discovery a few fathoms beneath the surface off the Oregon coast, just south of the Columbia River. This individual was diving from an outboard-equipped craft. With Scuba gear he made a dive just beyond the breakers, darting among schools of small fish. The figure came on at a steady plodding pace, pausing here and there for brief moments, his eyes behind the windowed mask straining in the murk in search of the remains of one of the many hulks lying in those shifting underwater sands. Almost unexpectedly he beheld what looked to be the remains of a long submerged ship which appeared as though it had been down for a century. Almost disintegrated, the old hulk was like the brittle skeleton of a human left to the elements. Curiously he dug with his hands in the sand of what had once been the deck of the ship. He unearthed bunks of metal rusted and red, what appeared to be a ship's stack and other debris—ghostly reminders of the forgotten past.

After 15 minutes more of exploring the shallow depths, he suddenly became extremely excited, his blood running fast and his heart beating sharply. Bubbles rose from his mask. Directly before him, less than a foot below the former sand level was a dull brown metallic bar. He quickly picked up a nearby shell, then bent over and scratched at the bar's surface. It gouged easily, exposing a bright yellow interior. It was gold—a solid cast ingot of pure gold!

Exhilarated by his find, he reasoned that there must be more, for gold bars are not usually singular in number. Placing the heavy metal object in a hastily contrived sling he started back for the surface trying desperately to hold down his excitement.

When he broke the surface he was pulled aboard by his wife and a friend, both of whom were also skin divers. Rieseberg identified the man as Robert Everett, a Scuba diver who dives for recreation only. Never in his diving days had Everett made such a discovery as this one. Instead of the boat heading back for shore and dinner on Clatsop Beach, it stayed on, and Everett

went down again and again. Five times he surfaced, each time with other gold ingots, and other relics including some Spanish coins.

By dusk the small craft had a small treasure trove on the bilge boards. The first pieces of underwater wreckage Everett had probed was of more modern vintage, the gold was from the reputed wreck of a Spanish ship lost there in ancient times and the accidental finding of the gold ingot and Spanish coins attested to this fact. According to old Indian legend handed down to the first white settlers, a winged ship had been wrecked along Clatsop Beach in the age of exploration.

On February 21, 1916, the little steam schooner **FIFIELD**, built in 1908 for the coastwise lumber trade, and of 634 tons, was wrecked against the south jetty of the Coquille River bar. The **FIFIELD** was built by Kruse & Banks on Coos Bay for the Arthur F. Estabrook shipping firm of San Francisco. She had a 500 hp compound engine, could handle 750,000 board feet of lumber and carried passengers. The wreck, within easy reach of beachcombers at low tide, was gradually smashed to bits by the high surf that sweeps along that sector of the Oregon Coast. Value of the vessel was $150,000 and her skipper was Captain C. Bakeman.

It all happened when Captain L. Westphal, master of the German bark **MIMI** mistook the Nehalem River for the Columbia River, 54 days out from Callao, in thick weather, the night of February 13-14, 1913. She ran hard aground on the north spit of the Nehalem River. The 1,984 ton vessel, formerly the **GLENCOVA**, and owned by H. H. Schmidt of Hamburg, held its composure after hitting the sandy beach, and immediately salvage operations were undertaken. No casualties thus far. The underwriters awarded a contract to Captain Charles S. Fisher of the Fisher Engineering & Construction Company of Portland. Under direction of Captain Albert Crowe of San Francisco, the work got underway with two four ton anchors placed well offshore, and barges mounting steam donkey engines to pull the **MIMI** seaward with steel cables. Against the warnings of Captain Robert Farley, head of the Tillamook Bay Lightsaving Station (Garibaldi), the salvagers removed the vessel's 1,300 tons of ballast. Starting at flood tide on April 6, in the face of storm warnings, against the wishes of Farley, the vessel was inched toward the sea and ultimate disaster.

Wrecked one mile north of Humbug Mountain, near Port Orford, Oregon, was the wooden steam schooner **PHYLLIS**, March 9, 1936. The venerable coaster was bound for Portland from San Francisco. Owned by W. R. Chamberlin & Co., the 1,266 ton vessel was built at Aberdeen, Wash. in 1917. All hands reached shore safely, and though the ship was a total loss, her cargo of oil (in drums) and general cargo was mostly salvaged through the use of a high-line rig similar to those used in logging camps. It was rigged on a high bluff and carried the cargo over a mile from the stranded **PHYLLIS**.

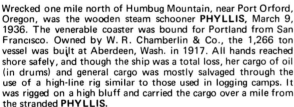

With 14 of the German crew aboard (three jumped ship in fear the night before), and a number of wreckers, including Captain Crowe, Captain Fisher and Russell Blackburn, (Fisher's secretary), the tall **MIMI** was inched out through the breakers. Suddenly she began to roll severely and capsized trapping all aboard inside a steel coffin. Despite three unsuccessful runs by Farley's surfboat, the welter of wreckage and huge surf prevented him from reaching the vessel. Through out the night a vigil was kept but the breakers mounted to 30 feet. Eighteen lives were lost, and only four saved including Captain Westphal, (master), Captain Fisher and two German crewmen. Captain Farley was unjustly blamed for cowardice by many onlookers. *Gregg photo.*

Needed, one large hinge! The steel steam schooner **ALVARADO** is seen breaking up in the surf eight miles north of the Coos Bay bar, March 17, 1945. All crew members including Captain Harold L. Kildall reached shore safely. The ship drove up on the shore in a storm and was short for this world when she began to break up. The 1917-built steel steam schooner, of 2,500 tons, is seen still in her wartime gray colors. The vessel operated for Moore Mill & Lumber Company of San Francisco.

But getting back to Bob Everett, Rieseberg said that his afternoon of underwater salvage work brought a return of more than $60,000.

This was but one isolated case of finds that have been made from the shores of Mendocino to Neah Bay. Occasional coins, silver goblets, and cannon have been found but the finders usually hush their discoveries.

Within reach of Scuba divers are many marine graveyards along the West Coast, and though gold and precious ores don't come easy, the challenge and the lore whet the appetite for further probing.

The best hunting grounds for lost ships are, of course, around the most used entrances from the ocean. Scores of ships lie rotting in Davy Jones' Locker in and around the entrance to the Strait of Juan de Fuca, the Columbia River, Grays Harbor, Coos Bay, Humboldt Bay, San Francisco Bay and along the Southern California coast. Alaska and British Columbia have well scattered victims along their rugged shores, many of which have never been visited by divers. Many wrecks lie in water too deep and treacherous even for the hard hat diver and will probably remain forever undisturbed.

Around some bar entrances, however, where ill-fated ships once went down in deep water, the constant battle between river and ocean has dredged up acres of sand forming new beaches and shoals above the water levels and leaving the location of some wrecks undetected and even landlocked.

Yes indeed, there is vast treasure on the wild and uneven floor of the Pacific slopes—gold and silver ingots, doubloons and pieces of eight. A silver goblet, believed of Spanish origin was long ago recovered off Yaquina Bay on the Oregon Coast. Buried treasure, as yet uncovered, supposedly was buried on Mt. Neahkahnie on the Oregon Coast and tons of beeswax from a Spanish ship has been unearthed from Nehalem

and Manzanita beaches within the shadow of that great headland.

Perhaps the best known and most told of all the intriguing tales of gold along the Oregon coast is the treasure of Neahkahnie. The treasure story some say is only legend, but the many clues and circumstances surrounding the legend leave little doubt that some kind of a chest was buried below or on the slopes of this great Oregon landmark. That one or more ancient ships did come there goes without saying, as the traces of at least two wrecks of unknown origin existed there. They were perhaps Spanish supply ships from Mexico or Manila galleons. Early pioneers told of the remains of a wreck on Nehalem beach not far from a place where tons of beeswax have been excavated from the sands down through the years. There is another ancient wreck claimed by commercial fishermen to be reposing in the depths just off nearby Short Sands Beach.

Since 1850, men have been digging holes on Neahkahnie mountain, following mysterious marks on so-called treasure rocks found by the first pioneers to arrive there. Some of the original marked rocks still remain.

About two miles south of Neahkahnie, just past Manzanita on the Nehalem sandspit lies a more authenticated tale. The Tillamook Indians (Nehalems) of old told of a violent storm, a huge ship caught in the surf, men with beards struggling in the breakers, and tons of beeswax washed upon the beach.

The Tillamook County Museum has a piece of this beeswax with the date 1679 carved in it, and in 1961 the Shell Oil Laboratory radiocarbon test dated the wax to an astonishing 1681, only two years variance from the branded mark. Some 12 tons of beeswax have been recovered in the Manzanita area. The Manila galleons, which followed the North Pacific current from Manila to Acapulco each year until 1815,

79

Look close.—In the sea mist rescurers can be seen chopping holes in the bottom planks of the gas schooner **RANDOLPH** to free a trapped engineer. Their efforts were rewarded. The wreck occurred near Bandon, Oregon in 1915 and three of the ship's crew perished. The **RANDOLPH** struck submerged rocks off the south jetty of the Coquille River bar close to the spot where the steam schooner **FIFIELD** struck a few months later. The **RANDOLPH**, built at Randolph, Oregon in 1910 was a total loss. *Courtesy Carl Christensen.*

carried such beeswax and also, spices, silks, gold, precious stones and pearls, hardwood chests and furniture and other items from the Orient.

Manila merchants saved their wares for an entire year or longer to place upon these immensely important (to commerce) ships and thus such wreckage, has very important significance. Historians can find only one Spanish Manila galleon after 1679 which is not accounted for: the *San Francisco Xavier,* which left Cavite in 1705.

Many early residents of Manzanita have found teakwood wreckage on the Nehalem sandspit and have used it for furniture. In addition, a small silver goblet was found in this area many years ago; it was believed to have been of Spanish origin.

There is another spot along the Central Oregon coast called Three Rox, on the north side of the Salmon River, where ancient Indian legend claimed that a ship with strange men was wrecked, that a treasure was buried and that a black slave was entombed at the site. Caucasian residents of later decades paid little mind to the legend until finding bits of an unknown wreck, and in a nearby shell mound, two skeletons, one of an eight foot Negro.

At least one historian believes that the Spanish wrecks along the Oregon coast were Spanish supply ships blown off course while coming to colonize California and to establish Catholic missions. One of these ships, the *San Jose,* is believed to have been lost on the Nehalem shores around 1769. With each of these ships there was small treasure, usually church adornment consigned to mission altars.

Among the many shipwrecks along the nearly 400 mile long Oregon coast have been such tragedies as that of the steamer *Francis H. Leggett* which foundered 60 miles southwest of the Columbia River with 67 persons aboard. There were but two survivors who lived to relate the shocking tale.

In December 1892, the small sailing vessel *Cornelius* went down off Cascade Head with her company of 50, and again reaching further back in history the SS *General Warren* draped her wooden hull over dreaded Clatsop Spit and was totally wrecked, claiming 42 lives, January 28, 1852.

The tanker *J. A. Chanslor* broke up on a reef off Cape Blanco on the southern Oregon coast December 19, 1919 and 36 members of her crew perished.

Other tragic Oregon coast losses included the schooner *Lottie* off Tillamook Bay in January 1892 with the loss of 32 lives; the steamer *Alaskan* went down off Cape Blanco on May 13, 1889 with the loss of 31 lives; the *William & Ann,* a British ship was lost on Clatsop Spit March 10, 1829 with the loss of 26; the capsized schooner *Sunshine* washed ashore near Coos Bay November 22, 1875 her entire company of 25 having vanished.

The steamer *South Portland* was wrecked on Blanco Reef October 21, 1903 with the loss of 21 lives and the steamer *South Coast* foundered off the Southern Oregon coast, September 16, 1930 with the loss of 19 lives, while the tanker *George Loomis* foundered near Port Orford in December 1918 with the loss of 18 lives, to name but a few.

The hand of God was apparent in the formation of the exceptionally scenic Oregon coast. The tourist thrills at nature's wonders where sea and land meet in dramatic display, but the mariner is more concerned with its notorious reputation and charts his course, giving a wide berth to the reefs, rocks and crags which dot the shoreline.

Good harbors are limited along the Oregon coast and most of the bar entrances and river channels that cater to heavy commerce, such as the Columbia River and Coos Bay stand as a monument to man's ingenuity in his struggle

80

against nature. It is a constant battle to maintain the bar entrances along the Oregon coast and none would be reliable except for the man-made jetties that prevent silting at the entrances, the constant dredging by Army Engineer dredges and the skilled pilots who take the ships across.

To the earliest navigators, the Oregon shores were forbidding—a seemingly endless line of breakers seen through the traditional Oregon mist. The old explorers and traders were plagued by persistent unfavorable weather and gazed with fear upon the bold landmarks that towered over the seething surf.

Though much deserved credit certainly goes to the ancient foreign explorers, yet it was the intrepid Captain Robert Gray who eventually found the fabled River of the West—the mighty Columbia River—opening to the world a great channel of commerce that today makes navigation possible far into the states of Oregon, Washington and Idaho. The busy ports of Portland, Astoria, Longview, Vancouver are the principle ports along the way.

Gray's ship, the *Columbia Rediviva* crossed over the Columbia bar at high tide May 11, 1792. The brig ran in between foaming breakers with seven fathoms beneath her keel. The *Columbia* floated quietly at the mouth of the mighty River of the West. A bucket went over the side. Only then was Gray certain the ship was actually in fresh water. Here was a river larger than any ever discovered on the west coast of North America.

Gray, jubilant over his discovery, but more interested in annexing a cargo of furs, named the river for his ship and charted landmarks on both sides of the channel. One day, well into the future, this river would become the natural boundary between the states of Washington and Oregon. The river entrance was also to become a graveyard of ships before man finally won his long struggle with the elements.

Let's face it, Oregon territory was, for the main part, Indian land in the middle of the last century. When the early white settlers arrived, forts had to be established to protect them. For hundreds of years red men had roamed at will over Oregon coastland and when they decided to war they warred against each other. When the white man came, they considered him an intruder and perhaps rightfully so.

The Lincoln Wreck

And so in the year 1851, we find the U. S. government transport schooner *Lincoln*, (also known as the *Captain Lincoln*), making her way north from California to Port Orford, Oregon in the bleak of December. Out of San Francisco with a contingent of 36 dragoons, the vessel neared her destination in a persistent storm which erased all semblance of a harbor entrance.

The vessel, under shortened sail was carried northward, her creaking timbers opening up and demanding a 24 hour effort at the pumps. For the next several hours the vessel took a terrible beating and there was no rest and no food for the ship's company.

By January 3, 1852, the gale had intensified, and had thickened so that the low hanging clouds took on the appearance of fog.

Wrecked in the fog, one mile north of Coos Bay, Oregon on September 8, 1892, in command of Captain Johnny O'Brien, the 265 foot long, 3,000 ton steam whaleback vessel **C. W. WETMORE** ended a jinxed career. The **WETMORE**, always more wet than dry, was driven ashore while en route to San Francisco from Tacoma with coal. Her crew of 22 was saved. Built on the Great Lakes, the vessel came around to the Pacific Coast for the coal trade and was lost the year after her arrival. *Courtesy Jack's Photo Service.*

Reduced to kindling, the schooner **ADVENT** is seen after being wrecked on the Coos Bay bar February 18, 1913. All hands were saved before the breakers did their dirty work. The 431 ton vessel was built in 1901 on Coos Bay by and for the Simpson Lumber Company. The wind failed as she attempted to cross the bar. Grounding on the spit, no tug in the area was powerful enough to get her free and the above was the result after the eight man crew was removed.

Amid the heaving breakers the vessel piled up on the beach, two miles north of Coos Bay. None were more surprised than that miserable company of men when they found their ship surrounded by sand. The tide had ebbed and taken the windlashed breakers back with it. No one aboard knew where they were.

The *Lincoln* was badly damaged and little time was wasted in deserting the vessel, none willing to risk the perils of a rising surf.

The ship's crew and the dragoons set up camp above the driftwood line and named it Camp Castaway—the first settlement of whites in the Coos Country. Ultimate plans were made for the overland trek to Port Orford. The Indians were soon on the scene bringing ducks, geese, venison and fish to barter for clothing, hard tack, rice and trinkets.

The camp lasted but four months when the last of the castaways packed his goods and crossed the sandspit to Coos Bay travelling the overland Indian trail down the coast.

The wreck lay a total loss, but at low tide the Indians plucked at her remains recovering metal for making knives and tools. The Indians had learned long before that the pickings were good whenever one of the white man's great winged ships was wrecked; and who better than they had a right to pilfer the goods?

The Fawn Incident

The ruggedness and isolation of the Oregon coast settlements in pioneer days was obvious. The little seaports existing inside unreliable bar entrances were wholly dependent on the intrepid and adventuresome seafarers who were willing to risk all perils as they brought their ships with supplies for the settlers. Such men could both take it and dish it out, but when they came face to face with the insurmountable odds of nature's wrath, they sometimes came out the losers.

On November 21, 1856, the brig *Fawn,* Captain Bunker, carrying stores and supplies to the newly established Fort Umpqua, was wrapped in the clutches of a gale. The storm howled unabated off the Oregon coast. As the *Fawn* neared the mouth of the Umpqua, the bar was a mass of white-lipped breakers. Aboard, besides Captain Bunker was a mate, four crewmen and three passengers.

Fort Umpqua had been established in July of the same year on a pine-covered flat some two miles from the mouth of the river in a wind-swept sand dune area. The post was created to help guard against the Siletz Reservation, for in the previous six years the Indians of southern Oregon had fiercely resisted the influx of miners and settlers in their area, and one of the main trails of overland travel for the Indians passed near the selected site of the fort. The Siletz Reservation stretched for 125 miles along the shore, surrounded on the north and east by the Coast Range.

Aboard the storm-tossed *Fawn* were supplies, uniforms and ammunition for the hard-pressed establishment. The *Fawn* had been tacking back and forth off the bar entrance waiting for the savage sou'wester to abate.

Tempest-tossed, the vessel fought a valiant battle with insurmountable seas. She was holding her own when suddenly a voluminous wall of water swept over the vessel, washing the mate and five persons into the sea. As the vessel slowly righted herself, heaving and groaning under the dead weight, three of the struggling men managed to regain the decks and were pulled aboard by their shipmates. The other three were never found. The vessel lost steerageway and the sails flapped and banged in terrifying crescendo as the wind lashed them. The canvas began to rip and the rigging tore loose from its fittings, in a welter of wreckage.

Strong winds and currents carried the helpless vessel northward, near Cape Perpetua ever closer to the dreaded shore. Soon the bowsprit, and

Twenty-five officers and crewmen of the steamer **CZARINA** clung desperately to the shrouds awaiting rescue that never came after their ship went aground on January 12, 1910. Outbound for San Francisco with coal, cement and lumber products, the Southern Pacific Railway Company steamer ran head on into a severe gale on crossing the Coos Bay bar. The seas were so severe that she was thrown out of control and dumped on the south spit. Anchors out, she drifted to the north spit. The local lifesaving station crew attempted to reach the wreck in vain. Breakers swept over the vessel, and the 24 crewmen and one passenger took to the rigging. Hour after hour they tenaciously hung on until only five were left, all the time the watchers on the beach unable to help them. Finally all perished, and the iron-hulled steamer succumbed to the sea's wrath. Captain C. J. Dugan, was lost with his ship. *Photo by A. M. Prentiss.*

WRECK OF THE CZARINA
COPYRIGHTED 1910, BY 46
A.M.PRENTISS, MARSHFIELD O.

Coos Bay motor lifeboat crew looks over the broken wreck of the SS **BRUSH** off Cape Arago, Oregon April 26, 1923. The freighter grounded while en route to New York. When salvage of the lumber cargo and the ship got underway she began to break up and finally parted amidships, the stern half sinking. Lumber was strewn in every direction littering the beach for miles. The 5,543 ton **BRUSH** was owned by Nawico Line. She had loaded at both Seattle and Aberdeen and was en route to the East Coast via San Francisco when the mishap occurred in the fog. All hands were rescued.

The powerful tug **L. H. COOLIDGE**, of the Upper Columbia River Towing Company stranded on the rocks on the Coquille River bar August 20, 1951, after her steering gear jammed. At the time, she was towing a barge full of peeler logs. The crew was removed, the barge later salvaged, but the tug's fate was sealed. An effort by the **SALVAGE CHIEF**, pulled her from the rocks but while being towed to the Columbia River for repairs, she went down off Yachats, Oregon and was lost. The 126 foot tug was valued at $300,000. The above photo shows her still aground on the Coquille jetty.

the foremast went by the board and the vessel was completely out of control. As shore loomed closer, the ship's master ordered the anchors dropped. They failed to hold and the vessel dragged her hooks until the chains could no longer stand the strain. Within less than six hours the *Fawn* was driven ashore near the mouth of the Siuslaw River.

As the wreck came to a standstill, digging itself deeper into the shoals, she was but a plaything in the hands of the surf throughout the bleak night. The crew and passengers, including Fort Umpqua's new surgeon and his wife, Dr. and Mrs. Edward Perry Vollum, were stranded on the vessel for 35 harrowing hours, fighting a desperate battle for their lives as one sea after another slammed into the wooden hulk. They might have perished with the ship except for a curious Indian who discovered their plight. This brave red man, whose name history does not record, launched his canoe in a perilous sea and came alongside to rescue the castaways from the battered wreck.

Other Indians soon appeared on the beach and aided the survivors; later these natives carried word of the tragedy to the fort. The urgent news brought response from the post physician, Dr. John J. Milhau and Captain Joseph Stewart, the post's commanding officer.

After a hasty overland trek they found the castaways near the wreck scene, in reasonably good condition, considering their long exposure to the winter storm. They were in the care of the Indians and the area's lone white settler, a former Hudson's Bay Company trader, Jean Baptiste Gagnier.

So pleased was Captain Stewart with the humane treatment accorded the castaways by the Indians that he recorded it in the post journal:

"They have acted most nobly in this case, evincing a sympathy for the sufferers and an anxiety to alleviate their miseries which have completely won their gratitude. When Mrs. Vollum was carried ashore, an old squaw met her and wrapped her up in her own blanket, and endeavored to impart to her, warmth and vitality by breathing on her, chafing her hands, etc., in the most kind and motherly manner."

En route from San Francisco to Seattle, the passenger liner **QUEEN** was off the Oregon coast on February 27, 1904, when fire broke out and burned furiously through the after part of the ship. Led by Captain N. E. Cousins, the crew fought a valiant battle against the blaze as a storm raged on the sea. For fear of the passengers lives, some boats were lowered. The first capsized drowning a woman. The second also capsized and four crew members were lost. Of the 218 persons aboard, four passengers and ten crewmen were lost. After four hours, the fire was brought under control, and Captain Cousins signalled the lifeboats to return. The vessel finally made Seattle under her own steam, as seen below. Captain Cousins was highly commended for such outstanding leadership in time of crisis, which might well have claimed many more lives. The 330 foot Pacific Coast SS Company liner, dating from 1882, first caught fire while off Tillamook Rock, and for awhile her plight was in doubt.

It was on December 5, 1887 that the steamship **YAQUINA CITY**, owned by the Oregon Development Company struck the bar, crossing over the Yaquina River entrance on the Oregon Coast. Engaged in the California-Oregon passenger and cargo business, the ship was intended to open a new portal in Oregon trade and to capture some of the Columbia River business. Her wreck and that of a second vessel a year later, the **YAQUINA BAY**, in virtually the same spot, ended high hopes of the company. The SS **YAQUINA CITY**, formerly in the Gulf coast trade as the **WESTERN TEXAS**, was a total loss, as was the **YAQUINA BAY**, ex **CARACAS**.

But though the Indians treated the survivors well, they looked upon the wreck as their property and wasted little time latching onto the spoils. They had a real Indian holiday requisitioning huge lots of supplies and clothing washed up on the beach. By the time the soldiers from the fort arrived to claim it, there was little to be found.

Some of the personnel of the fort were adamant over the Indian claims to the salvage, but few could deny them the right to the spoils of a

In 1937, the Puget Sound Navigation Company purchased several ex San Francisco Bay ferries for operation on Puget Sound. Among those ferries was the diesel electric **GOLDEN BEAR** which while being towed to Seattle by the tug **ACTIVE** encountered high seas off the Oregon Coast. Her superstructure drift bolts worked loose and damaged the exhaust system filling the engine room with carbon monoxide. Captain Louis Van Bogaert, in charge of the ferry crew directed removal of the engineers who nearly died of fumes. The towline then broke. The tug eventually got the ferry under control again and took her to Coos Bay where she was claimed a total constructive loss. Machinery was removed after the collapsed superstructure was cleared. The ferry became a cement barge and ended her days as part of a British Columbia breakwater.

wrecked ship especially in the light of their humane treatment of the survivors. Fort Umpqua suffered from the loss of supplies, but eventually was able to stock its empty shelves.

The wreck of the *Fawn* soon broke up and was sucked down in the sands near the Siuslaw.

A few years back L. D. Walgreave D. M. D., of Waldport, Oregon uncovered an ancient figurehead depicting an albatross or eagle's head, buried under the sand and driftwood ten miles south of Newport, Oregon. The figurehead is presently on loan to the Columbia River Maritime Museum at Astoria and it is not impossible that this unidentified carving might have been torn from the *Fawn* or the *Lincoln* when they fell victim to the surging seas well over a century ago.

Coast Guard Surfboat Capsizes

On Saturday, June 11, 1966 a large series of swells were moving in from offshore along the Oregon coast, and the Umpqua River bar had breaking swells of 25 feet and higher. Only the south part of the bar, the main channel, was passable; the middle ground area and the north side was a continuous line of breakers but small craft were navigating between the series of swells in all portions of the bar. A Coast Guard surfboat, the *CG-44303*, skippered by Chief Boatswain's Mate McAdams, along with a 36 foot surfboat were on patrol just in case one of the small private craft ran into trouble. At 11 a.m.,

Just a dot on the ocean. —Behind the rock in the center of the photo is the bow section of the ill-fated tanker **J. A. CHANSLOR** carried ashore by adverse currents in fog December 18, 1919, with the ultimate loss of 36 lives. En route to Pacific Northwest ports from California, with 30,000 barrels of oil in bulk, the vessel broke amidships shortly after striking the rocks. Only Captain A. A. Sawyer and two members of his crew managed to escape. The vessel, her cargo and most of her crew were claimed. The wreck was on the rocks off Cape Blanco, within sight of the lighthouse. The 4,938 gross ton vessel was built at Newport News in 1910, and operated for Associated Oil Company. *Carl Christensen collection.*

No shipwreck in Pacific Coast history has been more questioned than that of the British ship **GLENESSLIN** below Neahkahnie Mountain on the Oregon Coast. The ship crashed on the rocks, all sails set, on a clear day October 1, 1913. Out at sea 176 days from Santos for the Columbia River in ballast, the ship in command of Captain Owen Williams, was very mysteriously wrecked. Hundreds of pages of testimony were used in the following hearing, fought vigorously by the underwriters. Those on shore who aided in rather simple rescue of all hands, charged that many were drunk. The subsequent court inquiry in Portland held by the British Consul, found John Colefield, in charge of the watch, guilty and revoked his license for six months. Captain Williams lost his for three months and first mate Harwarth was reprimanded. The wreck was generally laid to green hands, incompetence, a windless pocket inside Cape Falcon and drinking. The iron-hulled **GLENESSLIN** of the DeWolf & Co. fleet was built at Glasgow in 1885 and held a sailing record of 74 days from Portland to Port Elizabeth. She quickly broke up after stranding.

the 44 footer was standing in to the south part of the bar at eight knots when a large swell series started to move in. The swells picked up in height as they approached the *44303,* and it became apparent to McAdams that the first series was going to break. He started to pick up speed and head straight in, in line with the swells, running away from them, but then the craft's bow began digging into the swell ahead.

"Looking over the stern, I could see we were in the curl," McAdams said. "I placed the engines in reverse, but it was too late—the bow was still digging in. The towing bit on the bow went under, then the bow, and then the handrails. My weight went forward in the coxswain's seat, but the seat belt held me fast. I told the crew to hang on, and then, over we went! The rush of water came in over my right shoulder and back; the pressure was terrific, and I about lost my grip on the wheel. The water around me then became reversed and confused; I could see nothing but darkness. I thought of being strapped in the seat, and if we did not right soon, I would have to unbuckle because I was running out of air."

"At first, the boat was wallowing in the swells upside down and it reacted slowly, but then the light coming through the water got brighter and brighter," McAdams related. "And then, swish! We were right side up! I was still strapped in the seat, and I turned around to see one of the crew, Ray Rensing, in back of me still clinging to the preventer screen. His safety helmet was gone but not before it had done its job. Rensing had been standing on the port side, in front of the hatch when we went over. He was thrown over me into the preventer screen, and there he grabbed and hung on."

His safety helmet had hit a steel brace on the overhead as he was thrown over McAdams. The helmet was dented in several places.

The other crewman, Seaman Don Powell, was standing on the starboard side when the boat end-for-ended, but the force of the water tore him loose as the boat rolled over. He came to the surface just in time to see the vessel still upside down, wallowing in the trough of the surf.

When the sturdy 44 footer came rightside up, both engines were still operating but had shifted to neutral. "We were still in large breakers," Chief McAdams continued, "We came about to pick up Powell and took another breaker broadside but we were not in the 'curl.' We went out of sight in the spray of white water as the 36 footer came in to help us—but seeing that we were still running and in good condition, they stayed clear to give us room to make the pick up. On the first try, we were headed toward the south jetty, and Powell was on the lee side of the boat. He was about ten feet from our side when another large breaker came down on us. I placed the engines in full reverse and nearly missed running him down as the wave washed us toward him."

The seaman in the water was picked up without further incident and he went right to work helping pick up some of the gear that was washed overboard and still floating.

"The *CG-44303* has been in scrapes like this before," McAdams recalled, "and in exactly the same water. On June 23, 1964, the same rough conditions on the bar prevailed— 25 foot to 30 foot breaking swells and small boats attempting to cross. Chief Boatswain's Mate Elmer A. Stevens was the coxswain, and was hove to near the south jetty, providing a lee and giving advice to a 16 foot skiff, when a 'sneaker' caught him and rolled the *44303* completely over. At the

En route from Los Angeles to Grays Harbor, the steam schooner **COTTONEVA** crashed on the shore in a 75 mile-an-hour gale during the night of February 10, 1937, off Port Orford, Oregon. Purchased just a week before at a foreclosure sale, by Charles R. Ayers of San Francisco, the 26 crew members were removed safely by breeches buoy. The **COTTONEVA** was built in 1917 as the **FRANK D. STOUT**.

Masts and rigging gone, decks a shambles, the schooner **ON-WARD** is lying hopelessly on the beach near the Coquille River bar after being wrecked February 25, 1905. The three-masted schooner, built in 1901 and hailing from Parkersburg was en route from San Francisco to Bandon and was wrecked while endeavoring to cross the tricky Coquille bar under sail. Her crew escaped. *Carl Christensen collection.*

Bound for Seattle from San Francisco to load for the Kuskokwim area of Alaska, the schooner **OZMO** struck a rock off Cape Blanco, Oregon. The damaged vessel was later taken in tow by the steamer **DAISY** and brought to Coos Bay. While crossing Coos bar, however, the **OZMO** became unmanageable and went aground on the south spit, later coming ashore near Empire. The wreck occurred May 18, 1922. The vessel was built at North Bend in 1904 as a sailing vessel. She was later given an auxiliary engine and was last owned by the Northern Commercial Company. *Courtesy Jack's Photo Service.*

While anchored one mile west of Tillamook Bay bar, Oregon on June 17, 1908, awaiting a tug, the schooner **IDA SCHNAUER** was carried ashore near Bayocean, after the wind shifted from the southwest to west. Her anchor cable had parted, and by the time the tug arrived she could not be budged from the beach. On the next high tide, the schooner began to break up and ultimately became a total loss. The 215 ton vessel was en route from Hobsonville, Oregon to Redondo, Calif. when wrecked.

This is believed to be the wreck of the schooner **CHARLES H. MERCHANT** which stranded on the beach near the entrance to the Nehalem River, Oregon August 11, 1902. Built by Hans Reed at Marshfield, Oregon in 1877, the **MERCHANT** was well known in the coasting trades. Badly battered by the surf, local salvage efforts a month later were partially successful and the hull was towed inside the bar and beached in Nehalem Bay where it was broken up. *Ray Lindsay photo collection.*

The most photographed shipwreck on the Pacific Coast is that of the British bark **PETER IREDALE,** part of which still reposes on the sands of Clatsop Beach, near Fort Stevens, Oregon. She is pictured here a short while after grounding October 25, 1906. Twenty-nine days out from Salina Cruz, Mexico, bound for the Columbia River, the vessel was wrecked under command of Captain H. Lawrence, The beautiful British four-masted bark after being abandoned by the underwriters was sold for a mere $500.

same time, the skiff overturned, broke in three pieces, and dumped its four occupants into the boiling sea. Once again, the *44303* was rolled over, and then Stevens, 'through superb seamanship and daring,' maneuvered the boat in the breakers in close proximity to rocks on the south jetty, picked up his lost crewman, and maneuvered to pick up the four other persons safely and without injury. Chief Stevens was awarded the Coast Guard Medal for his heroism, and the crew was given the Coast Guard Commendation Medal."

For many, many years, Coast Guardsmen have been masters at handling rescue craft in the treacherous waters of the Pacific Northwest.

Today, the Coast Guard self-righting surfboats are standard equipment at the stations on the Washington and Oregon coasts. Chief Boatswain's Mates Thomas D. McAdams and Elmer A. Stevens have dramatically demonstrated the seaworthiness of the boats and the skill of the twentieth century Coastguardsmen.

Saga of the Captayannis S.

Within the lengthy wreck log of West Coast ships, are a few that have escaped virtually certain destruction. One such ship that regained her freedom from one of the most treacherous shoals on the Pacific Coast was the Greek cargo ship *Captayannis S.* Her refloating is unique in salvage annals, though the vessel had been so badly damaged by heavy seas that some salvage experts believed it would have been better to have left her as a prize of the elements. Suits and counter suits only added to the misery of the ship's owner, charterer and insurers.

The *Captayannis S.* ran aground at the mouth of the Columbia River where scores of deep sea ships had fallen victim down through the years —Clatsop Spit. She was driven hard aground in the storm of October 22, 1967, and spent nine days stuck on a sandbar before being pulled off in a titanic drama of salvage.

The owner of the cargo of the Greek ship filed a $125,000 suit against the owners and charterers of the ship. Wilbur-Ellis Co., a California firm whose 3,400 tons of fish meal was ruined in the holds of the *Captayannis* S., filed their complaint in U.S. District Court against the Sarantex Shipping Co. of Panama whose main offices were in London.

Also named as defendants in the complaint were A. H. Basse, of Copenhagen, the time charterer, and Norsildmel of Bergen, the charterer. In their complaint, the Wilbur-Ellis Co. charged the *Captayannis S.* "was unseaworthy when she left Aalesund, Norway in September for Portland, and as a result was stranded off the mouth of the Columbia River."

Unseaworthiness was never fully substantiated and certainly the fact that the vessel did not break up under the terrible pounding was a credit to her builders.

Under her master, experienced Reino Mattila, the Astoria-based salvage vessel *Salvage Chief,* a powerful 204 foot salvage vessel, owned by Fred Devine, was primed and ready to take on one of the biggest challenges of her successful career. To her credit were many miraculous endeavors, but to salvage a large vessel from dreaded Clatsop Spit, a renowned devourer of ships, would be the ultimate, as the *Chief* neared the end of two decades of salvage work.

The *Salvage Chief* was converted from a World War II LSM (landing craft) in 1948 at Swan Island in Portland. Fred Devine, Portland diver and salvager had purchased it as a surplus hull from the government.

For many years Devine had dreamed of building a salvage vessel along new and different lines. He took his cue from the stranding in 1932 of the SS *Sea Thrush* at almost the same position which the *Captayannis S.* occupied. The *Sea Thrush* ran aground and was hammered by the surf for days while salvage men and insurance representatives argued about how to get the freighter free. Finally the menacing surf breaking over the shoal caused the ship's hull to crack, making salvage virtually impossible and the ship eventually was sucked down by the sands.

Fred Devine was there during those days and wondered why a big barge equipped with powerful windlasses and lots of heavy steel cables and heavy anchors, couldn't be constructed to anchor itself between a stranded vessel and deep water. Then, by pulling against its anchors and the ship at the same time, it could literally pull itself and the ship into deep water, Devine reasoned.

During the war, Devine did a great amount of diving and underwater construction work for a Portland shipyard taking only enough pay to keep his crew and himself, and allowed the rest of his earnings to remain with the company as credit owed to him.

After the war, Devine looked around for a suitable hull and hit upon the LSM as something he could use. He had the assistance of Kaiser engineers in designing and converting his LSM into the salvage vessel about which he had so long dreamed. The craft underwent conversion at Portland, inside and out. Where once it carried 300 persons, Devine had the accommodation altered for a salvage crew of 20. The tank deck was covered with surplus steel to form a new upper deck and installed were six big LST anchor windlasses in the former tank deck. Three of the windlasses faced forward, three aft. He installed three big diesel generators to provide internal power for the windlasses, pumps, and other deck equipment, added thousands of feet of 1½ inch and two inch steel cables, a set of big Eels anchors and other basic salvage equipment. With 3,600 horses in the two main propulsion engines, the *Salvage Chief* was ready to go anywhere in the world, and future assignments were to call her to the Far East, Alaska, Hawaii and up and down the West Coast.

During her career the *Salvage Chief* has pulled scores of vessels off beaches and sandbars. Notable were the salvage of the Liberty freighters *Yorkmar, Lipari* and *White Cloud* from the Washington and California beaches.

Devine once purchased a former Japanese motorship hull which was sunk during the World War II by American bombs on the beach at Kiska, in the Aleutians. His crew patched it, pumped it out and started back to Japan with the vessel, intending to sell it for a half million dollars. This time, however, Devine's luck turned sour for when they ran into heavy seas off Japan, the freighter's hull opened up, filled and sank in full view of Devine and his unhappy crew. They watched their treasure vanish but did gain some insurance money to pay for part of their gamble.

A breaker explodes against the side of the Matson Navigation freighter **MAUNA ALA** aground on Clatsop Spit at the entrance to the Columbia River. The vessel hit the sands 700 feet from shore, after being ordered back to port following the Pearl Harbor attack on December 7, 1941 while en route to Honolulu with 30,000 Christmas trees, automobiles and general cargo. She reached the Columbia entrance at night on December 10, a coastal blackout being in effect. Without navigation lights on the shore she ran hard aground and became a total loss after her 35 man crew was rescued. The sands soon swallowed her remains.

How not to operate a vessel ... the gas schooner **GOLDEN WEST** was literally thrown up by a huge bar swell and dropped rudely on top of the rubble-mound jetty while crossing the Coquille River bar. En route to Bandon from San Francisco, the little freight carrier was wrecked November 29, 1936. Her crew escaped, some of whom can be seen here revisiting the vessel, which ultimately was a total loss.

One of the tragic shipwrecks of 1915 was the stranding of the passenger and cargo steamer **SANTA CLARA**. After a checkered and jinxed career, the **SANTA CLARA** met disaster on Coos Bay bar November 2, 1915, the death toll given at both 16 and 21 lives. The 1,558 ton vessel which was built at Everett, Washington in 1900 as the **JOHN S. KIMBALL,** and later renamed **JAMES DOLLAR,** had seven owners in her 15 years of troubled service. She last operated for the North Pacific SS Co. replacing the fire-damaged **F. A. KILBURN** in Oregon-California coastal service. In command of Captain August Lofstedt, with about 60 passengers and crew aboard, she struck a newly formed uncharted shoal at the south entrance of Coos bar. She refused to back off, and her seams opened flooding the engine room. Six boats were lowered, one capsizing, the others maneuvering in the high surf finally reached the shore. The ship soon broke up and only her whistle remains today at the Weyerhaeuser mill at Coos Bay. *Rehfelds photo.*

This misfortune did not dampen the enthusiasm of the salvage vessel's owner. He firmly believed that if he had had the *Salvage Chief* before World War II he could have saved many vessels lost through stranding at the entrance to the Columbia River such as the liner *Admiral Benson*, the SS *Sea Thrush* and the Russian freighter *Vazlav Vorovsky.*

The salvage master was in Oakland, California on Sunday night October 22, 1967. His skipper Reino Mattila of Astoria received the word of the *Captayannis S.* grounding and got the *Chief* underway, while Devine hopped a plane for Portland, transferred to his pet purple Pontiac and hustled off to Astoria. This was the big opportunity for which he had so long waited.

By mid-afternoon on Monday, Captain Mattila had the *Salvage Chief's* anchors laid out, and the ship's helicopter had helped string a line to the stranded vessel. The *Chief's* crew was ready. Devine arrived to direct operations, fully confident. Work got underway, but the persistent wind and contorted surf did not cooperate.

Salvage operations on the Greek freighter remained at a standstill Wednesday after strong winds buffeted the *Salvage Chief* the previous night and broke two lines and one anchor cable.

The salvage vessel's crew was busy replacing the broken lines and clearing sand out of the sea suction intakes from the stricken ship so its generators could be operated.

Captain Mattila, reported the weather calm Wednesday night and hoped another attempt to pull on the 418-foot freighter could be made during the Thursday evening high tide.

The vessel "is really hard aground," he confessed and added that it might not be moved before the following week's nine foot tides. The wreck had not yet suffered too much damage, and only a little water had appeared in the holds, which boosted hopes of refloating her.

The master of the *Captayannis S.,* her chief engineer and two other engineers along with four men from the *Salvage Chief* were aboard the wreck Wednesday night. The chief officer had earlier been taken off by helicopter so he could go to the John Jacob Astor Hotel in Astoria to attempt to placate members of the Greek freighter's crew, unhappy and irritated because they were confined to their hotel rooms after removal from the wreck.

Reports that crew members had declared they would not go back on the ship even if it was refloated were heard in Astoria. The ship's agents, General Steamship Corp., Ltd., had offered the crew subsistence money, but it was rejected. They just wanted to go home.

Being aliens, the men were subject to deportation if they did not return to their ship. The owners would be required to pay the cost of their transportation back to Greece.

Indeed, the *Salvage Chief* had its greatest challenge for in the days to follow the seas barreled in, smashing with tremendous power against the freighter. She began to leak and as the hatch covers were torn off, the fishmeal in the holds was soaked and ruined. The ship ground on the bottom, her plates becoming dented and scarred. The *Chief* took a real beating but seldom retreated. It was feared that the *Captayannis* would break in two and for a long time it was touch and go. Devine's plan was almost foolproof as long as the wreck would hold together; but

On May 2, 1908, the steam schooner **MINNIE E. KELTON**, skippered by Captain James McKenna, was hit by a gale en route to San Francisco from Aberdeen with lumber. Off Yaquina Head the deckload shifted and smashed the fireroom bulkhead. The vessel shipped water in great quantities until the fires in the boilers went out and the vessel became waterlogged. Abandoning ship north of Yaquina Head, a huge wave carried the deckload of lumber overboard, part of the after housing and both boats. Eleven members of the crew perished. The others floundered in the seas and regained the vessel, taking refuge in the foc'scle. All through the night they held out until removed next day by the Yaquina Bay Lifesaving boat. The wreck was towed to Astoria, as seen in the above photo, where she was reduced to a rock barge, and later rebuilt as the steamer **ROCHELLE.** The vessel was originally a Great Lakes "lumber hooker." *Woodfield photo.*

would it? A couple of times it was budged but nine tormenting days passed before the badly pummeled Greek ship was pulled free and towed across the bar to safety.

Such a beating had she taken, that the insurance companies listed her as a total constructive loss, and many felt she should have been left to perish. Even the Greeks, for once, had no word for it. Devine had made his dream come true,

however, and if he could save a ship under such circumstances, he could save just about any stranded ship that could weather such an ordeal.

Fred Devine had exercised his brain, and his ship had exercised its muscles. It was a good combination and coupled with a knowledgeable skipper and experienced crew, the teamwork paid off.

Not hopeless afterall! The handsome British bark **BARODA**, went aground near the Coquille River on the Oregon Coast in 1894, and for several weeks it appeared that she would remain there. However, she kept her composure on solid sands, and eventually was refloated. The vessel is seen here in 1894, some of her upper rigging removed during salvage operations. The 1,417 ton vessel, built at Dunbarton, Scotland in 1891 was later cut down to a barge, and caught fire and partially sank with a cargo of coal at Esquimalt in 1910. Raised and repaired she was owned by the James Griffiths interests and was still afloat in the 1940s.

This photo of the classic old Russian merchantman **ILLITCH** was taken a few months before her demise at Portland, Oregon. While tied up at the port June 24, 1944, awaiting further repairs at the Portland drydock, the vessel suddenly heeled over on her side imbedding herself in the mud. Bids for raising her were called but rendered too high, and the wreckage, after a long period of litigation was raised by the Army Engineers, much of it remaining on the river bottom. The steamer was built as the **EMPEROR NICHOLAS II** at Germany in 1895 by the Kaiser as a gift to Russia. She is seen here painted in her war colors. *Joe Williamson collection.*

Torn apart by the breakers 20 miles south of Port Orford, near Gold Beach, the steam schooner **WILLAPA**, ex **FLORENCE OLSON**, became a total loss. Bound from Marshfield for San Francisco, the vessel was overwhelmed by a storm the night of December 2-3, 1941. Captain Oscar Peterson, master, was injured after the vessel, owned by Hart-Wood Lumber Co., struck. Flares were sent up and the Coast Guard responded dispatching a motor lifeboat to the scene. All hands were removed just before the vessel broke up. One of the survivors was first mate E. Stahlbaum who a few years earlier escaped from the wrecked **COTTONEVA** in the near vicinity. It was too rough for the 36 foot motor lifeboat to put the survivors ashore, so a local fisherman, James Combs, made several daring surf runs landing the **WILLAPA'S** crew two at a time. All 24 reached shore safely. The 1,185 ton **WILLAPA** was a total loss.

Stern of the barge **PORT OF PASCO (BARGE 510)**, owned by Upper Columbia River Towing Company, aground on the tip of the Coos Bay north jetty. Her back was broken, and she was declared a total loss by the underwriters December 12, 1953. Most of the deckload was still in tack when this photo was taken. Much of it was salvaged. The barge grounded while being towed across the bar. *Jack's Photo Service photo.*

Outbound with lumber for Crescent City, California from Coos Bay, Oregon the MS **ALASKA CEDAR** struck the north jetty of the Coos Bay bar, December 2, 1962, and stuck fast. Commanded by Captain N. F. Hall, the W. R. Chamberlin & Co. vessel was the target of an immediate rescue operation, the 24 man crew being rescued by breeches buoy, set up by the Coast Guard. All reached shore safely. The vessel, however, worked on the bottom and soon broke her back and had her bulkheads stove. Most of her two million board feet of lumber was scattered in every direction—little recovered in tack. The **ALASKA CEDAR** was built in 1944 as the **JOHN J. MANSON** and was last owned by J. J. Tennant of Portland for Chamberlin operation. In the above photo a helicopter hovers over the scene shortly after rescue operations.

Beyond salvage—the MS **ALASKA CEDAR** lies helpless, constant surf pounded her steel sides until they gave way under the assault. The vessel was another of the many that fell victim to the Coos Bay bar, leaving her bones to rust on the north jetty rocks in the grim winter of 1962. *Official Coast Guard photo.*

The ship's master and first officer of the steel steam schooner **COLUMBIA** were both qualified pilots. In the aftermath of the wreck it was learned that they were arguing on the bridge over who was going to take the vessel in. During the argument the ship struck the north jetty. The wreck occurred on February 17, 1924, the vessel having been employed on charter to McCormick Steamship Co., and last owned by Thomas Crowley. All hands on the **COLUMBIA** were rescued, but the vessel's back was soon broken and she became a total loss following fruitless efforts by the salvage steamer **HOMER**. Much of the cargo from the wreck came drifting up on the beach. The **COLUMBIA** of 1,923 gross tons, was built at Wilmington, Del., in 1912. *U.S. Coast Guard photo.*

One of the last puffs of steam was issued (in this aerial photo) from the stranded steel steam schooner **OLIVER OLSON** aground on the south jetty of the Coquille River bar on the Oregon Coast, November 2, 1953. The 307 foot freighter was caught in a strong cross-current while crossing the bar in command of Captain Carl Hubner. The initial impact jammed her rudder and screw, and holes were opened up in her bottom plates causing internal flooding. An emergency breeches buoy was rigged up, but the 29 man crew remained aboard for three days as the CG cutter **BONHAM** and the port tug **PORT OF BANDON** stood by awaiting favorable conditions to free the **OLIVER OLSON**. Finally, all hands were removed and the wreck sold to a California firm which removed deck equipment and salvageable items. A December gale put an end to the work, and being unable to remove the hulk, the Army Engineers filled it with jetty rock and incorporated it into the jetty. *U.S. Coast Guard photo.*

The 177 ton steam schooner **JULIA H. RAY,** a total wreck demolished by the breakers. The little vessel was wrecked on Coos Bay bar January 26, 1889. Her crew reached shore safely. The vessel was built for J. S. Higgins of San Francisco at San Francisco in 1884.

Emergency breeches buoy rigged between the Coquille River south jetty and the stranded lumber vessel **OLIVER OLSON** owned by Oliver Olson & Co. It was set up shortly after the vessel stranded November 2, 1953. All hands were eventually brought ashore safely. *Jack's Photo Service.*

Submarine? No! A voluminous greasy swell on the Coos Bay bar rolls over the sunken U.S. Army Engineers seagoing hopper dredge **Wm. T. ROSSELL,** sunk in a tragic collision with the Norwegian MS **THORSHALL,** September 10, 1957. The dredge had just dumped its last load and was inbound when the Thor Dahl-owned **THORSHALL** operating in the Pacific Islands Transport Line service, outbound from Coos Bay, traveling at a good rate of speed, plowed into the dredge opening up a gaping hole and sinking her almost immediately. Four men trapped below were drowned and seven seriously injured as they scurried topside to find the swells as high as eight feet combing the deck. Captain Carl Heil and the dredge crew managed to get four boats away, one being smashed and another capsized. Col. Jackson Graham, of the Army Engineers, visiting Coos Bay from Portland directed the rescue operations. Fifteen men were finally plucked from the rigging and stack of the sunken dredge by helicopter operated by Wes Lematta of Portland. The CG motor lifeboat and the cutter **BONHAM** also aided in the rescue. Another of the survivors later died of a heart attack, bringing the death toll to five. The officers of the **THORSHALL** attributed the accident to faulty steering apparatus. The ship limped off to the repair yard for an $85,000 bow repair job. *Photo by Bob Frenette and Drew McKillips.*

The Astoria salvage tug SAL-VAGE CHIEF standing by the sunken wreck of the Wm. T. ROS-SELL. The dredge was beyond salvage and eventually had to be blown apart as a menace to navigation. The ROSSELL was a 3,490 ton vessel, built at Chester, Pa. in 1923-24. Measuring 268 feet in length, the vessel was designed to carry 12 officers and 32 crewmen.

Some 80 per cent of her hull plates had to be replaced after the CYNTHIA OLSON, a lumber freighter of the Oliver Olson & Co. was freed from the Coquille River bar. The tug SALVAGE CHIEF towed her to a Portland shipyard for the major overhaul. The vessel hit a shoal on the Coquille bar on June 9, 1952, and for awhile it was feared she might end her days there. The CYNTHIA OLSON, of 3,117 gross tons, and 310 feet in length, was built at Flensburg, Germany in 1935, and one of the few foreign-build vessels ever used in the U.S. west coast lumber trades. *Photo supplied by Fred Devine, owner of the SALVAGE CHIEF.*

The local gentry come to look over the shattered remains of the four-masted schooner MARCONI. While being towed across Coos Bay bar outbound for Valparaiso, March 23, 1909, the towing hawser parted midway over the bar. The vessel drifted up on the south spit of the notorious Oregon bar and was pounded into submission. Built by and for the Simpson Lumber Co. at North Bend in 1902, the MARCONI came to grief at the entrance to the port where she was built, just seven years later. *From Coast Guard files.*

British bark **GALENA** hard aground on Clatsop Beach, where she stranded the night of November 13, 1906 inbound from Chili for Portland, under command of Captain J. J. Howell. The 2,294 ton four-masted vessel, built at Dundee in 1890, was to have loaded grain at Portland for the United Kingdom. Immediate efforts were undertaken to refloat the vessel, but all ended in failure and she was partially scrapped on the beach, her lower sections finally being covered by the sand. The **GALENA**, built for S. Galena & Co., was last operated by Thomas Shute of Liverpool. *Courtesy Chas. H. Fitzpatrick.*

This dramatic photo shows the evacuation of passengers from the furiously burning coastwise passenger liner **CONGRESS**, three miles off Coos Bay, Oregon. Some 428 persons were forced to abandon in a very orderly operation, under the direction of the ship's skipper, Captain N. E. Cousins. The $2 million palatial liner caught fire in the after hold northbound from San Francisco, and it spread rapidly in the cargo below decks. The flames were first reported off Crescent City, Calif., but the evacuation on the Seattle-bound ship did not take place until the fire reached major proportions. An SOS was sent out and the boats lowered with precision. Not a single life was lost. The date was September 14, 1916. Finally the ship got so hot that all hands had to abandon. She was soon ablaze from stem to stern. The salvage ship **SALVOR** was unable to get closer than 100 feet, even then, having all her paint scorched. For hours the fire continued until only the steel skeleton of the liner remained. Gutted almost beyond recognition, the vessel was finally towed to Seattle. Miraculously, much of her propulsion gear had been spared. The naked vessel underwent a complete and very costly rebuild, equal to her original cost. She emerged as the **NANKING** for transpacific passenger service. She later returned to coastwise passenger service of the Pacific Steamship Co. as the **EMMA ALEXANDER**. *Rehfelds photo.*

Finally cooling off after the drastic fire that swept her September 14, 1916, off the Oregon coast, the three year old passenger liner **CONGRESS**, of the Pacific Coast Steamship Co. was a devastating sight. Everything that wasn't metal burned; much of the metal melted. The terrible inferno rendered the ship a ghastly derelict, the davits all empty of their boats and the falls dragging in the water. The 7,793 ton, flagship of the Pacific Coast SS Co. was built by the New York Shipbuilding Co. at Camden, N.J. in 1913, with triple expansion engines and twin screws. The 424 foot ship was the ultimate in Pacific Coast passenger luxury, but was reduced from riches to rags. The ship carried 253 passengers and 175 crewmen.

On February 18, 1937, the Italian MS **FELTRE** was rammed and sunk by the SS **EDWARD LUCKENBACH** in the Columbia River, near Prescott, Oregon. The **FELTRE** is seen here after sinking to the river bottom. As pilots differed over the cause of the crash, and hearings got underway, salvage was begun to recover 365 bars of silver valued at $185,000 in the hold of the wreck. The silver was recovered, and on March 18, salvagers managed to raise the ship, but she sank again. Three days later they had her up again and she was towed to Portland for one of the largest repair jobs at a Portland drydock to that date. On May 13, the salvage firm filed a $200,000 libel against the ship. On June 9, she was sold to Pacific American Fisheries of Bellingham for a mere $55,000, and a $300,000 rebuild job was begun. The ship was renamed **CLEVEDON** and placed under American registry.

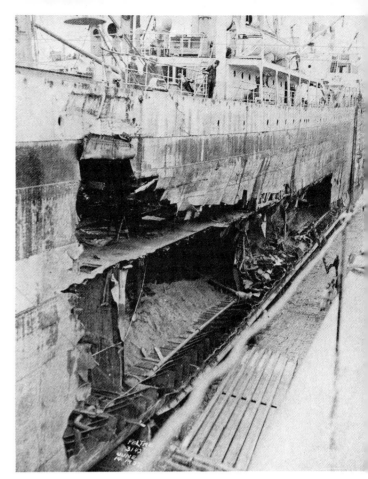

The ill-fated Italian freighter **FELTRE** in drydock at Portland, Oregon after being raised from the bottom of the Columbia River, where she was sunk by the **EDWARD LUCKENBACH** February 18, 1937. The gaping hole torn in the ship demanded a very expensive repair job and much litigation. After becoming the American MS **CLEVEDON**, for PAF, she was drafted as an Army Transport during World War II. On January 13, 1942 she caught on fire while loaded with ammunition at Yakatat, Alaska. The SS **TAKU** towed her away from the dock and beached her. She was then destroyed by a huge explosion. *Harold Brown photo.*

This was once a river sternwheeler, the **ANNIE FAXON**. The Columbia River steamer, in her 16th year of service and commanded by Captain Harry Baughman, exploded near Wade's Bar on the Snake River, April 14, 1893. Captain Baughman saw his companion in the wheelhouse beheaded and a moment later found himself blown to the river bank. Eight lives were lost and the vessel destroyed. *Captain Homer Shaver collection.*

Stranded on Clatsop Spit, at the mouth of the Columbia River in heavy fog, December 4, 1932, inbound to the Columbia River from Seattle, on the intercoastal run, the SS **SEA THRUSH** grounded because of erroneous navigation charts. Captain Ernest J. Landstrom was exonerated of blame. The crew of 31 plus a stowaway and a woman passenger were rescued by the cutter **REDWING**. Landstrom stayed with the ship till it broke up and was then removed by a motor lifeboat from Point Adams. The 5,538 ton **SEA THRUSH**, a unit of the Shepard Steamship Company, was built at Portland, as the **WESTLAND** in 1917. *Courtesy Charles Fitzpatrick.*

Wreck of the Annie Faxon

In a cloud of spray, 44 foot Coast Guard motor lifeboat goes through a practice run in the high swells near the Umpqua, in preparation for the real thing. Such self-righting craft often have to go through giant walls of water to make a rescue, where the ultimate in seamanship is demanded. Sometimes they take a complete 360 degree role and the men have to hang on for their lives in a watery nightmare. The most recent 360 role took place in November 1969 when a Coast Guard craft was endeavoring to aid a stricken Mexican tug, four miles off Cape Foulweather, Oregon. *U. S. Coast Guard photo.*

For 40 years, from her launching on the day of the San Francisco earthquake, until her last run on March 20, 1947, the **GEORGIE BURTON**, never gave anyone any problems. She performed her workaday existence on the Columbia River and on the Willamette, most of her latter days for Western Transportation Co. On her final voyage as a river workboat, Rex Gault of Western presented the old vessel as a gift to the city of The Dalles, to be preserved as a museum. But she never arrived at her final home. En route from Portland, roaring flood waters from the Columbia, rising to heights not reached since 1894, swept her from her moorings on Memorial Day, 1948. She crashed on a reef below the canal and broke her back, near Celilo, Oregon.

Several decades ago, before the motor lifeboat was widely used, lifesaving crews on the Oregon Coast still used the Dobbins boat and the surf boat. Here in 1910, a Dobbins type lifeboat, oars out, plows through a Pacific comber near Coos Bay bar. The iron men who manned them were brave indeed. The Dobbins boat was the forerunner of the 36 foot motor lifeboat. *Brown photo.*

The Greek flag freighter **CAPTAYANNIS S.** astride of the treacherous Clatsop Spit, where she grounded on October 22, 1967, after coming in to signal for a pilot. With a cargo of fishmeal from Norway, the vessel was inbound for Portland in command of Captain Ioannis Markakis. A dramatic rescue took place, removing the 22 man crew by Coast Guard helicopter as huge swells combed the decks. It was feared that the ship would be a total loss as had so many before her. Fred Devine, however, had his famous **SALVAGE CHIEF** dispatched to the scene and in a touch and go operation which lasted for nine days, the **CHIEF** gained her apex when she and her doughty crew succeeded in pulling the battered freighter free. So badly damaged was the ship that estimates of repair ran $1 million, more than three times her value. The cargo was mostly destroyed. The wreck was later sold at Portland and at this writing is lying idle in the Columbia River, a total constructive loss. *Jim Vincent photo (Oregonian).*

Blackened amidships, the Danish MS **ERRIA**, lies at anchor off Astoria, Oregon. While anchored to await the calming of the Columbia River bar, the East Asiatic Line ship, outbound from Portland for northern Europe with lumber, steel, pulp and general cargo caught fire and trapped 11 persons who burned to death. The passenger-cargo vessel had a total of 114 persons aboard, all escaping but the unfortunate 11, mostly passengers. The fire believed started from a shorted electric cable, was discovered at 2 a.m. when most were asleep. The Coast Guard and other vessels shoved the ship on the mud and fought the fire around the clock. The date was December 20, 1951. The 8,786 ton vessel, was built in Denmark in 1932 and was in regular berthline service. The wreck was finally towed to Portland, where a decision was to be made to rebuild or scrap her. The owners finally decided to have the big Dutch tug **ZWARTE ZEE** tow her all the way to Rotterdam where she was rebuilt as a freighter (without passenger accommodations), at a cost of $1.5 million.

The traditional Japanese junk though developed by a maritime people, was of poor design and performance. Beamy, heavily constructed, lugsail-rigged with two or three masts it had an inherent and dangerous defect; the open stern well, built to permit the raising and lowering of the rudder. It was responsible for the swamping and destruction of scores of such craft. Many disabled junks of old were carried across the Pacific by the Kuroshio and wrecked in Pacific Northwest waters.

Hard aground on the sands three miles north of Alsea Bay, Oregon the 92 foot fishboat **COLLIER BROTHERS**, September 21, 1979. The vessel was later refloated.

Steam schooner **BANDON** aground against the jetty of the Coquille River bar in Oregon about 1909. She was pulled free, one of the few lucky vessels to escape the clutches of the bar entrance. This was just one of six major strandings the vessel suffered during her years of service, 1907-1947, the last being near Trinidad Head in the winter of 1941, when declared a total constructive loss, but later was used as a barge. Bandon Historical Society photo.

Coast Guard air sea rescue operations have saved numerous lives. Here on the Oregon Coast the Umpqua River motor lifeboat **CG 44331** meets its aerial counterpart from the North Bend Coast Guard Air Base, **HELICOPTER 1373**. U.S. Coast Guard photo.

The British bark **PETER IREDALE** wrecked on Clatsop Beach near Fort Stevens October 25, 1906 has became a national attraction. The remains are still there at this writing. The photo taken 25 years ago shows the bowsprit still protruding upward. It has since fallen to the beach. Hale photo.

Pummeled by the elements, the stern section of the wooden fishing vessel **DEBONAIR** out of Shelton, Washington ends her days in a rocky cove October 31, 1981 near Gwynn Bluff, south of Yachats, Oregon. The vessel's skipper drowned in the incident.

Narrow escape from sinking. The U.S. Army Corps of Engineers ocean going hopper dredge **BIDDLE** is pictured assisted by the famous salvage tug **SALVAGE CHIEF** and the Knappton tug **BETSY L.** at the mouth of the Columbia River. The dredge was rammed in the fog by the Matson cargo ship **HAWAIIAN** August 9, 1977. Her starboard side was crumpled and she was taking on water fast. Hasty salvage efforts kept the ship from going down and she was towed to Portland for $2.4 million dollars in repairs. Licenses of both the pilot and skipper of the **HAWAIIAN** were suspended for two months at the subsequent hearing.

Coast Guard helicopter **1471**, an HH3 out of Astoria transferring a generator from isolated Destruction Island Lighthouse off the Washington coast.

Rising from the sands at Big Creek, midway between Yachats and Waldport, Oregon are what is believed the last vestige of the schooner **JOSEPH AND HENRY**, built for the lumber trade by Matthew Turner at his yard in Benicia in 1892. She was named for her owners, Joseph Harder and Henry Steffins of San Francisco. She was wrecked off Big Creek January 3, 1901 with the loss of her crew of six. Photo taken 1980.

103

CHAPTER FIVE

California Shipwrecks

California has one of the longest ocean frontages of any state in the union and its ramparts are marked by countless shipwrecks. Nowhere on the Pacific Coast has commerce abounded as much as in the Golden State which in 200 years has burgeoned into the most populous of its 49 counterparts, and become the cross-roads of the maritime Pacific.

Before California became part of the United States territory the Spanish, who had run rough shod over the

Four-masted schooner-**J.H. LUNSMANN**, sunk in a collision in San Francisco Bay July 12, 1913.

natives of what we now know as Mexico, maintained the only regular transpacific sea route. It had its beginning in 1565 when the little carrack *San Pablo* returned from the Philippines in command of Felipo de Salcedo, with the knowledgeable Friar Andres de Urdaneto aboard. He suggested using the more northerly route across the Pacific from the Spice Islands where the vessel could take advantage of the Kuroshio Current. It was a remarkable voyage of three and a half months, the cargo of cinnamon arriving safely at Acapulco.

Little did those sea pioneers know that the voyage would open the door to a trade that would last for more than two centuries under the flag of Spain. Neither did they know that next to Russia's early sea route between Siberia and Alaska, it would be one of the most demanding at that point in history. Voyages to Manila ordinarily required from 75 to 90 days, but the return to Acapulco and San Blas, owing to the necessity of sailing northward beyond the trade winds to the westerlies, generally required from seven to nine months of rigorous voyaging fraught with every conceivable hardship. It was said that no voyage of the earlier carracks and the later galleons was ever made without death en route. Though the largest galleons ranged up to 2,000 tons, most of those making the two annual transpacific voyages were 500 ton craft with crews of about 115 men, plus passengers.

Thousands of souls died of scurvy and beri beri in the Manila galleon era and several units of the Spanish fleet were castaway in remote locations, several of which vanished without trace. Others left clues along the California or Pacific Northwest coast affording grim reminders of shipwreck and in some cases massacre by savages. Though America was usually approached with a landfall at Cape Mendocino before the galleons turned southward, they sometimes, owing to crude navigation instruments or faulty dead reckoning, made a landfall off the Oregon coast. If the winds were contrary there was no guarantee they would not crash against hostile outcrops or near river entrances in little known territory, there to be forever separated from the then known civilized world.

Before and after—the sad tale of the old passenger liner SS **LA JENELLE,** of Panamanian registry. In the upper photo she is seen at her berth at the Port of Hueneme, California in 1969 summer. She had been purchased by a group who intended to convert her into a floating restaurant. The 467 foot long, 7,000 ton liner built at Quincy, Mass. in 1931, had served as the **BORINQUEN, BAHAMA STAR, AROSA STAR** and **PUERTO RICO,** mostly as a passenger and cruise liner on the East Coast and the Caribbean.

Then came the end. To conserve money, her owners anchored her in open ocean waters just off Port Hueneme with only two watchmen aboard. On April 14, 1970 a storm struck, accompanied by huge seas. The ship was swept up on the beach at Port Hueneme after those aboard had been unable to drop another anchor. They were rescued but the vessel rolled over on her side and lay like a great wounded whale. And there the once proud ship ended her days. *Upper photo by William Bitters. Lower photo by Lawrence Barber.*

Hard aground at Naples, California the four-masted schooner **ENSIGN** January 20, 1909. It was there the five year old vessel ended her days.

Perhaps the voyage to Mexico is best told by an irate passenger who made the trip in 1697:

"It was the longest, and most dreadful of any in the world; as well because of the vast ocean to be cross'd, being almost one-half of the terraqueous globe, with the wind always ahead; as for the terrible tempests that happen there, one upon the back of another, and for the desperate diseases that seize people, in seven or eight months lying at sea, sometimes temperate and sometimes hot, which is enough to destroy a man of steel, much more flesh and blood, which at sea had but indifferent food."

The early Spanish pinks and carracks were primitive forerunners to the galleon, or 'Great Ship' which was a new type of Spanish design meant to take over where the carrack left off. The galleon hull was more slender and graceful and the forecastle no longer overhung the bow but was constructed behind a ram-like projection called a beak head. Within that housing was contained the toilets for the crew which resulted in the term 'head', still used by modern sailors. The steering mechanism was a whipstaff, a type of vertical extension of the tiller on roller bearings in the 'steersman's hutch', a small cabin sunk in the poop deck. So called 'trees' were erected to protect the sail trimmers and fighting men in case of a battle at sea. The merchant galleons were not nearly as well protected as the fighting galleons, but all were armed, for even in the Pacific they sometimes were victims of British marauders.

Common seamen on the Pacific galleons were, for the most part, of Spanish extraction, or Filipinos, the latter, labeled as 'Indians'. Filipinos received considerably less pay than the Spaniards, were extremely subservient to their taskmasters and often treated with cruelty. Despite great risks and hardships it was easy to recruit hands for the galleons. When they died at sea, and scores of them did, they were often cast overboard without thought or ceremony. One of their worst enemies was the cold, for often the Filipinos, used to native tropical climates, were signed on without any clothing, nor was any given them in the cold latitudes at sea. As a result, large numbers perished. Said Los Rios, "...they are treated inhumanly and are not given the necessaries of life, but are killed with hunger and thirst. If he (the Filipino) were to tell in detail the evil that is done to him, it would fill many pages."

Gemelli Careri told of the callousness of the captain of his galleon, whose personal profits from a single voyage was from 25,000 to 30,000 pieces of eight. (an old Spanish dollar.)

".....the abundance of poor sailors fell sick, being

The San Francisco ferry **PERALTA** was gutted by fire after the Oakland peir where she was moored first went up in a blaze on May 6, 1933. The hull was later towed to Puget Sound and converted into the world's first streamlined ferry, the **KALAKALA**.

Panamanian cargo vessel **LIBERTY MANUFACTURER** aground 500 yards off Point Fermin, California, October 7, 1972. She was refloated about three weeks later by the Astoria-based salvage tug **SALVAGE CHIEF**, and continued her voyage to Yokohama after repairs were made. The vessel was owned by Chinese merchants.

expos'd to the continual rains, cold and other hardships of the season; yet they were not allow'd to taste of the good bisket, rice, fowls, Spanish bread and sweetmeats put into the custody of the master by the king's order."

Death was a grim reaper. On one vessel with 400 persons aboard, 208 died before Acapulco was reached. On another, the *San Nicholas*, 330 perished. On most galleon voyages the sufferings were terrible.

Careri leaves us with another account of life aboard a Pacific galleon:

"..... the galleon is never clear of a universal raging itch, as an addition to all other miseries...the ship swarms with little vermin, the Spaniards call Gorgojos, bred in the bisket; so swift that they in a short time not only run over cabins, beds and the very dishes men eat on, but insensibly fasten upon the body. There are several other sorts of vermin of sundry colours, that suck the blood."

Careri who was a cabin passenger, went on to tell that "rats had invaded every part of the ship, that the quarters were narrow and overcrowded and that along with other discomforts there were the "terrible shocks from side to side, caus'd by the furious beating of the waves."

The first recorded shipwreck on the Pacific Coast was that of the Spanish galleon *San Agustin*, under Captain General Sebastian Cermeno, with Francisco

Chavez serving as master. The vessel departed Manila on July 5, 1595 carrying a cargo of beeswax, various wearing apparel, porcelain and a small amount of gold, somewhere between 130 and 150 tons of cargo. Cermeno also had orders from King Filipe of Spain, via the magistrates in Mexico, to seek out harbors of refuge along the California coast where galleons could seek refuge from the enemy, en route to Acapulco. After making a landfall off Cape Mendocino, the vessel sailed south, and near Point Reyes, charted out what is presently known as Drake's Bay. While at anchor there with a partial crew aboard, the *San Agustin* was struck by a sudden gale, driven ashore and wrecked, two crewmen being drowned.

There was a determined effort to save a portion of the cargo, and after salvaging one of the ship's boats, they left much of the salvage behind, having fought with the natives over the spoils. Seventy-six survivors, packed like sardines in the open boat sailed southward along the California and Mexican coasts. After several rigorous days of hardship, they gained Acapulco, remarkably only one of their number dying en route.

A Japanese submarine torpedo zeroed in on the tanker **EMIDIO** off the northern California coast December 17, 1941, ten days after Pearl Harbor. The vessel drifted ashore and broke up. Five died and 31 survived.

On Thanksgiving Day, 1970, the former San Diego-Coronado ferry **SILVER STRAND,** while idle at Los Angeles parted from her moorings in a severe storm and was smashed to pieces on the Fish Harbor Los Angeles Breakwater. The vessel was built at Alameda, California in 1927 and once served on Puget Sound as the **ELWHA** and on San Francisco Bay as the **GOLDEN SHORE.** *Photo courtesy John L. Whitmeyer.*

Many tales of Spanish treasure and shipwreck exist along the coast of California, some based on truth others only fanciful myths.

Stories with some reliable backing include the following:

Units of the Manila galleon fleet that went missing somewhere in the Pacific on returning to Acapulco include the *San Juanillo* in 1578; *San Antonio* in 1603 and the *San Francisco Xavier* in 1705. They vanished with their entire crew, passengers and cargo. Galleons carried between 150 and 500 souls on most voyages. Other galleons of the fleet reputedly lost along the Pacific Coast include the *San Sebastian* in January 1754, probably off San Miguel Island or near Santa Barbara, California, and the *Santa Cecilia* and *Santo Domingo* also believed lost on the southern California coast. The only chronicled wreck of a galleon on the Pacific Coast was that of the *San Agustin* at Drakes Bay in 1595, but it is well established that early Spanish vessels were castaway on the Oregon coast, borne out by the finding of bits of wreckage and tons of beeswax, the latter a commodity carried by nearly all of the galleons eastbound.

Many tantalizing tales of the Spanish treasure wrecks are related by divers and treasure hunters. Some have segments of truth but mostly they are fanciful thinking. Persistent claims insist galleons lie in the depths off Cataline Island as well as in other areas. Of the 20 Manila galleons reported lost between 1565 and 1815 probably the larger percentage went down in the treacherous waters in and around the Philippine Islands.

When Captain Shigeo Fujime in the 6,519 ton freighter **KEN-KOKU MARU** steamed out of Nagoya for San Francisco, he missed his mark. The ship went aground in the fog 2½ miles north of Stewarts Point, 80 miles north of San Francisco, April 28, 1951, with 54 persons aboard. Despite several salvage attempts which ended in failure, the ship was finally refloated in early May 1951 and escorted to San Francisco in bad condition. All but one of her 16 compartments had been torn open, the hull badly gashed. After a long and costly overhaul the ship was returned to service, cheating Davy Jones out of a choice customer.

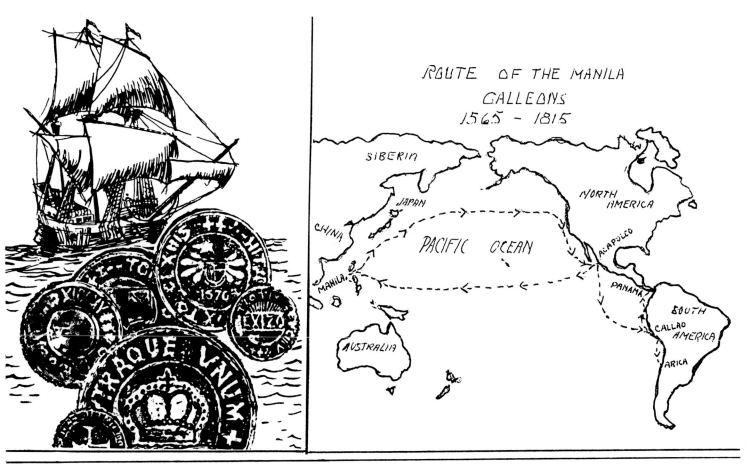

ROUTE OF THE MANILA GALLEONS 1565 - 1815

SIBERIA

JAPAN

CHINA

MANILA

PACIFIC OCEAN

NORTH AMERICA

ACAPULCO

PANAMA

SOUTH AMERICA

CALLAO

ARICA

AUSTRALIA

Route of the Manila galleons that gave Spain control of the Pacific for 250 years.

U.S. Milwaukee on Samoa Beach, Eureka, Cal. # 860

The USS **MILWAUKEE** hard aground on Samoa Beach, near Eureka, California where she became a total loss in 1917 after failing in an attempt to free the Navy submarine **H-3** which ran aground December 14, 1916. Flak flew in Washington D.C. over the loss of the 10,000 ton cruiser.

Other California treasure ships of the more modern vintage include the elusive 1865 wreck of the SS *Brother Jonathan* whose story is told elsewhere in this writing and the *City of Rio de Janeiro*, an American passenger liner wrecked about 600 yards off Fort Point, in San Francisco Bay, February 22, 1901. In this terrible fog-shrouded tragedy the vessel went down with $2,075,000 in gold, silver and cash, but also with the shocking loss of 129 lives including her master, Captain William Ward. Despite the fact that the wreck happened in San Francisco's own front yard, there were but 81 survivors. It appears that most of the treasure is figment of the imagination.

Unfounded reports claim $2 million in Chinese silver and $75,000 in gold, specie and bullion have reputedly been salvaged from the rusting hulk.

California's 1,000 mile plus shoreline, longer than that of Washington and Oregon combined, is marked with some natural harbors and many man-made harbors. Long the destination of world commerce, California, despite its sunny reputation has claimed a long list of ships, and the tragedies have been legion along its shores.

The Treacherous Farallones

Roll on, thou deep and dark blue ocean—roll!
Ten thousand fleets sweep over thee in vain:
Man marks the earth with ruin—his control
stops with the shore.
                              —Lord Byron:

Landfall light for ships approaching the Golden Gate shines out from the lofty rocky crest of the Southeast Farallon. If one has been fortunate enough to approach San Francisco by sea or by air, he may have seen the Farallones, even little known to most Californians. The ugly appearing but captivating Farallon Islands, 26 miles west of the Golden Gate, are the only points of land between California and Hawaii.

The fog that often obscures the Golden Gate further hides these miniscule and infamous islets except on clear days when from San Francisco they appear as small dark dots on the western horizon.

Rising like great shadowy ghosts from the Pacific's depths—only one of them has habitation and at this writing those few government employees that man the Coast Guard light station will soon be removed in favor of space age automation.

The name Farallon, interpreted from the Spanish means, "little pointed islets in the sea," which perhaps describes them well. Despite their inhospitable appearance, they hold a history of interest, though are best known for the scores of ships that have left their gnarled bones draped over their ageless outcroppings or deep in the surrounding, restless ocean.

The Farallones are not all bad, in fact even though the landlubbers of California know little of them, the commercial fishermen often visit there, and the seafarers on the endless string of inbound cargo vessels and passenger liners eagerly scan the horizon for the first sight of the islets. They listen for the foghorn, or by night search for the probing shaft of light. Naturalists, Coastguardsmen, U.S. Wildlife personnel and seabird lovers all know the place and have a personal regard for it. It was President "Teddy" Roosevelt, who in 1909, by presidential order, set the islets aside as a Wildlife refuge—Middle

On the rocks off Point Reyes, California, the wooden steam schooner HARTWOOD, 946 tons, after stranding June 27, 1929. She worked on the rocks until her bottom planks succumbed to the wrath of the surf. Her crew was rescued. The vessel was built at Hoquiam, Wash. in 1916 for the Hart-Wood Lumber Co. of San Francisco. She was fitted with a triple expansion engine of 650 hp and carried 1,250,000 board feet of lumber.

Farallon, the North Farallones and Noonday Rock. South Farallon and the rocks surrounding it, not part of the refuge, are under Coast Guard jurisdiction.

History-wise, Spanish explorer Juan Rodriguez Cabrillo first visited them in 1539. Later came Sir Francis Drake who came ashore to replenish his depleted stores of food with fresh sea lion meat. Then came the slaughter of sea otters and sea lions by both early Russians and Yankees who found the islets heavily populated with the mammals.

After the California goldrush of 1849 food was at a premium in San Francisco. Eggs were worth their weight in gold and imaginative individuals stormed the islets between 1850 and 1856 to rob the helpless seabirds of their eggs. In that six year period some four million eggs tickled the pallets of San Francisco gourmets—mostly those of the common murre. Those eggs sold for $1 apiece.

Not only did the poor seabirds suffer, but the greed of man to make an easy buck turned the islets into battlegrounds with brawls and shooting incidents over the eggs. Such practices continued till the turn of the century when government restrictions put a stop to the exploitation. By then the murre eggs had become very scarce. With the end of the Farallon egg wars the poor old murre was able to rebuild its greatly depleted army. Man had already eradicated the sea otter.

Today the islets have returned to the ways of nature and scores of seabirds of numerous varieties haunt them in peace and quiet. Sea lions live there undisturbed and whales haunt the surrounding waters.

Yes, the islets have returned to the way God intended them to be, still surrounded by wet fogs, confused currents and roaring breakers. The changeable weather conditions can make these grisly shores something that can throw real fear into the tempest-tossed or fog-plagued mariner.

Though modern aids to navigation have ended much of the fear of the Farallones inherent in the days of sail, constant danger still lurks and even today they claim unwary victims.

Hopelessly Aground

So close and yet so far away from home was the liberty transport *Henry Bergh* wrecked on the outlying fangs of California's Farallon Islands.

In addition to her crew of 100 officers and men, this vessel carried 1,300 Navy sailors homebound to San Francisco from the war-wracked South Pacific. The date was May 31, 1944. The time was about two hours after midnight.

In the stuffy confines in the 'tween decks the battle-worn sailors were either sleeping, playing cards, packing gear or just chewing the rag. They were excited as might be expected. For most, it had been endless months since they had last seen the United States.

To those too excited to sleep, dawn seemed an eternity away. Already fog was collecting over the ocean but this did not dampen the enthusiasm of the boatload of bluejackets. They could only visualize sweethearts, parents, family

Steam schooner **TIVERTON**, 557 tons, aground near Humboldt Bay bar, Calif., March 13, 1933. All salvage attempts failed, the crew was removed and the vessel left on the beach. The **TIVERTON**, built by Hitchings & Joyce at Hoquiam, Wash. in 1906, was one of the smaller steam schooners, carrying only 575,000 board feet of lumber. Her remains were later burned on the beach.

Some members of the crew can be seen at the right, having left the wreck of the wooden steam schooner **SEA FOAM** which ran aground on February 23, 1931, without loss of life. The vessel was built at Aberdeen, Wash. in 1904, and wrecked at Point Arena, Calif.

and friends standing at dockside cheering the ship's arrival.

In the impenetrable darkness the second mate stood quietly on the bridge, his coat pulled up tight around his neck to keep out the cold that penetrated like a wetted knife. Between the fog and the bleakness of night the ship seemed but a little world on an eternal sea. The mate listened for the sound of a foghorn in the distance. Instead, he heard only the frequent sonorous blasting of the *Bergh's* whistle.

Inside the pilot house the helmsman stared dead ahead, the light from the compass lining his face. The clock above his head read 0430. If the skipper's calculations were right the ship should be entering the Golden Gate in another three hours and the voyage would be over.

The fog closed in as a southwesterly breeze picked up from astern. The ship moved along at a little better than 10 knots. Wartime blackout regulations were in effect and the ship as well as the area for miles around did nothing to suggest a landfall. The fog was too thick anyway.

Inside the pilot house the ship's master, Captain Joseph C. Chambers, paced nervously,

awaiting a break in the weather or the sound of a horn. He stepped out on the port bridge wing where the second mate was keeping a lookout.

"We should be picking up the diaphone on Farallon soon," he said. "Should be abeam of it before long."

The mate looked down at the direction finder. "We should pass it about 10 miles off," he answered.

The captain blew some warm air into his hands and stepped back in the pilot house.

It was calm on the water and the ship rolled ever so gently, approximately 30 miles off San Francisco in a northwesterly direction. Somewhere out there in the murk lay the three deadly Farallon Islands, one of which was the location of the lighthouse, and the fog signal. Around the bosom of those islets was a notorious graveyard of ships. Void and barren, these upheavals of rocks had no population except the Coast Guard personnel which manned the station on the Southeast Farallon. These obstructions have always been like the fabled sirens of the sea that beckoned the ancient mariners to their deaths.

The persistent overcast and fog had prevented any celestial bearings, and the ship had been navigated only by dead reckoning for more than 36 hours. The blackout and communication restrictions had done little to aid the situation.

Captain Chambers was an experienced mariner with a quarter of a century of seafaring behind him, ten of which were in the capacity of a deck officer. He was familiar with the approaches to San Francisco but under such circumstances any master mariner could go astray. He had, he thought, laid a proper course allowing for wind and current.

Liberty ships were generally considered slow war horses, but for some undetermined reason the *Henry Bergh* had been making better time than her officers had imagined. She was doing almost 11 knots. This had not been allowed for, and the current and wind had set the ship north nearly ten miles. She was directly in the path of the Southeast Farallon.

Down in the deep recesses of the ship the 2,500 horsepower steam engine was purring along under watchful eyes. The chief engineer dropped in for a quick look around and finding everything in proper order departed for his cabin. Just as he stepped into his quarters he suddenly heard the throb of the engines cease. He was informed that the lookout had reported hearing a ship's whistle dead ahead and had signaled the pilot house. Due to the fog, the ship's engines were stopped and for a few minutes she drifted silently forward. Her whistle sounded but no answer came back. The time was 0445. The chief started for the engine room but changed his mind when he heard the engines start up again.

Five minutes later both the mate and the watch on the bridge detected a faint whistle signal off the starboard bow. They listened intently that they might get a bearing on the direction of the sound.

The *Bergh's* whistle gave out with another blatant blast.

Captain Chambers was growing more concerned when suddenly dead ahead the thick mantle of fog parted for a brief moment. Directly ahead of the ship loomed a bold, black pillar.

"Breakers!" shouted the bow watch. "Land, dead ahead!"

Pandemonium broke loose in the wheel house. The captain grabbed the telegraph and rang full astern.

"Hard right!" he shouted to the helmsman. But it was too late. The ship crashed onto the razor sharp reef that sliced the hull plates to ribbons. Before the engines could get into full reverse the ship was hung up and mortally wounded, water rushing into her lower recesses like a dynamo.

As the general alarm reverberated throughout the ship, the sailors below rolled out of their berths like bees evacuating a disturbed hive. The ship shook violently. Scurrying topside the men had to hang on to keep their balance.

Hopelessly aground, the 7,600 ton vessel was open to the full thrust of demanding breakers striking from three directions.

Out from the radio room went urgent distress messages immediately intercepted by the Coast Guard. The lives of 1,400 men were in jeopardy. The *Bergh* was already showing signs of breaking up. Time was a factor.

None could be sure that rescue vessels would arrive in time. Fog remained thick. Captain Chambers was gravely concerned over possible evacuation across the breaker-swept 200 yards to the islet. It was a devil's cauldron, an obstacle course, pock-marked with jagged chunks of rock waiting to puncture any lifeboat accepting the challenge.

The captain remained calm using all the common sense at his command. The responsibility for the entire ship's company lay on his shoulders, but all hands cooperated. The battle-tired sailors were used to emergencies. With orderly dispatch they went directly to their lifeboat stations to await the skipper's command. The total capacity of the boats was not equal to one third of the personnel aboard but they were swung out in readiness dangling in the davits.

At 5:20 a.m. the command to lower away came from the bridge. The captain personnally supervised the lowering of each boat. Though the seas were high, by skillful handling, one after another, the craft were cleared away each holding 25 men. The last of the eight were cast off just as dawn sent its eerie pall over the murky waters. They followed the lead boat in command of Chief Officer Mark Franco who, before leaving the ship, had discussed the course to follow with Captain Chambers.

Those still aboard the wreck watched as the lifeboats were swallowed up in a white shroud. The lifeboats had a long, hard pull, those at the oars digging in to cope with the strong currents

At picturesque Point Carmel on the Monterey Coast of California, the wooden steam schooner **FLAVEL**, on the bottom with water up to her main deck, after wrecking without loss of life on December 15, 1923. Throughout her brief six year career she was owned and operated by the Hammond Lumber Company of San Francisco. She was built by the Bendixsen Shipyard at Fairhaven, California in 1917 for hauling lumber. The **FLAVEL** was of 967 tons.

and tide rips that swirled about tentacles of rock. It required 45 minutes for the craft to find the hidden cove shown on the charts, but at last a landing was perfected and shouts of joy from the survivors were so exuberant that they could be heard by those remaining on the wreck.

The emptied boats with only those at the oars started back to the wreck for the next load of survivors. By 0800 through splendid oarsmanship and boat handling 600 were safely ashore and the rescue efforts continued.

The personnel at the Coast Guard Light Station were soon on the scene with hot coffee packed over the rugged terrain in five gallon jugs.

The news by now had reached San Francisco and a gigantic air-sea rescue had been launched. Fog still prevailed and rescue teams had no way of knowing the extent of the disaster nor the fate of 1,400 men. A mixed armada of military and commercial ships were passing out through the Golden Gate, bound for the Farallones. The first of the rescue ships to heave to off the wreck signalled its presence with a series of whistle blasts.

Those still on the *Bergh* took solace in the fact that their chances of survival now took on more affirmative aspects should the vessel suddenly slip off the reef and go down.

While the larger vessels remained well off the reef, smaller boats felt their way to the side of the stricken *Bergh* and took scores of men out to the waiting ships.

By 1300, the evacuation was nearly completed except for a skeleton crew who remained with the wreck in the faint hope of salvage. Shortly afterward, a salvage tug moved in as close to the wreck as possible and fired a messenger line across the vortex to the stern of the transport. Those aboard the wreck reeled it in and brought up the attached 8 inch hawser. The line was made fast about a stern bitt and the tug began to take up the slack. The line soon grew taut as a fiddle string. The wreck refused to budge. Then there was a muffled crack and the deck plates and the hull buckled and cracked across No. 4 hold.

By 1430, the men remaining aboard the transport were taken aboard a rescue launch. Captain Chambers was last to leave. He took a quick look about his dying charge and satisfied that he had done all he could, relinquished his command to the elements and boarded the launch. It is indeed a dark hour for any ship's master when he loses his ship, regardless of the circumstances, but Captain Chambers had gained the respect of all who were under his command. The evacuation of 1,400 men without a single casualty was a record of achievement.

The war-time restrictions on aids to navigation were in a large way responsible for the loss of the *Henry Bergh* which joined a long list of victims lying in the depths around the perilous Farallones.

Loss of the Schooner Exact

This is the story of a stout little two-masted schooner whose name is destined to live for time immemorial—the *Exact*. Among her claims to fame was the bringing of the first white settlers to what was to become the great metropolis of Seattle.

Perhaps more dramatic and at the same time tragic is the little known account of the loss of this sprightly schooner on the northern coast of California in 1859.

The *Exact* was built at Glastonbury, Conn., in 1830 for owners in Hartford. In 1841 she was operating out of Nantucket under the ownership of George H. Folger, Levi Starbuck, and Henry

Down in the surf, the steam schooner **THOMAS L. WAND** is pictured wrecked south of Point Sur, Calif., September 16, 1922. Built in 1906, the **WAND** was almost lost near Ketchikan, Alaska, May 5, 1914, but was refloated. The vessel was built at Aberdeen, Washington by John Lindstrom and was of 657 tons.

Liberty transport **HENRY BERGH** hard on a jagged reef of the Farallon Islands. She is pictured here in an official U.S. Navy photo a few hours after the last of the 1,400 men aboard were evacuated. The transport was bound for San Francisco from the South Pacific, when in the fog she went aground May 31, 1944 and shortly after broke up.

Aground on the rocks near the Cliff House at the entrance to San Francisco Bay, the Union Oil tanker **LYMAN STEWART** is pictured after a collision with the SS **WALTER LUCKENBACH** in thick fog October 7, 1922. The tanker, badly gored and disabled by the freighter, drifted ashore and became a total loss, outside the port where she had been launched seven years earlier.

WRECK OF S.S. BEAR

Looking down from the cliff onto the wreck of the SS **BEAR**. On June 14, 1916, en route to San Francisco from Portland, Oregon, she grounded off California's Sugar Loaf, near Cape Mendocino, at night. The coastal passenger liner carried 100 passengers and 82 crew, most of whom evacuated in the boats. Five lives were lost and several others injured in landing the boats. Many of the survivors were taken aboard the **BLUNTS REEF LIGHTSHIP** until rescued by the steamer **GRACE DOLLAR**. The wreck occurred in heavy fog when Captain L. N. Nopander, mistook Sugar Loaf for Mendocino. The ship, valued at $1 million, was operated by the San Francisco and Portland Steamship Company and was built at Newport News in 1909. She was of 4,507 gross tons.

After the Canadian salvage steamer **SALVOR** was forced to give up in unsuccessful attempts to refloat the coastwise passenger steamer **BEAR**, the breakers eventually broke the ship in half and she became a total loss in the bleak waning months of 1916.

Coffin. A decade later, like a thousand other ships full of gold-thirsty individuals, the *Exact* sailed into San Francisco where the Bay was a mass of abandoned windjammers from the far corners of the earth. Their passengers and crew to a man had gone to seek their fortune. Under Captain Norton the *Exact* arrived with a cargo of bricks, lumber, hardware and general merchandise.

Unlike most of the idled fleet at San Francisco, the *Exact* found employment along the coast. Her owners were listed as her master, Captain Isaiah Folger, George Folger, Henry Coffin, Edward Morton and Ovid Starbuck.

According to official government records the *Exact* was a square-sterned schooner 73 feet in length with a registered tonnage of 73 tons. She had a beam that barely exceeded 22 feet and was a swift and dependable sailer.

And so it was a few months later that we find the *Exact* making her famous voyage that will forever perpetuate her name. As morning caressed the eastern horizon over the timbered shores of Puget Sound, a heavy drizzling rain fell from a pearl, gray sky. A persistent breeze was whipping across the water. Plowing southward through the foaming waters was the *Exact*, eight days out of Portland, Oregon, with 12 adults and an equal number of children as passengers. This small group was to become the first settlers of Seattle. The date was November 13, 1851 and Captain Isaiah Folger was in command on this epic voyage. The schooner dropped her hook off Alki Point at the southwesterly entrance to Elliott Bay.

As the rain pelted down, one by one the dampened apprehensive settlers scampered into a small skiff and were rowed toward the shore. The boat landed on the sandy beach backed by a green stand of tall evergreens. The only reception committee was an occasional curious Indian peeping out of the bracken attracted by the white man's "big winged canoe."

Among this founding group were Arthur A. Denny, John Low, C. D. Boren, William N. Bell, Lee and Charles Terry and their families.

At first, the landing spot was named New York, at Low and Terry's suggestion but this name soon succumbed to Alki, a Chinook word which means "Bye and Bye." In the course of time, the names New York, and Alki gave way to the great friend of the white man, the Indian chief Sealth—hence the name Seattle. Today the landing spot only is still known as Alki Point. As additional pioneers came to Seattle they settled at the head of Elliott Bay. Following in the wake of the *Exact* a few weeks later, came the brig *Leonesa* to load the first commercial cargo of piling in the area. Then came a Coast Survey ship which sounded Elliott Bay for the making of navigation charts. In 1855 the Sloop-of-War *Decatur* saved Seattle from an Indian attack and later still the 200 Mercer girls were landed to bolster the small female population.

Yes, all of these historic events transpired by water in the wake of the Pacific Northwest's little Mayflower—the *Exact*.

But what became of the *Exact?* After she brought the Seattle settlers, the craft seemingly eluded historical records. But from the early re-

After stranding on Humboldt Bay bar, California, the gas schooner **CORINTHIAN** appears at rest here after her entire 12 man crew was claimed by death. The date was June 11, 1906. The 94 ton two-masted wooden vessel, engaged in coastal trading, was a total constructive loss. In the above photo, citizens of Eureka come out to look her over.

The wrecking steamer **GREENWOOD** stands by the hopeless wreck of the steamer **POMONA** which stranded on the rocks off Fort Ross, California, March 17, 1908. The vessel's stack had already fallen into the sea when this photo was taken. The passenger-cargo steamer became a total loss. The vessel was of 1,264 tons. *Meiser photo.*

No friendly welcome here. The British freighter **ORTERIC** aground on Fish Rocks, 70 miles north of San Francisco Bay and ten miles north of Point Arena. The wreck happened in thick fog on December 11, 1922, while the ship was en route to San Francisco from Puget Sound to complete loading for Australia. Valued at $750,000, the vessel was a total loss. In the service of the Bank Line, she was owned by Andrew Wier & Co.

ports of the U. S. customs office at San Francisco, pages yellowed by time, we find the account of the *Exact's* final and somewhat tragic voyage.

The schooner had just loaded a cargo at Crescent City, California, consisting of 300 barrels of salmon and ten tons of potatoes. Anchor was weighed and the *Exact* stood out to sea. After crossing the bar, a terrific gale unloosed its lungs and blew with great fury from the southwest. Aware of his precarious situation off the inhospitable northern California coast, Captain James J. Higgins who owned half interest in the vessel, elected to drop both anchors and hope the schooner would ride out the blow.

The *Exact* bucked like a bronco, as huge lunging seas slapped at her, sending great avalanches of water scudding across her deck. For hours all hands worked at the pumps and tried every way to hold out the sea. As the black of night came on, both anchor chains parted. Terror gripped the hearts of the crew as the vessel was swept toward the hostile shores. In desperation, the schooner's master tried to make sail but every sheet was ripped to shreds as it was hoisted. There was nothing left to do but to fill the sky with distress signals.

The flares were sighted by some shore dwellers who immediately organized a rescue crew from among the citizens of Crescent City. Their valiant pioneer spirit came to the fore; after hours of toil they got a stout open boat down to the beach opposite where the flares had been sighted. With the break of day they could see the *Exact* wallowing in the surf. Challenging the elements, a rugged group of oarsmen negotiated

the surf and finally managed to reach the wreck which by now was hard aground. It was a difficult piece of seamanship, but this volunteer crew, most of whom were wise in the ways of the sea, managed to remove every man from the *Exact* and bring them to safety. They were cheered hardily by the people of Crescent City who had gathered on the beach to witness the courageous effort. And none too soon had the boat reached the *Exact,* for within a few hours of the rescue, the schooner heeled over on her beam ends and quickly went to pieces under the pounding of the crashing breakers. The date was March 21, 1859.

So ended the career of the gallant schooner *Exact*. Not so much as a splinter of the vessel was saved for posterity's sake.

It is doubtful that Seattle's early citizens received the news of the tragedy for many weeks afterward, as information traveled slowly in those days. The population of Seattle was less than 300 persons when the *Exact* came to grief. Seattle's population today is well over 600,000 persons, largest city in the Pacific Northwest and all because of a little schooner which well over a century ago brought a handful of hopeful pioneers to a new frontier.

Brother Jonathan Wreck

According to the Annual Report of the Superintendent of the U. S. Coast and Geodetic Survey 1869-70, the locale where the gold-laden pioneer steamer *Brother Jonathan* went to her doom, is called Jonathan Rock. Partly submerged and awash during low tide this submarine obstruction near the western extremity

118

Lashed by huge breakers, the Associated oil tanker **ROSECRANS**, after battling a gale, became unmanageable and was driven ashore on the rocks at Alcatraz, California, 22 miles north of Santa Barbara, where two seamen lost their lives trying to launch a boat. The vessel was given up as a total loss after she went aground March 12, 1912, but in a remarkable salvage job was eventually refloated and back in service six months later. She suffered several holes in her hull including one measuring 25 feet. In September of the same year the **ROSECRANS** burned almost to oblivion at Gaviota, California. Rebuilt at something equal to her original cost, the **ROSECRANS** came to her final end January 7, 1913, on Peacock Spit, on the Columbia River bar, with the loss of 31 members of her crew. Only three were saved. Captain L. F. Johnson, who was lost with his ship had mistaken North Head Light for the lightship, which caused the stranding, ending a hectic career for the vessel which was built originally at Glasgow, Scotland in 1884.

The little schooner **EXACT** which brought the first settlers to Seattle in 1851 was wrecked near Crescent City, California on March 21, 1859. She is pictured here in an artist's conception done by Harry Anderson.

A little publicized incident of World War II was the stranding and eventual destruction of the huge 800 foot drydock **YFD-20** off Bolinas, California in 1943. The monster drydock broke loose from the tug that was towing it in rough seas. The drydock had been built only a few months earlier at Eureka at a considerable cost to Uncle Sam. Those aboard were rescued before the dock broke up.

of Point St. George's Reef has been labeled in the past as Crescent City Reef and Dragon Rocks. It is about eight miles from Crescent City in a northwesterly direction and approximately four miles and a little east of south of Northwest Seal Rock. Yet nobody is exactly sure where in the immediate vicinity the ship went down, and its wooden hull containing much wealth and the bones of scores of unfortunate shipwreck victims has eluded the most dedicated efforts of would-be salvagers for well over a century.

The *Brother Jonathan* was a staunch wooden steamer of 1,181 tons, built in 1850 by Perrine, Patterson & Stack at Williamsburg, New York, for New York shipowner Edward Mills. Measuring 221 feet in overall length with a 36 foot

beam she was a study in fine woods, built of live oak, locust and cedar and her white oak decking was 14 inches thick. Her steam plant was accompanied by a rather unorthodox sail rig, square-rigged on the foremast with two yardarms, schooner-rigged below the foreyard; and a schooner-rigged mainmast.

Her massive enclosed paddlewheels were 33 feet in diameter and were driven by a vertical beam engine with 72 inch diameter cylinder and an 11 foot piston stroke. Power was provided by a 400 horsepower single acting low pressure engine.

The $200,000 vessel carried 350 passengers in all, but the elite traveled in the deluxe cabins, 24 of them, a dozen on either side of the main

One of the remarkable feats of salvage was performed on the Associated tanker **FRANK H. BUCK** which went hard aground at Point Pinos, California near the entrance to Monterey Bay, May 3, 1924. Straddling the rocky outcroppings, it was believed that she would break up. The salvage ship **HOMER** was called to the rescue of the 6,067 ton tanker and with a crew of expert wreckers, the **BUCK** was eventually refloated, but with considerable bottom damage. She met her demise 13 years later when rammed off the Golden Gate by the SS **PRESIDENT COOLIDGE**, going aground near Point Lobos. *Heidrick photo.*

lounge with access to both lounge and outside deck. Her plush accommodation was not to last for long, however. Edward Mills placed her on the New York-Panama run until March 1852. Then Cornelius Vanderbilt purchased the ship for transfer to the Pacific but not before it received an overhaul increasing her accommodation to 750 passengers, for the "goldrush run" between Central America and San Francisco. A third mast was added, a square-rigged foremast with three yards instead of the former two, and a schooner rig below the foreyard; a yardless mainmast and a schooner-rigged mizzen. The foreward section was enlarged and the forecastle formed by the changing of the cabin superstructure. A near vertical bow replaced the clipper bow and the stack was relocated further aft. The saloon, which measured eighty feet in length below the main deck was surrounded by staterooms with paneled gilded doors.

Demand was so great for passage to San Francisco that the *Brother Jonathan* was rushed through her overhaul and hastily departed New York for San Francisco on May 14, 1852, flying the Vanderbilt houseflag. By mid-summer she was solidly on the run between San Juan del Sur, Nicaragua and San Francisco.

Overloaded with passengers every voyage, the *Brother Jonathan*, despite heavy competition, did well, and Vanderbilt saw the money pour into his many bank accounts. By early 1853, the liner passed to the Accessory Transit Company, the firm that was transporting travelers across Nicaragua by mule, stage, river and lake steamers depending on what mode of transport the individual could afford.

So the *Brother Jonathan* joined the parent firm's Nicaragua Steamship Company and ran for them until 1857, carrying droves of eager pioneers into San Francisco Bay to seek their fortunes and returning with disappointed men, many broken in spirit and health.

The *Brother Jonathan* was one of the favorite ships on the run and her appointments were elegant with considerable gingerbread work. But the most inviting of all were the excellent meals. Freshly slaughtered cattle, pigs, sheep and fowl were kept on ice aboard the vessel. The finest in fresh green vegetables, dried fruits and nuts, fresh fish, lobsters, and crab, as well as a menu full of more delicate items, turned the most finicky of passengers into gourmets, except when overcome by seasickness.

John T. Wright organized the Merchant's Accommodation Line in 1857 and purchased the *Brother Jonathan* for service between San Francisco Bay and the Pacific Northwest in competition with Pacific Mail Steamship Company. The new owner made a few alterations and renamed his acquisition *Commodore*.

Cashing in on the Fraser River goldrush, which was of short duration, Wright also added the steamer *Pacific* the following year to aid the overloads traveling between San Francisco, Puget Sound and British Columbia.

Until this time, all had gone well for J. T. but about the time the *Pacific* was assigned to the run in the summer of 1858, the *Commodore* failed to make her scheduled appearance at Victoria, B.C. The word finally reached the Canadian city that the vessel had met with heavy weather two days out of San Francisco and was forced to return to port with several feet of water sloshing her holds and boiler room. The clogged pumps found ship's personnel forming a bucket bailing brigade. The disconsolate passengers and angry miners cornered owner Wright when the badly damaged ship limped into port, demanding their money be returned. Wright was forced to pay refunds of $12,000.

The shipowner's cash reserves dwindled and in December, before the ship made another voyage, he sold her to the California Steam Navigation Company for $40,000. The once popular ship which had gained a bad reputation from that one unfortunate incident then received a major overhaul. On a San Francisco drydock her frame was strengthened with 6,000 new bolts, refitted with new furnishings, a new decor and later returned to the San Francisco, Columbia River and Puget Sound run.

Through the morning seamist, the Norwegian SS **TRICOLOR**, owned by Wilhelmsen Steamship Co. of Hunsberg, Norway, is seen in grave trouble after stranding July 26, 1905 in a heavy fog. The 6,590 ton vessel laden with 5,000 tons of coal was outbound from Oyster Bay, B. C. in command of Captain Wold. She was built on the Tyne in England just 11 months before this, her final demise. Locale of wreck, north of Cape Mendocino, California.

An avalanche of water cascades into the side of the stricken wooden steam schooner **SEQUOIA** trapped in the breakers off Humboldt Bay, California, January 14, 1907. Her crew got off safely, but the vessel which was built at Fort Bragg, California in 1898 was totally destroyed. The 519 ton steamer was engaged in the redwood lumber business.

As the Merchant's Accommodation Line withdrew from the North Coast route the California Steam Navigation Co. stepped in and the *Brother Jonathan,* (her old name restored), continued to serve coastal ports under her new owners.

In 1860, Major Samuel J. Hensley who had been acting as agent for the California Steam Navigation Co. in San Francisco purchased the steamers *Senator* and *Brother Jonathan* after CSNC went into the river transportation exclusively. He paid $200,000 for the two steamers. The *Jonathan* made calls at Southern California ports on occasion but mostly ran opposite the *Pacific* to the Pacific Northwest from San Francisco.

In May 1861, Hensley sent the *Brother Jonathan* to North's Shipyard near Mission Rock, in San Francisco for a complete overhaul. New boilers were installed, old timbers replaced and two keelsons were bolted on. The ship's bottom was completely recoppered. Oregon oak was used in the hull, Douglas fir for the spars and California redwood for the cabins.

Additional cargo space was created by cutting down on passenger accommodations, allowing a 900 ton cargo capacity. Family suites and double berths were installed with all cabins on the main deck. The steamer was cut down to a two deck vessel and a new dining saloon, 120 feet long, was built on the upper deck to replace the old one. Some $100,000 was spent on the vessel affording one of the largest overhaul jobs yet performed on a liner on the West Coast.

The end result detracted much from the former handsome appearance of the vessel but she was comfortable and ornate. After seven months of face-lifting she was ready in December 1861 for the San Francisco-Portland-Victoria run. San Francisco advertisements read:

"The new and splendid steamship *Brother Jonathan* built expressly for this route with unequaled accommodations for passengers and freight, Samuel J. DeWolf, commander, will leave Pacific Street Wharf for the above ports on Thursday, December 19, 1861, at 4 o'clock p.m. For freight or passage apply on board, or to S. J. Hensley, Washington Street, opposite the Post Office, upstairs."

The liner lived up to the boast of her advertisement for three and a half years.

Watery tombstone. Sinister view of the SS **ALASKA** jutting above the cruel sea, which turned from a raging monster to a complete calm after claiming this ship and 42 of her company August 6, 1921. The coastal passenger liner of 3,709 tons, in command of Captain Harry Hovey, and on charter to the San Francisco & Portland Steamship Company from Alaska Steamship Company, struck the outlying rocks off Blunts Reef. Tearing open her hull below the waterline she listed to starboard and went to the bottom in 15 minutes. The first boat lowered was crushed against the ship's side and all drowned. The second and third boats got away safely and the fourth turned turtle. In response to an SOS the James Griffiths' steamer **ANYOX**, 15 miles away, responded, and this ship and her crew performed an heroic piece of rescue work saving 96 passengers and 70 crewmen who might otherwise have been drowned. Captain Hovey was killed when the **ALASKA'S** stack fell on him.

On July 28, 1865, the vessel was berthed at San Francisco taking on cargo in excess of her capacity. In fact, even the casual waterfront observers were commenting at how low the *Brother Jonathan* rode in the water. The cumbersome cargo included such heavy items as woolen mill machinery, mining machinery and such oddities as two camels, some horses and a Newfoundland dog. And among the more prized treasure, locked securely in the ship's safe, was a $200,000 payroll for the troops at Fort Vancouver.

Well beyond her 900 ton freight capacity, Captain DeWolf became slightly enraged about the preponderance of cargo the owners had accepted for the voyage. The safety of more than 200 passengers, including important San Francisco and Portland business men, entertainers, government employees and miners was at stake.

Some heated words were expressed by the ship's master but the company officials told him if he did not like it he could easily be replaced. It was a moment of decision for the skipper, and as it turned out he should have followed his better judgment and walked off the ship. Nevertheless, the *Brother Jonathan,* after the usual dockside amenities, dropped her lines at high noon on July 28, 1865 and with a sonorous blast of her whistle moved slowly down the bay, deeply laden. Once out of the Golden Gate she ran smack into a nor'wester blowing down the California coast and creating nasty seas which caused much unpleasantness and seasickness aboard. Captain DeWolf was still seething over the demands of the profit-hungry company officials as his ship labored in the rough seas.

The coastwise passenger liner **ST. PAUL** is pictured aground near Point Gorda, California after stranding in the fog on October 5, 1905. Sixty-one passengers and crew members made successful their escape from the 2,442 ton liner, which later broke up. The **ST. PAUL** was built in 1898.

The McCormick steam schooner **KLAMATH** was caught like a spider in a web after going aground in an 85 mile-an-hour wind near Point Arena, California February 4, 1921. En route to the Columbia River from San Francisco, the vessel was in command of Captain Jamieson. He and his passengers and crewmen were landed safely after some harrowing moments. The vessel was a total loss.

Off Crescent City about noon on July 30, the liner gave her usual salute of one cannon shot and continued her northerly run fighting against increasingly heavy seas and stiff headwinds. As the situation worsened, the ship's master decided to turn against the sea and seek the refuge of Crescent City harbor.

Headed east by south, the vessel was driving full into the gale endeavoring to fight her way to safe haven when a frightening grinding impact brought her to a jarring halt ripping open her bottom timbers. The ship had run up and over an underwater obstruction throwing passengers to the deck. A massive geyser of water gushed in just forward of the engine room and the foremast came crashing down on the deck, cradled by the foreyard.

At a position a few miles from Crescent City, three cannon shots were fired to alert the landsmen of the ship's peril. On shore many scurried to the high bluff above the town, Indians among them, to witness the death throes of the vessel.

Most of the passengers were below deck or in their staterooms at the moment of impact. They were rudely awakened, dashing from staterooms clad in night clothes. There was confusion, terror and panic all mixed into one terrible drama in a fight for survival. The raging seas offered no hope, but nevertheless, because there was no other way to turn, six boats were launched and all but one were promptly swamped by voluminous seas before clearing the ship. The one craft that managed to get clear was in charge of the third mate James Patterson. At the time of the

Port of no return—the little coastal wooden freighter **LA FELIZ** on her beam ends on solid rock, shoulders a punishing breaker three miles north of Santa Cruz, California. The 102 ton vessel stranded October 1, 1924.

Local folks living on the Monterey Peninsula come to observe, some brave salvagers walk the twisted remains of the veteran wooden steam schooner **CELIA**, which was wrecked at Point Joe, immediately south of Monterey, California August 28, 1906. She was under the ownership of Swayne & Hoyt. Built by Matthew Turner at Benicia, California in 1884, the **CELIA** was one of the pioneer steam schooners of a vast coastal lumber fleet of about 300 vessels. She started out carrying vegetables from the Ventura area but eventually entered the redwood trade. The 173 ton vessel was a total loss, but her crew all reached shore safely.

On March 3, 1937, in a heavy fog off the Golden Gate, the Associated Oil tanker **FRANK H. BUCK** was struck by the passenger liner **PRESIDENT COOLIDGE,** receiving a mortal wound. As her crew abandoned, the tanker drifted toward the fogbound shore and went hard aground near Point Lobos within view of San Francisco's Cliff House, coming to rest within 50 feet of the remains of her sister tanker, the **LYMAN STEWART,** wrecked under identical circumstances in 1922. Both ships were built side by side in San Francisco in 1914 and came home to die, side by side. Some of the engine room casing and other wreckage of the **LYMAN STEWART** was still visible, (as seen in the photo), when the **BUCK** came to rest in the same watery plot.

crash he had been awakened from a sound sleep but came on deck in time to take charge of the boat. With him were 19 persons, five women, three children, ten crewmen and the mate. Those not at the oars bailed frantically to keep from being swamped. As it turned out, this was the only boat that escaped, reaching Crescent City about 4 p.m.; the lone survivors of the 232 persons on the ill-fated *Brother Jonathan.* The broken wreck slipped off the reef and plunged to the bottom within 45 minutes of stranding.

As the numbed survivors were cared for, a Sunday fleet of small boats had set out to sea to search for other survivors. Big fires were kept ablaze on the shore as a light of hope.

A few days later, excited Indians reported sighting a large group of people on distant Seal Rocks. A boat was provisioned and rowed 12 miles to the site only to find that the supposed survivors were only a herd of sea lions.

The handful of escapees had Captain DeWolf's last words ringing in their ears. "Tell them that if they had not overloaded us we would have got through all right and this would never have happened," he had cried mournfully as he watched the boat depart from the wreck.

One of the survivors, the ship's quartermaster, gave this account of the disaster:

"I took the helm at 12 o'clock. A northwest gale was blowing and we were four miles above Point St. George. The sea was running mountain high and the ship was not making headway. The captain thought it best to turn back to Crescent City and wait until the storm had ceased. He ordered the helm hard aport. I obeyed and it steadied her. I kept on due east. This was about 12:45. When we made Seal Rock, the captain said southeast by south. It was clear where we were, but foggy and smoky inshore. We ran until 1:50 when she struck with great force, knocking the passengers down and starting the deck planks. The captain stopped and backed her, but could not move the vessel an inch. She rolled about five minutes, then gave a tremendous

A half a ship is no ship at all. The steam schooner **GIRLIE MAHONY** is seen here a total wreck off Albion Harbor, California. She drove aground after her anchor fouled a buoy, December 23-24, 1919. The 382 ton wooden-hulled vessel, built at Aberdeen, Washington in 1903, was last owned by Olson & Mahony, of San Francisco, who purchased her less than two years earlier and changed her name from **JAMES H. HIGGINS**, to the more feminine **GIRLIE MAHONY**, for a member of the owner's family. *From Carl Christensen collection.*

thump and part of the keel came alongside. By that time the wind and sea had slewed her around until her head came out of the sea and worked off a little. Then the foremast went through the bottom until the yard rested on the deck. Captain DeWolf ordered everyone to look to their own safety and said that he would do the best for all.''

One of the first dispatches to go out after the news of the wreck reached shore went to General Drum of San Francisco informing him of the death of General George T. Wright, his staff, and the loss of $200,000 in military payroll money. Wright had been on his way to Fort Vancouver, Washington Territory to take command of the newly created Department of the Columbia.

The West Coast maritime world was stunned. The *Brother Jonathan* was one of the best known passenger ships on the Pacific and many persons had close friends or relatives among the deceased.

Captain DeWolf who bravely went down with his ship was held in the highest esteem and was almost deemed a martyr for having sailed under protest.

When passenger James Nisbet, editor and part owner of the San Francisco Bulletin realized the hopelessness of his situation, he is said to have calmly sat down on the deck of the foundering vessel and composed his will, and that will was later to be recovered from his dead body. It read:

At Sea on Board Brother Jonathan
July 30, 1865

"In view of death, I hearby grant my brother, Thomas Nisbet, at present engaged on the Pacific Railroad, near Clipper Cape, California, my sole executor, with instructions to wind up my sole estate, real and personal, and convert the same into cash with all convenient speed but so as not to sacrifice the same, and to pay over and divide the same equally between himself and my sole sister, Margaret Nisbet, now residing in England; and under burden of the payment of a legacy of five thousand dollars in gold to Almira Hopkins, wife of Casper Hopkins, insurance agent, San Francisco, California. And I desire that my brother, said Thomas Nisbet, shall not be asked to give security for his intromissions with my estate.''

At the time of the wreck, Nisbet had been en route to Victoria to obtain evidence in a libel suit.

With this will containing a note to Hopkins's wife, the penciled document was placed inside his breast pocket as he wrapped two life preservers about himself. His body was discovered two days later, the document removed and dried and a copy sent to his brother in San Francisco in care of a police officer. The will came before the California courts but it was later alleged that the brother took undue personal advantage of his position as executor.

For days after the catastrophe the beach was patrolled in search of both survivors and bodies. The currents caused corpses to wash ashore from Humboldt Bay north to Oregon's Rouge River. Some 45 were recovered in the Crescent City area alone. Many of the bodies had life jackets strapped to them. There was a varied array of ship's wreckage, cabin doors, pieces of flotsam and jetsam, furniture, luggage, etc. Some of the bodies were in ghastly condition. Even the remains of a horse and one of the camels carried in the ship's hold were found intertwined with seaweed.

Estimates of the loss of ship and cargo were never accurately established but it was conservatively placed at between $300,000 and $500,000. All that remains today are a few desecrated graves marked by old tombstones on a bluff overlooking the scene of the wreck, the memory of which time has never been able to completely erase.

Wreck of the New York

On March 13, 1948, a large group of Californians gathered on the shores of Halfmoon Bay, California to pay homage to the last living survivor of the ship *New York,* wrecked 50 years earlier on Friday March 13, 1898.

Among the invited guests were Earl Warren, governor of California, James Dean, state director of Finance and three members of Congress.

The man being honored was Paul Scharrenberg who for many years was affiliated with the Sailors Union of the Pacific.

His story of the wreck as recorded in the 1901 Christmas edition of the Coast Seamen's Journal follows:

"The American full-rigged three skysail ship *New York,* Captain Peabody, sailed from New York early in May, 1897, for a 159 day voyage to Shanghai via Cape of Good Hope. Besides the master she carried a crew of two mates, cook, steward, carpenter and sixteen able seamen.

All the crew, except four A. B.'s left the ship at Shanghai. A motley non-English speaking crew of Chinese, hired for the run then helped to sail her to Hongkong.

While in Hongkong harbor, the *New York* received a thorough overhauling; she was drydocked, painted inboard and out from keel to truck. But when Captain Peabody commenced to look for a crew he found that

After escaping enemy raiders and submarine torpedoes, during her valuable service to the allies in World War I in the English Channel, the SS **HARVARD** of the Los Angeles Steamship Co. succumbed to a foe of another kind when she ran aground in heavy fog, May 30, 1931, four miles north of Point Arguello, California. The swift turbine steamer, of 3,818 tons was evacuated by her passengers, officers and crew, without loss of life. Salvage experts were dispatched to the scene to see what the chances were of saving the vessel. All came up with negative answers; the vessel was a total loss. The **HARVARD** was built at Chester, Pa. in 1906.

Headed back to rescue more of the passengers lining the decks of the stricken passenger ship CORO-NA, a boat braves the surf as straining arms and backs lay to the oars. This photo shows the actual rescue operations after the liner straddled the north jetty of the Humboldt bar in the face of driving wind and strong, confused currents, March 1, 1907. Despite the hazardous situation only one life was lost. The volunteer surfboat performed brilliantly.

sailors were not as plentiful as Chinamen in that part of the world, and it became necessary to include two Japanese in an already cosmopolitan crew.

Finally on January 14, 1898, the *New York* sailed from Hongkong, bound for San Francisco with a cargo of general merchandise. The first part of the voyage passed by without any notable incidents. After clearing the Yellow Sea, the wind hauled astern and we were running before a gale with our main yardarms alternately touching the briny deep. The rolling and tossing kept the Chinese cook busy lashing his pots to the stove. He in turn kept us guessing about our coffee and tea, which were so much of the same flavor that we could not for our lives tell one from the other.

When about nine hundred miles off the California coast, we ran into a gale of exceptional fury. On the second day the fore topgallant mast carried away, breaking the fore

upper topsail yard in two and snapping the main skysail mast just above the royal yard. It took many hours of hard work to get things straightened up, and as there were no extra spars aboard we had to let her go under the new rig with a skysail on the mizzen and lower topsail on the foremast. Her steering had been bad enough before, but from that night the good ship could not be made to readily respond to her helm.

On March 12 we sighted the California coast, somewhere near Pigeon Point. There was a strong northwest wind and we made long tacks off and on. Very little headway was made, and the next day we were abreast of Halfmoon Bay.

Toward evening a light fog settled over the coast, and with an increasing northwest wind the old ship crawled along under her topsails at little more than three miles an hour. We stood inshore at about four o'clock, and when the watch was called four hours later to wear

128

ship, it was blowing a moderate gale. The weather was hazy, and we could neither discern the shore nor see any lights. According to calculations, we were supposed to be somewhere in the vicinity of Point Bonita Light.

The captain had been aloft himself and since he was evidently not quite sure of his whereabouts decided to wear ship and stand-off for the night. We had just commenced to square the after yards when the lookout shouted that he thought there were breakers ahead. The ship was slower than usual in answering her helm, and before we knew what was coming the *New York* was in the first line of breakers. Heavily pounding, the doomed vessel was driven broadside on the beach and the *New York* was at the end of her last journey—a hoodoo day—Friday 13, 1898.

For the next hour it was impossible to walk or stand on the decks because of heavy pounding and grinding. However, as she slowly settled in the sand there was a chance to make our way to the afterdeck. The captain's wife and little daughter were standing in the door of the charthouse, calm and prepared to meet the worst that might come. The little girl proved herself a genuine heroine; not a cry did she utter during the long hours of that night. Her thoughts seemed to be for the safety of her father and mother only.

Morning after the wreck. The full-rigged three skysail ship **NEW YORK** grounded at Halfmoon Bay, California on Friday March 13, 1898. All hands, including the ship's master, Captain Peabody reached shore safely. The 266 foot long vessel was built at Philadelphia in 1883, and was formerly known as the **T. F. OAKES**

Fifty years after being wrecked in 1907, the SS **CORONA** retains her own grave marker above the sands. Her mast is seen off Humboldt bar near an aid to navigation. The spot where she now lies was once inundated by water.

The wind continued with the same velocity, while the weather became clearer and a few stars appeared. We could also see the glare of a big fire on the beach right opposite the vessel. In the early hours of the morning we made preparations to launch the after boats. The two boats on the offshore side were smashed to splinters the moment the old craft turned broadside to the breakers. The first boat with the captain's wife and daughter and eight men, in charge of the mate, landed safely with the assistance of scores of men, who had gathered on the beach, attracted by the fireworks.

The hull of our good ship acted as a breakwater for the heavy surf; nevertheless our second mate managed to get the only remaining boat broadside to, when hitting the beach, and the cook under her with a broken leg—the only injury during the night. We made several attempts to launch the boat again and rescue the three men, including the captain, who were yet aboard the ship, but the surf continued to break heavily and not until daylight did we succeed in bringing the last three men ashore.

The old *New York*, better known as the *T. F. Oakes*, under which name she sailed for fourteen years and made some of the longest and most notorious voyages in the annals of the American Merchant Marine, stuck to the bottom until the wreckers and breakers made scrap iron of her and left her a more or less unpleasant memory to deepwater sailors the world over."

Paul Scharrenberg has since passed on, and the wreck of the *New York* and other sailing vessels of her breed remain little more than a memory.

Losing her way in a dense fog, the SS **OHIOAN** of the American Hawaiian Steamship Company, crashed on Seal Rocks outside the Golden Gate, off San Francisco, October 6, 1936. Swung broadside to the beach, several holes were stove in the vessel's hull just after she struck. Captain Tom Mac-Farlane, pilot on the ship and the rest of the officers and crew had to come ashore by breeches buoy. The freighter was bound for the East Coast from San Francisco when she grounded in a spot from which few ships have ever gained their freedom. The 5,153 ton steel freighter eventually broke up after salvagers removed deck gear and cargo. The vessel was built in 1914.

There were many red faced members of the high Navy goldbraid in this mishap. The 10,000 ton **USS MILWAUKEE**, a first class fighting ship, is seen hard aground at Samoa Beach, California in 1917, after Coast Guard and Navy personnel removed all 438 sailors and officers. It all started on the morning of December 14, 1916, when the U.S. Navy submarine **H-3** grounded in the fog on Samoa Beach. In a mounting surf, Coastguardsmen rigged up a line and breeches buoy and after many harrowing hours, managed to get the 27 crewmen ashore. Efforts by the CG cutter **McCULLOCH**, U.S. monitor **CHEYENNE** and Navy tug **ARAPAHOE**, combined, could not free the submarine. Bids were put out to private firms, but to no avail. The Navy then elected to use the **USS MILWAUKEE**, and her 24,504 horses to free the submarine. The result was the running aground and total loss of the **MILWAUKEE**. The submarine was eventually freed by digging a channel in the sands.

A seagull's eye view of the distressed steam schooner **ALCA-TRAZ**, wrecked May 2, 1917, ten miles north of Point Arena, California. One of the earlier steam schooner types, the 255 ton vessel was built by C. G. White at San Francisco in 1887 for the L. E. White Lumber Company. One of the best known and most successful units in the lumber trades, the little vessel never sailed again after going aground, as seen in the above photo.

It would have seemed as though there was no hope for this two-masted schooner wrecked near Point Arena, California January 24, 1901. The **BARBARA HERNSTER** was almost written off the books as a total loss, but persistence paid off, and several months later the battered wreck was refloated. Later rebuilt as a gas powered schooner, she finally left her bones to whiten at Bald Head at the entrance to Plover Bay, Alaska, July 28, 1905.

On the black night of July 20, 1907, the wooden steam schooner **SAN PEDRO** collided with the much larger passenger liner **COLUMBIA** off Shelter Cove, south of Mendocino Cape. The **SAN PEDRO** stuck her bow firmly into the side of the liner tearing a gash 30 feet wide. In a mad moment of terror, the **COLUMBIA** careened sharply and as her whistle emitted calls of distress the 200 passengers, some clad only in night clothes, scrambled to the decks. Counting the crew, the **COLUMBIA** had 249 persons aboard. So quickly did the liner go down that many terrified passengers never had a chance. In only five minutes the liner was gone, and when the death toll was finally released, the number lost was 87. The **SAN PEDRO** was also badly damaged. She lost her mainmast, part of her cutwater and her battered bow was filled with water. Despite this, 70 survivors of the **COLUMBIA** were taken aboard, many of which can be seen huddled on the boat deck aft, adding more weight to the little 400 ton vessel. The SS **GEORGE W. ELDER** finally came to the rescue, picking up the survivors. The **SAN PEDRO** was towed to port. Masters of both ships were found guilty, one for not being on the bridge after being called by the watch officer, the other for travelling at excessive speed in fog-patched weather. The 2,721 ton steel liner **COLUMBIA**, built in 1880, was the first vessel in the world equipped with electric lights.

This was a steam schooner? After a few weeks of assault by Pacific breakers, five miles south of Point Gorda, California this is what remained of the steam schooner **MERCED**. She went aground in adverse weather on October 15, 1913. The picture tells the rest of the story. The **MERCED** was built at St. Helens, Oregon only a few months before her loss, for the McCormick Lumber Company. She was on her second voyage.

The Pacific Coast liner **ALAMEDA** is believed in this photo to be aground near the Cliff House, off the Golden Gate. The gravity of her grounding was such that all-out efforts were made to get the liner free, efforts that proved rewarding for the rugged 1883-built vessel. The date was about 1906.

Two ships are not better than one. In this photo the SS **SANTA ROSA** has cracked in two near Point Arguello, California, an area that has a sinister reputation as a killer of ships. The **SANTA ROSA** stranded on July 7, 1911, and there were some touch and go operations in getting the passengers ashore. The Pacific Coast Steamship Company vessel, built especially for West Coast service, had a shallow draft to allow her to clear the San Pedro Harbor entrance. Originally twin-stacked, the vessel was overhauled in 1904 eliminating one funnel. The 326 foot iron-hulled steamer was built at Chester, Pa., in 1884. *Aston photo.*

Written off the books as a $300,000 loss, the steamer **SANTA ROSA** is seen here in her death agonies after breaking up near Point Arguello in the summer of 1911. Seas are seen roaring through her forward section. *Aston photo.*

Foremast, bow section and funnel askew, holds full of water, the Norwegian freighter **QUEEN CHRISTINA**, dies a slow, tormenting death on the rocks off Point St. George Reef on the northern California coast. She went on the rocks in October 1907, and is pictured here several months after grounding. The crew of the freighter reached shore safely. *Courtesy Carl Christensen.*

The first commercial ship to become a victim of Japanese submarine action along the Pacific Coast during World War II was the General Petroleum tanker **EMIDIO.** She was first under fire by the Japanese submarine **I-17**, which sent a 5.5 inch shell against her steel sides, 20 miles off Blunts Reef, north of San Francisco. The unarmed tanker radioed she was under attack, while the submarine fired four more shells, most of which landed on the tanker's boat deck, doing little damage. On approach of two U. S. Army bombers, the submarine dived and launched a torpedo which crashed through the tanker killing two men in the engine room. Three others were drowned in the launching of a lifeboat. Two boats carrying 31 survivors, (six injured), safely reached the Blunts Reef Lightship. The mortally wounded tanker, down by the stern, refused to sink, but half inundated drifted to the north some 60 miles, finally grounding at the harbor entrance of Crescent City. It later became necessary to blow up her remains to clear the harbor entrance. A piece of the hull with an account of the ship's loss was placed on the beach front as a memorial.

Full cargo of muck. This photo was taken by Carl Christensen in March 1954, showing the remains of the steam schooner **YEL-LOWSTONE.** The vessel foundered on the Humboldt bar March 1, 1933, and the wreckage came up on the beach. The vessel ended her days within a short distance of the spot where she was built, at Fairhaven on Humboldt Bay in 1907. The 767 ton vessel was built for the lumber trade.

The remains of four of seven U. S. Navy destroyers can be observed in this awesome photo. Enveloped by a steep bank of fog, the naval squadron was steaming in formation at a speed of 20 knots, and what was worse, as later developed, 30 miles off course. Off the Honda, 75 miles north of Santa Barbara, California, the flagship destroyer **DELPHY,** seen in foreground, scraped bottom, then heaved crazily on an outcrop 500 yards offshore. The destroyers all steaming in formation went aground one after another in one of the greatest peacetime losses in naval history. The date was September 9, 1923, and 22 sailors lost their lives. The other destroyers that piled up on the treacherous rocks were the **S. P. LEE, YOUNG, NICHOLAS, WOODBURY, CHAUNCEY** and **FULLER.** An enemy could not have done a more perfect job. Hundreds of Navy personnel finally reached safety after hours of rescue work.

No spot for a three-masted schooner. The **ALICE McDONALD,** poked her bow up on the beach near Point Loma, California in 1910. Though the era of sail had begun to wain, salvage efforts were undertaken and the vessel refloated and returned to service. The aging schooner, which is still carrying her wooden-stocked anchors in this photo was built at Bath, Maine in 1888 by John McDonald for Flint & Co.

Neglect of the use of the lead and foggy weather were given as the reasons for the wreck of the British four-mast bark **GIFFORD** which stranded in late September, 1903, at Mussel Rock, San Francisco, (now Daly City area). Inbound for San Francisco from Newcastle with a cargo of coal, the vessel became a total loss. Built in 1892, the steel-hulled **GIFFORD,** owned by Weir & Co., was of 2,245 tons. *Courtesy San Francisco Maritime Museum.*

Two beach walkers observe the pitiful remains of the five-masted schooner **WILLIAM H. SMITH,** which had last earned her way as a fish barge off the California coast. She is pictured here after being driven aground off Monterey, California, April 14, 1933. The vessel was originally built at Bath, Maine, in 1883 as a full-rigged ship.

The power of God's hand and the punyness of man is exemplified in this photo. It shows the Greek freighter **IOANNIS G. KULUKUNDIS** after stranding on a sandbar five miles north of Point Arguello, California, July 11, 1949. The 422 foot, 7,000 ton Liberty type ship, was under command of Captain G. Mastrominas, and carried a crew of 32, all of whom were rescued by the Coast Guard. Two salvage attempts were undertaken to free the vessel, but she held fast. Aboard was 9,000 tons of grain, valued at $600,000. The ship was valued at $500,000. This photo was taken at 4 p.m., four hours after the vessel stranded.

Like a waterfall, water drains from the wreck of the Greek freighter **IOANNIS G. KULUKUNDIS** as a breaker retreats, five miles north of Point Arguello. The cascading seas played havoc with the Greek Liberty ship. The crew was still aboard here. One man can be seen looking down on number four hatch. Steam is still up, smoke coming from the stack. The vessel was a total loss. The date was July 11, 1949.

Powerful wave explodes on bow section of the lumber steamer **COOS BAY**, which earlier ran aground in the fog, October 22, 1927, near Lands End, at the entrance to San Francisco Harbor. Note the rock puncture in her hull at the waterline. The crew of the **COOS BAY** was rescued but the ship soon broke up, beyond chance of salvage. Built in 1909, as the **VULCAN**, the vessel was owned by Pacific States Lumber Company of San Francisco, and was of 5,149 gross tons. *Courtesy Mike McGarvey.*

Cargo salvage work is underway in this photo. It shows the Waterman Line's SS **CHICKASAW** aground on Santa Rosa Island, off the California Coast; the barge **PT&B 402**, the powerful salvage ship **SALVAGE CHIEF** and Columbia Helicopters' copter. Fred Devine, owner of the salvage vessel was hired to remove the cargo after hopes of saving the freighter were dismissed. The **CHICKASAW** stranded in a rainstorm February 7-8, 1962 en route to Los Angeles from Japan. Most of the ship's cargo was successfully removed. The helicopter flew lines back and forth, piloted by Wes Lematta. The **CHICKASAW**, after being claimed a total loss and abandoned to the underwriters was sold by auction in May 1962. The 439 foot long C-2 type freighter, built at Kearny, N.J. in 1942, left her bones to rust on the tentacles of the lonely Pacific isle.

Commercial and amateur divers alike have for decades hunted for the remains of the SS **CITY OF RIO DE JANEIRO** which during the early morning darkness of February 22, 1901 crashed aground near Fort Point at the entrance to San Francisco Bay in heavy fog. Amid often bloated stories of treasure reputedly aboard the vessel, the hunt for the wreck goes on even today. In that awful maritime disaster, right at San Francisco's front door, the vessel went down with 129 passengers and crewmen, one of the greatest marine tragedies in California's history. There were only 81 survivors. The liner is pictured below, a few years before her demise while in the transpacific service of Pacific Mail Steamship Company. Slightly off course, due to the swift currents, the rocks of Cantil Blancos suddenly showed their sharp black fangs at the time of impact. Amid frantic blasts of the whistle, the ship went down in less than 20 minutes as night clothes-clad survivors struggled in the frigid waters. Among those lost was the ship's skipper, Captain William Ward. Some experts believe that the wreck of the **RIO DE JANEIRO** drifted under the sea projection called Arch Rock which was later dynamited as a marine obstruction, which in turn could have completely covered the wreck with shale. *Courtesy San Francisco Maritime Museum.*

CHAPTER SIX

Alaska Shipwrecks

Who could count the number of wrecks that lay scattered over the hundreds of miles of harsh shoreline that composes Alaska, that giant among states, where they say that even today there are many spots that have not been fully explored.

Though the Spaniards and the British get credit for most Pacific exploration, the Russian role in the Pacific was also significant. Though they may not have been as far ranging, yet in their endeavors to establish new trading posts in North America they were forced to operate in the world's most troublesome and fickle waters where the storm gods would blow out their lungs. Countless ships were snagged on the rocky crags jutting out from the perilous Aleutian isles. Virtually unpopulated, they are like giant stepping stones dividing the Bering Sea from the North Pacific Ocean.

The ancient Russian mariners sailing from Siberian ports followed along the Aleutian chain and often became their victims when swept ashore in mountainous seas and driving snow storms.

One of the most famous of the Russian ships to fall victim along this perilous route was *the Three Saints.* This was the ship that carried Gregorii Shelekof to Kodiak Island in 1784 where the Russian merchant established the first permanent colony at Three Saints Bay.

Then in 1790, while taking the infamous Alexander Baranof, Shelekof's chief manager to Russian America, *The Three Saints* was wrecked somewhere off Unalaska Island. After a bitter winter on Unalaska, Baranof continued his journey to Three Saints Bay—600 miles away in a native skin boat.

Recently (1969), Ted Bank, a Michigan scientist working under the banner of the Explorers Club, believed he had found the grave of *The Three Saints.* The site is on the north side of Unalaska Island, and should the wreck turn out to be the 200 year old *Three Saints,* it could be one of the greatest shipwreck discoveries of modern times.

Alaska—the very word—reminds one of vastness and ruggedness. One of the stormiest regions of the entire world exists between Yakutat Bay and the Arctic Ocean. This is particularly true of the middle and outer Aleutian Islands. Heavy weather with rain or snow is a common occurrence. Clouds are often very low, and dense fogs are frequent. Temperatures are moderated, however, to the southern edge of the Bering Sea by the transport of warm water into this area through the Japan Current system.

By contrast Southeastern Alaska is made up of a myriad of islands, islets, mountains and valleys representing one of the most fascinating inside water passages in the world, equal to the fjords of Norway. Population, even in this day is sparse and air and water transportation are the only means of transport between the islands where many of the towns and cities are located. This remarkable waterway is frequented by freak tides and currents and only the most experienced of navigators should challenge its waters.

Commercial fishermen and tugboat operators respect the inside passage and realize that though it is deceptively beautiful it can also be extremely dangerous. A few mute reminders of the countless ships that litter the shores of Southeastern Alaska can still be seen.

The outside passage to Southwestern Alaska from the Strait of Juan de Fuca is some 1,340 miles via the North Pacific. The barometer is jumpy in that part of the world and weather patterns are uncertain. The winds come from every direction over the Aleutians and strong gales are the most severe from the north. The average wind force in the Aleutian Islands latitude strip for January is Beaufort force 5, up to 21 mph, but force 12 winds above 65 mph are not uncommon when the weather sours.

The williwaw is the name given to the violent winds which frequently occur on the leeward side of the mountains of the Aleutians and western Alaska. It is an especially dangerous wind due to the suddenness of its occurrence as well

Stark drama in the making—the Canadian Pacific liner **PRINCESS SOPHIA** cradled on Vanderbilt Reef, her lifeboats swung out, October 24, 1918. The wind-whipped waters prompted the delay of the rescue till a more opportune time. That night, the steamer slipped off the reef and went to the bottom with her entire company of 343 persons. *Winter Pond photo.*

as to its violence and extreme gustiness; it occurs when the air dams up in great quantity on the windward side of a mountain and then spills over suddenly as an overwhelming surge. The local topography determines the direction from which williwaws will blow. When for example a well developed low pressure area lies near and just south of Dutch Harbor or just south of Adak Island and a large high pressure area dominates the Bering Sea, then the strong northerly and northwesterly winds are likely to cause williwaws over many of the leeward coasts of the Aleutian chain. The violence and turbulence often raises giant seas, in this, one of the more remote sectors of the world.

The long coastal area of Alaska, north of Bering Strait is considerably smoother in general than the Alaskan coastline to the south. It is also less rugged, the portion from Icy Cape eastward being comparatively flat with no elevations as high as 1,000 feet within 100 miles of the coast.

The hitherto lonely Arctic has taken on new meaning in recent years with the fantastic oil discoveries on the North Slope centered at Prudhoe Bay, and the long frozen Northwest Passage, though the season is extremely brief, may someday become a well used passage for merchant ships. In bygone years, only the whaling ships, government ships and an occasional trader would venture to these frozen wastes.

Princess Sophia Disaster

Of the scores of shipwrecks in and around Alaska, the most tragic from the standpoint of loss of life was that of the Canadian Pacific passenger liner *Princess Sophia* in Southeastern Alaska's inside passage. The trim steamer draped herself over dreaded Vanderbilt Reef in October of 1918 and when she later slipped off that reef she went to Davy Jones Locker with her entire complement of 343 passengers and crewmen. There was but a single survivor, a bedraggled half-crazed dog.

The appalling tragedy claimed 218 men, 33 women and 17 children — totaling some 268 passengers plus 75 officers and crew members.

The scene of the terrible disaster was in Lynn Canal, 40 miles from Juneau and four miles west of Sentinal Island. Sentinal Island was the spot where another Canadian Pacific liner, the *Princess May* grounded just eight years earlier under remarkably similar circumstances. After evacuation of her passengers she was refloated and eventually repaired. The similarities in the wrecks perhaps brought about less concern for removing the passengers from the *Sophia* than might otherwise have been exercised.

And another strange coincidence was that the lighted buoy that was to have marked Vanderbilt Reef, replacing a can buoy, was aboard the lighthouse tender *Cedar* which was among the vessels that answered the distress calls of the *Sophia*. Those distress calls were received in Juneau at 2:15 a.m. at the U. S. wireless station there, just 15 minutes after the *Sophia* stranded on the reef, October 24, 1918.

In all, seven vessels responded to the call for assistance including the *Estebeth, Amy, Lonefisherman, King & Winge, Elinor, Elsinore,* and the *Cedar.*

Captain J. P. Locke, master of the *Sophia* sent out a dispatch to F. F. W. Lowel, general agent for CPR in Juneau, that the stranded *Sophia* was in no immediate danger and he was confident of no serious problem inasmuch as the ship was double bulkheaded and had a double bottom.

Due to prevailing rough seas it was decided inadvisable to remove passengers but it was decided that they would be transferred to the *Cedar* as soon as weather conditions permitted.

Occasional snow began to fall and the greybacks raised their hoary heads. The appearance of the weather became grim and some of the smaller standby vessels were forced to move to more protected areas. Soon the inky darkness came on with a veil of impending doom. It was during that howling blackness, between 8 o'clock the evening of October 24 and 7 a.m. the next day that a terrible drama of death was enacted. Unseen by any of the would-be rescue ships, the *Sophia* suddenly slipped off the reef in a grinding, screaching movement, immediately filled, and plummeted to the bottom trapping all hands inside the steel coffin. Her last message— "For God's sake, Come! We are sinking!" Within moments it was all over.

With the first pale glow of dawn the *Cedar* relayed the grim message to Juneau.

"Sophia driven over reef during night. Only masts showing. No survivors. Will cruise Lynn Canal to leeward. Blowing storm. Started snowing this morning. *King & Winge* assisting."

The *Cedar* had moved slowly through the contorted sea into the northwest gale as near the reef as possible but could find little trace of the liner nor any survivors. The bitterly cold and blinding snowstorm and near zero visibility made conditions nearly impossible. Unable to find any survivors the *Cedar* was forced to seek shelter where she remained at anchor until Saturday morning. On returning to the scene of the wreck only the tips of the *Sophia's* masts remained above the water.

Several hours before the *Sophia* went down, the late Captain L. H. (Kinky) Bayers, was returning from Peril Straits in the gas schooner *Anita Phillips* when he was "flagged down" at Shoal Point by Capt. Ed McDougal of the *Amy* and informed of the *Princess Sophia* being astride the reef. He followed the *Amy* to Lincoln Island and then lost sight of her in the snowstorm raging near Vanderbilt Reef. The *Anita Phillips* proceeded to the scene of the disaster, arriving there on Thursday night.

"We picked up the lights of the *Cedar* cruising nearby and made out another vessel as the *King and Winge,"* said Captain Bayers. "We bucked the storm up to a point between the wreck and the buoy intending to drop the hook and ride her out until morning, but could not hold bottom, so made a run for shelter in Tee Harbor. It was pretty tough crossing the canal as we fought a blinding snowstorm and heavy northwest wind, accompanied by giant seas, but we were able to make it with only two broken windows on the port side of the wheelhouse. Come daylight, we left Tee Harbor and had fairly good going to Vanderbilt Reef. The lighthouse tender *Cedar,* the *King & Winge* and *Estebeth* were there, but due to their size were unable to get within hailing distance of the *Sophia.* I saw a small flat-bottomed skiff leave the *Estebeth.* It's occupant was able to row nearly to the *Sophia,*

There was not a single survivor aboard the stranded passenger steamer **PRINCESS SOPHIA** when a few hours after this photo was taken she slipped from perilous Vanderbilt Reef in Alaska. There was, however, a dog carried on the vessel that survived the ordeal, of this, the worst of all Alaska shipwrecks.

Caught on a pincushion of rocks —the passenger liner **AL-KI** aground off Point Augusta, Alaska, Nov. 1, 1917. All hands were rescued but the 1,259 ton vessel became a total loss. Built at Bath, Maine in 1884, the vessel spent most of her years on the Puget Sound-Alaska run.

but then was forced to turn back. At this time it would have been an easy matter to launch all of the lifeboats of the *Sophia* and come to where we could have picked them up. I ran the *Phillips* up to within 100 feet of the *Sophia* and spoke to Captain Locke, her master. I told him to launch his lifeboats and we and the *Estebeth* would pick them up by the buoy, but he refused saying that the *Princess Alice* (a passenger ship of the Canadian Pacific Railway Company) would arrive the next day and that he was in no immediate danger.

"We cruised around until about noon, when the wind began to pick up again," continued Captain Bayers. "We were again forced to run for shelter in Tee Harbor, where we had to work on the engine. Saturday morning we again left Tee Harbor for Vanderbilt Reef. The weather had flattened out pretty good. When we arrived at the reef, only the masts of the *Sophia* were showing. We began cruising around Lincoln and Ralston Island, looking for possible survivors, but saw none, so we left for town to get gas and supplies as we were about out. On the way, we picked up 48 bodies floating in an oil slick between Shelter Island and Shoal Point."

The *Monaghan,* Captain Robert O. Griswold, arrived in Juneau from the scene of the wreck with 26 bodies which she recovered in the vicinity of Shoal Point, Douglas Island.

Captain Griswold and Deputy Marshal Harry F. Morton, visited the scene of the wreck and examined Vanderbilt Reef at low tide. They found that the rocks had been worn and broken by the weight of the *Sophia.* The part of the reef where the bottom of the vessel rested, was worn as smooth as glass by the action of the ship and was white from the grinding. The bow of the sunken liner was facing in the opposite direction from where she struck the rocks, with her foremast sticking up and with her guy ropes taut. The theory was expressed that the heavy storm quartered on the vessel's stern, which was free from the reef, swung her slowly around, the bow holding until the vessel faced in the opposite direction. With only her bow holding, the *Sophia* floated free and filled from a hole in the forward section.

Eighty-seven employees of the White Pass & Yukon Route, comprising the officers and crews of ten steamers operated by the company on the Yukon River, were among the passengers lost in the *Princess Sophia* disaster. The steamer crews were coming out of the North for the winter, navigation having closed with the freezing of the river.

Others lost were William Scouse of Seattle and Dawson, who was reputed to have hoisted the first bucket-full of gold-bearing gravel on fabulously rich Klondyke Creek; Mrs. F. Benson, one of the first white women in Iditarod City; Walter Burns, wealthy hydraulic operator in the Yukon gold country; John F. Pugh, collector of customs of the Alaska district; Mrs. F. Featon, wife of the discoverer of the Iditarod claim and Thomas MacMahon, a merchant of Flat City.

Lynn Canal, scene of the loss of the *Princess Sophia,* is one of the most dangerous areas of all Alaskan waters during the winter season. It has

142

been the scene of numerous wrecks. In 1898, just after Christmas the little steamer *Clara Nevada,* after landing a group of gold seekers at Skagway and Dyea, was lost with a toll of 38 lives about 11 miles north of Vanderbilt Reef in just such a snowstorm as was encountered by the *Princess Sophia.*

Another early wreck in Lynn Canal in the same vicinity, was the steamer *Ancon,* a small vessel, which was pounded to pieces in Lynn Canal in 1889. The schooner *W. H. Dimond* went on the beach at the head of Admiralty Island on Bird Island about 20 miles south of the scene of the *Princess Sophia* and became a total loss in February 1914.

Theoretically, it was believed the *Princess Sophia* had over-run her time from Eldred Rock, due to strong tail winds, and was unable to pick up the buoy or fix her position due to the blinding snowstorm. Ironically enough, as was mentioned earlier, the lighted buoy which was to replace the old can buoy marking the reef, was on board the lighthouse tender *Cedar,* and would have been placed in position with a break in the weather.

For many years, bodies were found on the Alaska beaches by fishermen, hunters and others, most presumed to be victims of the *Princess Sophia* disaster. Today, persons strolling through the Juneau cemetery may see a plot containing more than a hundred mounds with small wooden numbered stakes as headstones, marking the last resting place of the unidentified dead from the ill-fated liner.

The tragedy has never been forgotten and it was revived again only a few years back when two Alaskan divers descended on the wreck and came up with some bits of wreckage including

the teredo-eaten wooden steering wheel. The wreck lies scattered over the ocean bottom as it has for the past half century, an underwater tombstone to those who perished on that regrettable night.

The wreck of the *Sophia* brought about 15 years of litigation, ending in the U. S. Supreme Court which refused to review the ruling of the Circuit Court of Appeals limiting liability of the owners to $643 for 227 victims' estates. The claims of their survivors aggregated $2,095,000. It was claimed that up to 40 pounds of legal papers were hauled into court by the defense attorneys.

Destruction and Resurrection of the Islander

Many years ago there was an aged prospector that lived in a shack on the beach near Juneau. Every week or so he would come in to town with enough gold to buy his grub stake. He was frequently asked where he got his gold but refused to divulge his secret. Certain people got curious and went out to spy on the old prospector. To their amazement they found him panning it right off the beach near Lynn Canal.

When the *Islander* was raised in 1934, after nearly 33 years in the depths off Douglas Island, the anticipated loot was not to be had. The amount of gold recovered was not enough to cover the expenses of the salvage undertaking. What happened to the treasure on this ship which sank with a loss of 42 lives after striking an iceberg August 15, 1901?

It was surmised that the gold dust the old prospector was panning off the beach might have been swept from the ship by strong underwater currents.

Salvage operations are underway here on the U. S. Army Transport **ELNA,** which ran aground in the Kuskokwim River area of Alaska in June, 1943. She was pulled 2,000 feet by the **USS DISCOVERER** and freed with the ice breakup, only to be totally lost at Wide Bay, Alaska December 27, 1943.

Plaything for the vicious Alaska surf—American (barkentine) sailing vessel **CATHERINE SUDDEN** breaking up near Nome after stranding on September 7, 1900 in a violent storm. Built at Port Ludlow, Washington in 1878, the vessel was valued at $50,000. *Nowell photo.*

This is all that remained of the famous Alaska gold ship **IS-LANDER** after she was dragged ashore from her sea grave near Douglas Island. In a novel salvage effort a cradle was rigged between two barges, with slings placed beneath the ship's hull. The extreme tides were used to aid the process of getting the wreck to shallow water. That was in 1934; the **ISLANDER** went down in 1901 after supposedly striking an iceberg. Forty-two persons lost their lives in the tragedy. The purpose of the salvage, for the most part, was to recover the huge amounts of gold the vessel carried. Only a portion was recovered.

The SS *Islander* was the pride of the Canadian Pacific Navigation Company. A sturdy 20-knot queen, she was easily the finest thing on the Alaska run.

The *Islander* pulled out of Skagway en route to Vancouver, B.C. on a summer evening carrying a large passenger list, and a quantity of gold from the fields at the other end of Stampede Pass. Just how much gold the *Islander* carried seems never to have been properly recorded. Most think it was about $1,250,000, but the total swelled to $3,000,000 after the ship went down.

People have a way of contorting such things. The ship's owners claimed only $250,000.

Aboard the *Islander* were 183 persons, including 81 crew members and three stowaways trying to get free passage to the "outside." There was much revelry aboard the ship for the fever of the Gold Rush was still very much in swing.

A happy crowd celebrated until the vessel made her usual stop at Juneau a few hours later.

In command of Capt. H. R. Foote, the *Islander* steamed out of Juneau around midnight. Many of the passengers had turned in but others were living it up in the ship's saloon. The smoking room also was full of gay passengers playing cards for high stakes and guzzling down hard liquor.

The captain was enjoying a midnight snack. He was a bit perturbed with his pilot who had come on duty slightly inebriated and had caused him to stand an extra long watch on the bridge.

As he was downing his coffee, the liner suddenly slipped into a pall of glacial fog.

The whistle sounded a warning in the restricted visibility but the *Islander* continued her 15-knot clip. The whistle blew again but the passengers appeared little concerned.

The bow watch pulled his coat up around his ears and shivered in the frigid night air, eyes watering as he stared straight ahead. Suddenly before him a great blue mountain of ice rose like a gigantic phantom from the depths of the sea. He blinked once and then again. His hair almost stood on end. "Iceberg!" he shouted, "Iceberg dead ahead!"

The quartermaster heard the chilling cry and hastily put the helm hard over.

There were a few terrifying seconds before the impact and then the vessel plowed into the towering berg. It had broken off of Taku Glacier after the summer currents had swept against the bosom of the glacial flow.

The jar awakened the passengers who were asleep and those who had not retired were thrown into utter confusion. Captain Foote dashed out of the saloon and made a beeline for the bridge. On the way, he encountered the somewhat sobered pilot who informed him that the ship had struck an iceberg but that all the watertight compartments had been closed off.

Since the building of the *Islander* in 1888, she had been advertised as an unsinkable ship due to the innovation of watertight compartments, and this statement had become an advertising standard for many years. The *Islander* was the ultimate on the Alaska run ... alas, they said the same things about the Atlantic greyhound *Titanic* eleven years later.

The whiplash action of the *Islander* against the ice had jammed many stateroom doors shut. Rudely awakened passengers started banging on them trying to get out. A mild panic broke out in various corners of the ship. The stewards were running from door to door assuring the occupants that there was nothing to worry about—the ship was unsinkable. "Go back to bed and forget it," they would tell them, "We'll take care of the doors at daybreak."

In the engine room, optimism was waning. The chief engineer reported water pouring in faster than the pumps could throw it back out.

The ice (or obstruction) had torn a gash for several feet below the waterline, allowing water to enter several of the watertight compartments.

In a hasty parley with his officers, Captain Foote, reluctantly admitted that the damage was extremely serious. A rescue party was organized, and armed with fire axes went below and began freeing passengers by hacking down stateroom doors.

The passengers in night clothes crowded into the passageways pushing and shoving endeavor-

These twin screws once propelled the Canadian steamer **IS-LANDER**, and were still intact when the vessel was raised by the Curtis Housemoving Company in 1934. The vessel, which went down on August 15, 1901, yielded only a portion of the suspected gold aboard and the entire salvage endeavor came out in the red.

ing to get topside. The lights flickered off and on and panic grew. There appeared no order—everybody running in different directions. The ship's officers attempted to quell the fears of the passengers but it was like trying to stop a stampede of cattle. There were many pokes of gold aboard and the safe contained more. Some of the passengers forgot their loot in favor of their lives, while others tightly clutched gold dust and nuggets leaving all else behind.

As the ship settled deeper, boats were lowered, every man looking out for himself. Some of the lifeboats were unceremoniously dropped from the davits partially filling as they hit the water. One with a capacity of 40 got away with seven persons in it. Another carried only seventeen while dumbfounded souls walked about the slanting decks, dazed.

The *Islander's* stern suddenly began to lift and those still aboard grabbed for anything solid enough to help them keep their feet. Families and loved ones hovered together. Haunting sounds of weeping and hysterical screaming echoed over the dark waters, mingled with the mournful death call of the ship's whistle. The *Islander* was going down fast.

The bow slipped under the water and the ship's twin propellers fanned the air with a terrifying whrrrr. Then there was an explosion as the frigid sea water wrapped its clutches around the red hot boilers.

Lifeboats were rowed frantically away as the spinning propellers and the suction of the ship going down almost imperiled their escape. Trembling violently from stem to stern the giant steel coffin slithered into the vortex and those aboard leaped in desperation into the disturbed waters. Some were drowned immediately, others, the blood frozen in their veins, struggled to find a piece of wreckage. One man had jumped overboard with a suitcase filled with gold. He went down like a rock.

Then with one final hissing of boiling steam the *Islander* slipped from sight and only the last cries of the doomed settled over that black sea of death.

The lifeboats drifted from the scene and when they returned two hours later, the sea was void of struggling humans.

At dawn, a party of survivors led by chief engineer Brownlee, walked along the beach toward Juneau in search of help. They reached Treadwell Mine where the steamers *Flossie* and *Lucy* lay with steam up. The ships immediately took the survivors on to Juneau.

Rescue boats lingered about the grave of the *Islander* but found only a few bloated bodies. The toll stood at 42 dead or missing.

When the SS *Queen* delivered the news to the "outside" three days after the *Islander* had plunged to her doom, newspapers came out with bold headlines of the disaster. As soon as the list of obituaries was run, the interest turned from death to gold, 'and for years after the disaster men dreamed and plotted how to get at the treasure hidden within the recesses of the *Islander,* lying over 300 feet below the surface.

Many salvage plans were devised without success, but in the summer of 1928, Captain Thomas P. Quinn, went north as pilot and nautical

The rugged little two-masted schooner **CHALLENGE** ashore at Nome, Alaska at the turn of the century. Homeported at Unalaska, the vessel was built at Seattle in 1885. *Lomen Bros. photo courtesy R. E. Mackay.*

Resting on the bottom of Sumner Straits, Alaska after striking an uncharted rock, the steam schooner **DELHI** became a total loss. Owned by the Pacific Coast Steamship Company, the **DELHI** was commanded by Captain C. P. McCarthy. The wreck occurred on January 18, 1915. Salvagers finally succeeded in towing the wreck to Prince Rupert where it was rendered worthless, a huge hole torn out of the bottom timbers. The loss was set at $140,000. The vessel was built at Winslow, Washington in 1906.

adviser with the Wiley expedition. He descended to the *Islander* wreck several times in a revolutionary diving bell designed by Carl and Albert Wiley of Olympia. It was an 1,800-pound cast iron mechanism 40 x 48 inches and capable of holding one man with sufficient air for a period of one hour. It had been tested to a depth of 750 feet. There were inch thick glass observation portholes in the bell and an arm extending from it containing a large claw which could be worked from inside the bell. This diving chamber could be lowered on a heavy cable from the side of a ship.

Initial goal of the Wiley expedition of course, was to locate the *Islander's* safe, said to contain fabulous wealth. On being lowered to the wreck, Quinn described the *Islander* lying in the murky depths, as weird and ghostly, heavily encrusted with barnacles and other marine growth. The stacks and masts were gone and much of the upper housing. The vessel had been badly shaken by the implosion that occurred after she went down in the depths.

Bad weather eventually hampered operations but the claw on the diving bell did recover several relics from the wreck including the ship's cash register, a German revolver, a watch, a sugar bowl, field glasses and some women's stockings. These articles were displayed at Seattle and Vancouver, B.C. and only tended to stir a stronger desire to locate the gold.

But the *Islander* was in such a position that it would take more than a diving bell to gain anything of value. The ship would have to be raised.

In 1934 when the depression was hitting hard, a Seattle company figured they had little to lose by going all out in a desperate effort to raise the *Islander* and recover her gold.

Though Canadian Pacific Navigation Company, owner of the *Islander* at the time of her loss had always maintained that the vessel did not have any great quantity of gold aboard, that claim failed to dim the determination of treasure hunters. It was a known fact that many of the passengers were returning from the gold fields when they took passage on the *Islander* and some had pokes stashed away in places other than the safe. But the greater part of the treasure appeared to have been loaded on the vessel after it sank.

On the other hand, 19 affidavits from 19 passengers were sworn to. Each of these survivors swore that they saw three million dollars in gold put aboard the liner at Seward.

There is another account of a Los Angeles group who claimed to have gone down to the wreck in a diving bell in 1915 and to have extracted $100,000 in gold dust from various compartments of the ship. However, there is little to substantiate this claim and it probably was as overdone as the amount of gold reputed to be on the vessel.

To get back to our story—the expedition to raise the *Islander* in 1933-34 was headed by Frank Curtis of the Curtis Housemoving Company of Seattle. They purchased for a paltry sum, two old ships, the barge *Griffson* and the barge *Forest Pride*, (a former barkentine rigged sailing vessel), and towed them to Alaska. A diving bell also went with the expedition.

At the start, the water was full of silt from Taku Glacier. This made visibility difficult under the water. Strong lights were rigged to the diving bell but it was several days before the hulk could be viewed with any clarity in her ocean grave.

147

Port of no return—U. S. lighthouse tender **ARMERIA** aground at Cape Hinchinbrook, Alaska May 20, 1912. Note the flag of distress and a boat leaving the vessel. Her crew all escaped safely but the ship and her gear were totally lost. The sum came to $400,000, she being one of the finest government lighthouse tenders of her day. The **ARMERIA** was built at Camden, New Jersey in 1890 and was of 1,052 tons.

When the water cleared sufficiently for further work, plans proceeded for placing cables around the hull of the wreck. It took one solid month of 18 hour days to perform this task.

The *Islander* lay off Douglas Island, almost 12 miles south of Juneau, but for reasons of contour of the sea's bottom the wreck had to be dragged to Admiralty, a mile and three quarters distance as against a half mile had it have been taken to the nearest beach. It was a tremendous job prying the wreck loose as it was under 14 feet of silt.

Though a month was required to get the first cable around the *Islander,* the other cables were placed much more rapidly. A rather simple method was used. There were 40 winches on the decks of the *Griffson,* 20 on each side. They handled the cables that went under the wreckage and were cinched up at each low tide, thus allowing the barge to move the wreck closer to the shore with each full tide.

There was one long flat stretch of beach. A line was cinched on a big rock on shore and this permitted the *Islander* to be pulled along the bottom almost a half mile in a single night.

But the summer ended all too soon and the wreck was still well submerged though in comparatively shallow water. She was then securely anchored in position and buoyed until the raw winter storms ran their courses.

The weeks dragged by slowly. The Curtis outfit were overly anxious to get back to work and drag the *Islander* ashore where they could search her confines for the lost gold.

In the spring, the operation continued. Then one day the superstructure of the wreck struck the keel of the *Griffson.* The bottom was becoming shallower and a new problem arose. The wreck lay beneath the salvage barge. What to do?

This is when the experts of the outfit came up with a practical solution. They put the *Forest Pride* to work and built a cradle between the two ships. Instead of 20 lines running to 40 winches on the barge *Griffson,* half of the lines were left on her and the other half placed on the *Forest Pride.* This permitted the *Islander* to be cinched up between the two ships with each tide. By this method the wreck was run right up on the beach.

Due to the extreme tides, the treasure ship was completely exposed at low water and virtually covered on the flood tide. She was a solid mass of slime, seaweed and barnacles from stem to stern. Some of the barnacles exceeded 14 inches in length. When exposed to the air the stench was almost overpowering. People in nearby villages to the windward, complained.

But now, alas, the *Islander* had been raised and a systematic search of her mutilated remains was begun. Inspection turned up strange, humorous and tragic bits of evidence.

The reader should keep in mind that the ship had been on the bottom for almost 35 years. There were cases of the finest champagne which was as fresh and bubbly as the day it was brought aboard. Not so good were the bottles of whiskey. Salt water had seeped in around the corks of many of the bottles and overly anxious salvagers naturally had to sample it. Disappointed, they spat it out with distaste.

Teredo-eaten ship's blocks and tackle were strewn about the decks. A wrench worn almost paper thin by rust was found in the engine room. A kerosene lamp was found still swinging in its gimbel and filled with oil. A salvage man lit a match to the wick and it burned. Some men's suits were found with the press still in them and shoes still polished were found under a berth.

The mute remains of a coal passer in one of the ship's bunkers was discovered. He had evidently been trapped after the ship struck the iceberg. A bunker door had slid shut and locked itself as the ship listed and sank. The passer was imprisoned in the dark and must have died a horrible death. Evidence showed he had tried to pry the door open with his shovel, probably becoming frantic, as the handle was broken in two.

Oh, yes, the reader wonders about the gold. In the ship's safe which was somewhat battered, $7,000 dollars was recovered, in paper, gold and silver. A 17-pound poke was found in the men's lavatory plus tidbits of gold here and there. The contents of the entire ship were run through improvised sluice boxes but the take was most discouraging.

The Curtis people were none too happy over their undertaking. Conservative estimates say they recovered about $40,000 in all. It was a poor return when one considers that nearly a quarter of a million was sunk into the venture. The disappointing conclusion to an adventurous undertaking made many people lose their thirst for seeking gold on sunken wrecks.

There were offers to purchase the battered hulk to put her on exhibition, but none cared to foot the bill to move the wreck elsewhere. After souvenir hunters picked her bones, scrap cutters came in and stripped her bare.

Despite the outcome, it was nevertheless one of the great salvage feats of our century, though one that was doomed to failure, financially speaking. Most everything was there but the $3 million.

Since the *Islander* went to her doom, fantastic stories of how the gold disappeared have been

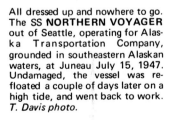

All dressed up and nowhere to go. The SS **NORTHERN VOYAGER** out of Seattle, operating for Alaska Transportation Company, grounded in southeastern Alaskan waters, at Juneau July 15, 1947. Undamaged, the vessel was refloated a couple of days later on a high tide, and went back to work. *T. Davis photo.*

Trying to climb an Alaska mountain is quite a job for a ship, but that is just what the MS **ZAPORA** endeavored to do after grounding on the desolate western shore of Admiralty Island February 12, 1937. The little freight and passenger vessel, operating between Seattle and southeastern Alaska, became a total loss. Seven passengers and nineteen crewmen survived.

One of numerous major strandings in the life of the Alaska Steamship Company passenger liner **NORTHWESTERN** was when she grounded in Wrangell Narrows, June 12, 1919. They refloated her from the awkward position she found herself in here. The **NORTHWESTERN** was built at Philadelphia in 1883, as the **ORIZABA**. During her long Alaska service she logged no less than 18 strandings, none of which proved fatal, a credit to her builders—the Cramp yard.

Indestructible ship—The SS **NORTHWESTERN,** survivor of numerous strandings, was serving as a barracks ship at Dutch Harbor, Alaska when the Japanese bombed that port June 3-4, 1942. She took a direct hit amidships, while nobody was aboard. The bomb left the vessel buckled and smoldering, but unbowed. She still floated, and is seen here after being towed into nearby Captains Bay and grounded. The Japanese claimed they had destroyed a first class fighting ship. Maybe they were not so wrong after all.

Hard aground on two sharp rocks at Cape Ilitugitak, Alaska is the SS **GOLDEN FOREST.** She eventually broke up and became a total loss. The freighter was en route from San Francisco to Yokohama when she ran aground at Avatanak Island July 24, 1929. Refloated with the aid of the Coast Guard cutter **HAIDA,** the vessel had to be put aground on Akutan Island to prevent her sinking. Refloated again, she stranded, as seen in the above photo, and that was the end. Her crew was rescued and some of the cargo was retrieved, among which were several phonographs. Operated by the Oceanic and Oriental Steamship Co., the **GOLDEN FOREST** was built at Portland, Oregon in 1919 as the **WEST TOGUS,** 5,658 gross tons.

Skeleton of a dying ship—the steamer **BERTHA** after burning at Uyak Bay near Kodiak, July 18, 1915. She was owned by the Pacific Alaska Navigation Company.

numerous. Gold from the ship is reputed to have turned up in all sectors of the world but probably all of these tales were but fabrications. The writer holds to the belief that if any gold escaped from the sunken vessel prior to her being raised, it was probably found among the sands by the old prospector mentioned at the beginning of this story. Considerable gold dust may have been carried ashore with the tidal currents sweeping through the confines of the wreck after it plummeted to the bottom.

That the *Islander* was probably off course when she sank was indicated by the fact that some survivors said they saw Captain Foote take his own life in the wild melee following the tragedy. Some of the eye-witnesses on the ship just after the crash, claimed to have seen the rocky edges of Point Hilda, disclaiming the oft-accepted iceberg theory. Absolute truth remains unknown, however, as it was shortly after midnight and there was also a heavy fog prevailing when the *Islander* put out from Skagway and reached her port of no return. She carried a total complement of 183 persons. Forty-two perished.

Last Hours of the Tahoma

Turbulent seas are no respector of ships or men. Even vessels carefully contrived for the sacred role of protecting maritime commerce sometimes fall victim to the elements.

In the diffused light of the revenue cutter *Tahoma's* chart room, Captain Richard Crisp stirred in his chair. Suddenly he rose stiffly to his feet, and loped into the pilot house.

As the dark September night came on, the clouds scudded along under a voluminous black ceiling that smelled ominous and threatening over the rockbound port of Aggatu.

The captain thought to himself, 'what a God-forsaken place this Aleutian settlement.'

It was near 2100 hours when executive officer Molloy joined the ship's master. The two began a discussion of a trial to be held aboard the revenue cutter the following morning, when the quartermaster broke in unceremoniously.

"Begging your pardon sir," he said, "We just received a radiogram."

Captain Crisp took the paper and returned to the chartroom to read it. Molloy followed after him.

"Mr. Molloy," he said sharply as he glanced up, "We're departing for Unalaska with the break of dawn. See that all is in readiness."

Without questioning the order the executive officer saluted and exclaimed, "Aye Sir!"

"We should get out of here tonight," said the captain, "but its better safe than sorry. We'll wait till dawn."

"Night captain," said Molloy as he smothered his cigarette in the nearest ashtray and then wandered out into the night.

At the first ray of dawn there was much scurrying about the decks of the *Tahoma*. Indications of good weather were evident and at 0630 the revenue cutter was underway. As she moved out of the harbor, constant soundings were taken. Periodically through the forenoon soundings continued as the ship rimmed the thousand-fathom curve.

It was when no bottom was reported that the cutter changed course and headed in an E.S.E. direction calculated to carry the vessel to a point thirty miles outside and to the southward of a pair of hazardous reefs, the kind which being inundated much of the time, make navigation a dangerous occupation.

Captain Crisp refused to leave the bridge all that day, keeping a constant vigil for kelp, or other signs of broken water. He had downed three mugs of coffee while dodging about the Semmeche Aggatu Passage. Still no sign of foul ground.

Anxiety subsided. Soundings were unfathomable and normal routine continued. Toward evening the wind freshened and the sea began to kick up its heels. It was then that the cutter's master decided to go below for some hot dinner to warm him.

Over on her side burning furiously—steamer **BERTHA.** She grounded at Harvester Island while in command of Captain Glasscock and later caught on fire, the master and his crew of 24 being cared for by workers at a nearby cannery. The vessel was later left on the bleak shores of Uyak Bay, a total loss. The incident took place in July 1915.

One of the most famous of Alaska shipwreck photos is this one of the SS **PRINCESS MAY** of the Canadian Pacific fleet. She ran hard aground on the Sentinel Island rocky outcroppings August 5, 1910, within full view of the lighthouse there. The passengers were safely evacuated (note the lifeboats all lowered). With the aid of high tides, the **PRINCESS MAY** was eventually refloated, bottom damage coming to more than $20,000. *W. H. Case photo.*

He dined with U. S. Marshal Hastings, a passenger on the vessel who had been trying cases of federal offenses when the cutter had been ordered to sea.

The two ate a leisurely dinner and then indulged in a contest of cribbage.

The roll of the ship and the constant pitching indicated that the sea was mounting, but the engine purred, undisturbed by the action of the ocean. The clock struck two bells in the ward room.

Then it happened. With the flash of a bolt of lightning the *Tahoma* crashed with a frightening noise against an unknown assailant. The bow lifted high in the air. The captain jumped up and fell backwards at the same time. The cribbage board fell to the deck and the little pegs scattered in all directions.

Two drinking glasses rolled off the table. One broke and the other rolled against the bulkhead.

The ship's keel ground along a ledge of unrelenting rock—piercing, tearing, grinding.

While the marshal was struggling to regain his feet, the captain was already rushing out the door in a frantic dash to the bridge. The ship's telegraph uniting the bridge and the engine room

sounded like a bell ringer's serenade as it repeated messages back and forth. The sounds were intermingled with the general alarm bell warning all hands to take emergency stations.

As the captain reached the bridge ladder, he ran into Lieutenant Molloy.

"Prepare to lower away the boats," he panted. "Hold them at the rail and standby for further orders."

As he ran into the pilot house he shouted as he went, "Molloy, order an immediate inspection of the fore, main and after compartments."

Amid the chaos, word soon came back that all watertight doors had been closed and the holds, engine room and fire room were free of water.

So intent was the commanding officer on the fate of his ship, he was for the moment oblivious of the mounting gale pushing in from a southerly direction. Seas were striking the reef where the *Tahoma* lay imperiled, lifting her up and slamming her down like a hammer against a spike.

The chief engineer was at his post in the bowels of the cutter prodding his men to keep the propulsion equipment operative. The big steam engine was taxed to the limit as it was shoved repeatedly from full ahead to full astern. Inspite of its full power output the propeller might just as well have been fanning the air. It was obvious that the *Tahoma* was going nowhere.

The ship shuddered from stem to stern. Sea after sea slashed at her, canting her this way and that. She worked hard on the reef and her position offered little in the way of encouragement.

The blackness of night did little to quell anxiety and fears. Then to make bad news worse, Lieutenant Molloy reported to the commanding officer that the rudder post had been driven up through the spar deck.

All the time the glass was dropping and a canopy of black scud cloud spread over the stricken ship scarcely higher than the masts. The wind was blowing furiously and the seas raising great liquid avalanches which roared and rumbled.

The perplexed ship's master pondered his situation wondering what was his best course of action. Here was his ship aground in one of the most remote ocean sectors of the world. Dispatches of distress were to little avail for it would be days before a ship could reach them.

Just then the executive officer entered the pilot house. "Captain," he said excitedly, "The chief reports the main steam pipe has torn loose from the bulkhead and is leaking badly."

A look of consternation came over the commanding officer's face. He could see the handwriting on the wall. He appeared in a daze as Molloy went on to tell him that water was pouring into the forward hold. Plates were buckling on the starboard side. It appeared but a question of time. The steel ship was no match for an unyielding rock barrier. To add to the serious situation, some of the pumps were reported choked and inoperative.

"Very well, Mr. Molloy," said the captain, "drop the port anchor and take every precaution against losing men overboard. I want soundings taken too."

The two men departed company.

The night was an eternity and with the breaking of dawn it was steel gray with no let up in the gale. The cutter had a definite list now and the decks slanted precariously. It was a sleepless night for all hands. The vessel was pounding itself to death. Seepage was everywhere. Plates were buckling, the heating system was inoperative, steam pipes had burst and the ship felt like the inside of an icebox.

The pounding kept up until water began rushing in. The quadrant room was filling. The fire room just forward the air lock suffered a split seam on the starboard side and water rushed in unchecked.

Captain Crisp had done all in his power to save his ship, but he was fighting a losing battle. Not one for sharing his woes with others he bravely bore the brunt of the responsiblity and turned all attention to saving the blue clads under his command. Hope of saving his ship was virtually gone.

The lifeboats and workboats had all been stocked with food and water and had been swung out in the davits. Boat crews were standing by awaiting their superior's bidding.

Soundings had been taken around the vessel. The average was but two and one half fathoms and no channel appeared to exist fore or aft. This meant that if the vessel was scuttled and rested in shallow water, she might be kept from pounding herself to pieces.

In the wireless room, "Sparks," sat patiently awaiting an answer from a ship or station. As yet none had been received. This was a lonely sea plied by few ships.

Then, suddenly there came an answer like a bolt from out of the blue. *Tahoma's* messages had been picked up at distant St. Paul Island and

This Winter & Pond photo shows the **PRINCESS MAY** on Sentinel Island reef from a stern quarter view. The fact that the **PRINCESS MAY** was refloated probably had a big bearing on not evacuating the passengers from the SS **PRINCESS SOPHIA**, which ran aground in much the same fashion, eight years later on Vanderbilt Reef, resulting in the loss of 343 persons.

In command of Captain Henry Burns, the Alaska Line freighter **DEPERE** crashed into the reinforced buttress at the base of Prowly Light in Wrangell Narrows in a blinding fog on August 6, 1939. Here she is seen beached nearby to prevent her sinking. The tug **SALVAGE KING** and the cutter **CYANE** aided in salvaging the vessel, robbing Davy Jones of a tasty 3,475 ton morsel. The vessel, built at Oakland, California in 1920, was en route to Juneau from Ketchikan when the accident happened. Alaska Steamship Co. owned the ship.

relayed to the Japanese freighter *Takoma Maru* which was soon proceeding to their aid. The freighter expected to reach the position of the *Tahoma* within 36 hours, but in those mounting seas they might well be off on their timing.

Any optimism by the men on the cutter was not shared aboard the Japanese freighter. The latter's skipper, noting the impossible character of the gale-lashed waters felt as he altered course, he too might be sending out a message of distress.

In desperation, Captain Crisp summoned all his officers to the ward room for an emergency consultation. He told them that by sinking the ship in the surrounding shoal water she might have a slim chance of holding together should future salvage efforts be possible. "I consider it wiser to take to the boats and attempt to reach land," he reasoned.

Boldir Island was the nearest land but the captain warned that landings there would be highly dangerous in most any sea.

"Aggatu is our best chance," he said.

With preparation for abandonment, the bedraggled crew now moved more rapidly drowning their fears in the thoughts of escape.

Several spars were lashed together and lowered over the ship's counter affording a place where the boats could make fast before beginning the long voyage.

The sea cocks that could be reached were opened. One of the officers went below with a rifle to shoot the glass out of the portholes to allow the water to rush in more quickly.

The *Tahoma* was now settling fast, and all hands were at their boat stations awaiting the final command. Lower and lower the cutter settled.

Then at last the resounding and somewhat chilling command, "Abandon Ship! All hands!"

One after another seven open boats creaked down the falls and detached themselves from the mother ship. The seas leaped up at them slopping generous portions of frigid water into the laps of those at the oars. Others bailed frantically. It was a delicate operation and except for the protection of the listing ship, the boats might have instantly swamped. Skilled hands, however, handled the situation well, despite the 45-degree list of the *Tahoma*.

The last boat was lowered at 1600, and the captain seeing that all had been safely evacuated stepped into the gig, and the *Tahoma* was left to die in solitude.

The boats rendezvoused at the lashed spars and made final plans for the perilous voyage that lay ahead, bouncing like corks as they tried to keep their positions. It was just an hour after the evacuation of the *Tahoma* that Captain Crisp gave final directions and orders. All waved farewell and started their gruesome battle against the sea. It was like abandoning a long time friend as the sailors watched the outline of their ship grow smaller and smaller and then disappear below the horizon.

Night came on with all the misery of the far northern latitudes. A near freezing rain soaked every thing and every one. Food and blankets were wet and misery and cold plagued all hands.

154

The southwest wind riling up the ocean refused to abate one iota. Despite the cold, however, the seamen obeyed orders explicitly.

The captain sat in the stern sheets of his boat, steering oar in his hand. He kept track of the other boats during the night only by the feeble kerosene lanterns burning in each. It was a long, night and before the first pink glow of dawn it was a crew of stiff, cold and miserable men pulling on their oars in erratic fashion. The morbid tempo of the operation was given somewhat of a morale boost at 9 a.m. the following morning when rations were doled out. The men in each boat received a biscuit, a sausage and a cup of water.

The captain took some sightings and calculated that they were ten miles north of the latitude where lay the wreck. Then came the break the men had waited for. The seas began to moderate. This meant a reprieve from the oars and a chance to hoist the sails. The men in each boat worked with a will and soon had the canvas bent to the wind.

The day passed with intermittent weather and toward the second nightfall the seas were again kicking up and the bailers worked fast and hard.

Another meal passed but there was grumbling and cursing, and notes of pessimism. The food had become soggy and the sailors' clothes were continually wet.

Lines of concern masked the captain's face. The thought of the loss of his ship was beginning to tell on him. The wind slewed around to the northeast as night wore on and he ordered all the craft to take in their sails and batten everything down to ride out the storm. By morning

they had all drifted apart and every craft was on its own pursuing a separate course—eight officers and 61 enlisted personnel.

The seas continued cantankerous. Day passed and another indescribable night of discomfort. Many got violently sick. In the captain's boat some lay suffering on the bilgeboards. Water slopped over the gunwhales as the wind roared like a lion. Giant acclivities formed at their outset. Some vegetable oil was broached and an oil bag was rigged and run out on a drogue line to calm the surrounding water.

Two days and three nights was a long time in an open boat but the ordeal was far from over. Real misery and mental strain was now hanging over the survivors. The captain's boat, now alone on a boundless ocean, was having difficulty and making little headway. The men picked at each other over trivial things and argued and sobbed over their chances of survival. There wasn't a dry thing in the boat.

Thursday broke like the other days, raw and ominous. Each meal seemed to give the men a slight lift but there was always the driving winds and heavy seas.

For the next two days it was a slow repetition of everything that had come before. The captain's craft sailed on. At last, a let up in the weather. Sail was hoisted and again taken in, the average forward progress being about two knots. Another night and a day and the craft lay becalmed. Suddenly a ray of sunshine broke through the eternal cloud barrier and the men cheered. The warmth was like a gift from heaven. They had ridden out the storm.

Swollen hands and feet, chapped lips and

The SS **ALASKA** of the Alaska Steamship Company, en route to Cordova from Yakutat was driven aground in a storm at Orca Bay, where rocks punctured her hull filling No. 1 hold with 22 feet of water. She slipped from the rocks and nearly sank but Captain Percy Selig guided the vessel safely into Cordova Harbor where rescue vessels removed the passengers and salvage work on the ship was begun. The accident happened February 2, 1947. The vessel was pumped out, temporarily patched and returned to Seattle for repairs. The **ALASKA** was built at Tacoma, Washington.

One of the most tragic shipwrecks of recent decades in Alaskan waters was that of the passenger liner **YUKON** of Alaska Steamship Co. The forward half of the vessel is seen above, after the ship grounded in a severe gale on sharp rocks off Johnston Bay, 40 miles southeast of Seward, February 3, 1946. En route to Seattle, the vessel carried 371 passengers and 124 crew members. After she struck, tremendous icy breakers up to 50 feet, crashed over the ship and broke her in two. Eleven persons were carried to a watery grave. The others were later saved by heroic efforts of seven rescue ships led by the Coast Guard cutter **ONONDAGA**. Some of the survivors were removed from a narrow beach below a 300 foot rock wall cliff. The ship's master, C. Trondsen, who survived, was first charged with negligence but later exonerated of all charges. The 5,863 ton vessel, dating from 1899, was one of the best known liners on the Seattle-Alaska run.

numerous aches and pains were checked by the ever vigilant boatswain. Clothes were hung about to dry. A variety of small jobs were thought up to keep the sailors' minds occupied.

On Friday evening after riding another long period of mounting seas, the bow man shouted, "Light off the port beam!"

It was as if a firecracker had been lit in the captain's boat. The sleeping, suffering, seasick and heartsick men rose to their feet. Sorrow was turned to joy.

Up from the craft went flares arching their reddish glow into the gathering dusk. Sail was hoisted and the drogue was tripped and hauled aboard. A search light from the approaching steamer probed its beam over the leaden waters. They had sighted the flares and were coming fast. That chill fall day of 1914 was drawing to a close and for the survivors it would be a day they would never forget.

It was a slow, tormenting process before the men were taken aboard the rescue ship for there they knew, hot coffee, food, and dry blankets awaited them.

On the bow of the steamer was the name *Cordova,* a freighter of the Alaska Steamship Company, that had made an epic voyage to perfect the rescue of these unfortunates. She had steamed 2,000 miles through perilous seas under the able hand of Captain Thomas Moore. The *Cordova* had turned the tables, a merchant vessel rescuing the crew of a ship whose mission it was to save other ships in peril.

The remaining lifeboats of the *Tahoma* had drifted far and wide and all had endured untold hardship and suffering. Some made Aggatu Island and were encamped when their signals were sighted by the *Cordova.* Eventually all the survivors were rescued and in spite of the rigorous experience not one life was lost.

There was a grand reunion aboard the freighter when the *Tahoma's* crew was reunited. For the 1,200-ton *Tahoma* there was no reunion, however, not even with the salvagers. She was written off the books as a $310,000 total loss.

Meanwhile the *Cordova* returned to Seattle with the survivors, arriving October 21, 1914. She had steamed some 7,902 miles in 59 days, a voyage that has never been forgotten in the annals of the maritime world.

Star of Bengal Tragedy

Space would never allow coverage of the hundreds of tragic shipwrecks that have occurred on Alaska's deadly outcroppings. Perhaps none is more grisly than that of the American bark *Star of Bengal.* While returning from Wrangell she was left to the mercy of a great storm and high seas as the two vessels towing her to sea cut the towlines and ran for safety to prevent their own destruction. Some 111 persons, mostly Oriental cannery workers perished in the awful wreck on September 20, 1908, off Helm Point near Coronation Island, when the 262 foot long bark broke up on jagged rocks.

An army of cannery workers and crewmen were thrown into the vortex to fend for themselves among 40,000 cases of canned salmon, hundreds of oil drums and a welter of rigging and wreckage.

When the veteran iron-hulled square-rigger departed for San Francisco from Wrangell she had either 132 or 133 persons aboard. Only 22 persons survived and among them was Captain Nicholas Wagner, her master, who was falsely blamed in the following court of inquiry but later exonerated on appeal.

The vessel was owned by the Alaska Packers Association of San Francisco. The terrible account of her loss has never been fully told, for dead men tell no tales.

156

The Foundering of the Panoceanic Faith

There have been many bizarre tragedies in the North Pacific in recent times, despite modern navigation aids and use of compartmented vessels of welded steel.

Many have involved heavy losses of life, some with no survivors. In the incident presented here there was only a handful of survivors, five to be exact, which miraculously clung to life after long immersion in the icy waters in the Gulf of Alaska. Of the crew of 41, these five alone were left to tell the tale, and that tale was a long time in coming as it took considerable time to thaw out the survivors following their rescue.

The freighter in question was the SS *Panoceanic Faith*, overly-laden with fertilizer, bound for Yokohama from Oakland. She departed the California port on September 29, 1967 in command of Capt. John S. Ogles. Following the Great Circle route, the vessel ran into stormy seas off the coast of Alaska. For nine days she fought her way through surging seas which continually mounted higher.

Finally the tarpaulin secured on the No. 1 hatch was observed to be loose. So dangerous were the conditions forward of the bridge that the ship's master failed to effect prompt repairs which ultimately resulted in the hatch being rudely opened by the boarding seas, filling completely with salt water and forcing out tons of fertilizer. Speed was cut, but the seriousness of the situation was perhaps not fully estimated by the skipper, as he did not heave to for repairs. Down by the head and listing 15 degrees, the situation worsened and at last it became obvious that the ship might go down. The first distress call intended to alert vessels in the vicinity as to the ship's condition was made at 0618 on October 9. Then an SOS, sent out at 0958 gave the *Panoceanic Faith's* position some 15 miles in error. Of seven ships, 53 to 165 miles away, the farthest ship was the first to reach the scene—after dark and more than 12 hours after the sinking. All the ill-fated ship's officers had long before perished.

The ship's 15 degree list had prevented successful launching of the 65 person motor lifeboat. Even so, the lifeboat's motor was inoperative. On September 30, a lifeboat drill had not included the required engine start and lowering of the boat to rail level. There had been no instructions given during the drill on handling of the ship's 25 person inflatable liferafts.

Three seven-man and two twelve-man rafts were dropped by a U. S. Navy aircraft over the scene after the *Panoceanic Faith* sank, but the Marine Board of Inquiry later found that swimming crewmen left to fend for themselves prob-

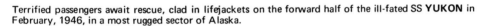

Terrified passengers await rescue, clad in lifejackets on the forward half of the ill-fated SS **YUKON** in February, 1946, in a most rugged sector of Alaska.

Unscheduled port of call—by the steam schooner **THOMAS L. WAND.** On May 10, 1914, she went ashore in the fog, near Ketchikan, Alaska, but was eventually refloated without major damage. Her final end came September 16, 1922 when she grounded south of Point Sur, California. She was owned by Olson & Mahony, for whom she was built at Aberdeen, Washington in 1906.

Portland Tug & Barge Company's barge **P.T. & B Co. 1651** astride of Louis Reef, 3½ miles north of Ketchikan, Alaska, February 26, 1947. The rail cars she was carrying for the Alaska Railroad were salvaged but the barge became a total loss.

ably were able to inflate only three. Seven crew members boarded one raft, but the raft's hand-cranked blinking distress light broke down and no other light was available. The lights of three ships were sighted during the night, but only three of the seven men were still alive when taken aboard a rescue ship the next morning. It was a harrowing experience and one of which the survivors spoke little.

The other two survivors of the 48 degree water clung to pieces of wreckage—one of them attracting a rescue ship with a flashlight he had in his pocket.

The cargo vessel went down some 500 miles south of the Aleutian Islands after progressive flooding. A large motor lifeboat fell by the bow during a futile launching attempt, throwing crewmen into 20 to 25 foot seas, and the ship's inflatable raft broke loose and drifted out of reach when it was not controlled alongside. Four crewmen in an air-dropped liferaft, which at times was within sight of three rescue vessels, died during the night hours.

On investigating the cause of the disaster, the National Transportation Safety Board listed the probable cause of sinking as ". . . failure of the Master to have the tarpaulins secured on the No. 1 hatch when they were observed to be loose" two days before the sinking. "Neglecting to effect prompt repairs ultimately resulted in this hold being open to boarding seas and complete flooding."

The National Transportation Safety Board found it "possible that the Master's concern about the fuel supply, and slow speed, may have influenced his actions" in not heaving to for repairs. "He obviously underestimated the seriousness of these conditions," the Board found.

As the Board continued its review of the case, it was told how the *Panoceanic Faith* in addition to her cargo of fertilizer carried, 4,162 barrels of oil. Minimum fuel for such a voyage was between 4,500 and 5,000 barrels. The Safety Board found that at departure, the ship "was overloaded" and "was not in all respects fit for this voyage." Inasmuch as the skipper went down with his ship such salient facts were hard to record. Problems were encountered in a boiler, the main condenser, and the lubrication pressure system during the first days at sea.

The veteran freighter **COLDBROOK** grounded on Middleton Island, Alaska, June 16, 1942 while loaded with military supplies. The scene of the wreck was about 75 miles south of Cordova, Alaska. The Hog Island type freighter, garbed in wartime colors, was built in 1919 and was of 5,104 tons. She became a total loss.

SS **CITY OF SEATTLE,** popular Seattle-Alaska passenger steamer grounded in Tongass Narrows, near Ketchikan, August 15, 1913. Refloating efforts are underway here and the vessel, which was built at Philadelphia, came off her perch with only $1,200 damage to her hull.

Few cargo vessels in the marine history of Alaska suffered more strandings than the steamer **NORTHLAND.** She is seen here ashore on Pond Reef, ten miles from Ketchikan. She grounded September 7, 1912 but was refloated, damages amounting to only $1,500. She was finally lost on the Umpqua River bar in Oregon, May 16, 1924, as the SS **ADMIRAL NICHOLSON.**

At the midnight hour while the SS **OLYMPIA** was steaming to Valdez from Cordova, she ran into a howling gale and went aground on Bligh Island Reef in Prince William Sound, Dec. 12, 1910. The following day, 75 passengers aboard the wreck were removed and salvage efforts were begun. Finally, Captain Daniels and his crew had to quit the ship and when she could not be refloated she was stripped of her wares. The wreck remained, and for years Alaska navigators set their courses by the derelict until it finally slipped from the reef and sank. The **OLYMPIA** was a former blockade runner in the Russo-Japanese war and was later converted to a cargo-passenger vessel for the Seattle-Alaska run.

After surviving several strandings in the northland, the SS **YUCATAN** was wrecked in Icy Strait, Alaska February 16, 1910. She was refloated in a major salvage effort, only to be lost three years later for good, in Alaskan waters.

"She foundered in sea conditions which, while severe, were not unusual for the area and time of year," the board reasoned.

The Safety Board's listing of causal factors included, "Failure of the Master to recognize the critical condition of his vessel and to request assistance earlier." His first distress call, "intended only to alert vessels in his vicinity as to his ship's condition."

It isn't often that in such a case of foundering that so many negative results are brought out on a ship that was supposed to have been shipshape in every category.

In addition to the marine survival problems shown by the accident, the Safety Board cited as causal factors the failure of the automatic radio alarm systems on the *Panoceanic Faith* and other nearby vessels to alert them of her distress and the failure of maritime emergency communications system "to effect the arrival of potential rescue vessels at the *Panoceanic Faith's* position prior to her sinking, or before darkness."

The *Panoceanic Faith,* built in 1944, was owned by Panoceanic Tankers Corp. (Spiro Polemis Sons Ltd.)

Sole survivors of the tragedy were John Kirk, Oscar Wiley, Edwin Johnson, Gordon Campbell and Lewis Gray, Jr.

But the disaster, nor its findings, could not restore the lives of 36 seafaring men who perished on that storm-tossed, pulsating sea. Nor could it erase the nightmare that five doughty men lived through—a seemingly endless, black eternity. Nor could it bring back a freighter and her full cargo. Indeed Davy Jones claimed a valuable addition to his well-stocked locker when he received the *Panoceanic Faith.*

'Wouldst thou, —so the helmsman answered,—
'Learn the secret of the sea?
Only those who brave its dangers
Comprehend its mystery!'

—Longfellow

On June 18, 1913 the SS **YUKON** of the Alaska Coast Steamship Company was wrecked on Sanak Island, bound for Seattle from the Kuskokwim River area, in command of Captain Archie McKay. The vessel and her cargo were valued at $170,000. The ship came to the West Coast under the name **M. F. PLANT,** having been built originally at Philadelphia in 1879. The waters where she struck were then being surveyed by the Coast & Geodetic Survey. The six passengers and the crew were rescued by the revenue cutter **TAHOMA** and the survivors taken back to Seattle by the SS **VICTORIA.** The **YUKON** often tabbed as a hoodoo ship, was a total loss.

"Goodbye; we are slipping from reef and sinking; we are abandoning!" Those were the final words sent out by the wireless operator of the SS **MARIPOSA,** one of the finest passenger liners on the Alaska run. This is how the liner appeared after being abandoned to the elements. She stranded November 18, 1917 on Strait Island off Point Baker, five miles west of Wrangell. The speed queen of the Alaska Steamship Company, the **MARIPOSA** was commanded by Captain Johnny O'Brien, who was in his cabin at the time of the mishap. The vessel, in charge of pilot H. Selness was en route to Seattle from Anchorage, when strong currents carried her off her course. She struck at 9:30 p.m. with 265 passengers and 1,200 tons of copper ore plus 25,000 cases of canned salmon aboard. She eventually broke in two.

Alaska Steamship Company's SS **EDITH** in command of Captain E. B. McMullen foundered off Cape St. Elias, after leaving Nome and Latouche Island with a cargo of copper concentrates. Her cargo shifted in heavy seas causing her company to abandon. The cargo vessel, with 37 aboard, is seen here in distress and slowly sinking. The ship was valued at $250,000 and her cargo at $150,000. Built in Sunderland, England in 1882, the steel freighter was of 2,369 gross tons. The SS **MARIPOSA** put a towline aboard the derelict in the Gulf of Alaska but the attempt to save her had to be given up. The date was August 30, 1915.

Deep in the snows of Alaska, the wreck of the steamer **SADIE** at Cape York. Owned by the Alaska Commercial Company, the vessel, a steel oil burning sidewheeler, after a conversion from a tug, had been placed on the mail run between Cape Nome and Kotzebue, in charge of Captain Rickmers. She reportedly struck an uncharted rock on September 4, 1904, ending her days near Cape York, north of Teller. The 276 ton craft was abandoned, her value placed at $77,500.

Going down—the SS CURACAO, at Warm Chuck, Prince of Wales Island. In command of Captain William Thompson, the passenger-cargo vessel foundered on June 21, 1913 and went down in deep water, after all hands abandoned. Laden with coal and cannery supplies, the ship was valued at $225,000. The last lifeboat can be seen leaving the vessel, at right. The vessel became the target of a major salvage endeavor.

Victim of the Alaska surf at Cape Carew, near Yakutat, the steam tug KAYAK broke up after running aground December 19, 1913. This vessel also acted as a cannery tender and was one of the craft that abandoned towing the sailing vessel STAR OF BENGAL in 1908 in heavy seas off Coronation Island, which resulted in the wreck of the BENGAL with 111 of her company.

Up from her sea grave she arose; the SS CURACAO was raised in 60 days after a cofferdam was built around her. Only $110,000 insurance was carried on the ship. She went down in 78 feet of water and is pictured here after being raised from her grave, Davy Jones being robbed of a precious gift. The vessel was towed back to Seattle and repaired in 1913. In later years she operated strictly as a freighter to Alaska. In 1940 she was purchased by Greek interests, renamed HELLENIC SKIPPER, and while bound for the Orient, mysteriously exploded and foundered 125 miles northwest of Grays Harbor, Washington, July 10, 1940. Her crew escaped.

Wrecked near Katalla on Controller Bay, the famous Alaska gold ship PORTLAND. She struck an uncharted rock off Martin Island in a blizzard November 12, 1910, in command of Captain Moore, en route to Cordova. The skipper backed her off and ran her aground two miles away, with ten feet of water in her holds. Her passengers, mail and all but 30 tons of her cargo were salvaged. The vessel, dating from 1885, became a total loss. She brought the famous ton of gold to Seattle, July 17, 1897, which launched off the fabulous gold rush to Alaska and the Klondike.

Steam schooner DESPATCH aground at Naket Inlet, Alaska in 1916. Owned by Border Line Transportation Company, the vessel was later removed from her rocky perch and repaired. Still later, she became the SS ADMIRAL RODMAN of Pacific Steamship Company. The vessel was built in 1899. *From Joe Williamson collection.*

Aground and two-thirds submerged at Wards Cove, five miles from Ketchikan, is seen the steam schooner **CHATHAM** after being partially destroyed by fire August 31, 1938. The Ketchikan fireboat and Coast Guard cutter **ALERT** put out the blaze after two firefighters were overcome by smoke. The vessel was abandoned but a few years later was patched up and towed off the beach and brought to Seattle for conversion to a barge. The plans failed and in 1947 the hulk was towed to Oyster Bay, B. C. to become part of a breakwater. In the above photo, when the **CHATHAM** caught fire she was Seattle-bound with a cargo of salmon and ore, under Alaska Transportation Co. and was loading fertilizer at Wards Cove when the blaze broke out. She was in command of Capt. Olaf H. Hansen. The 179 foot vessel was built at Everett, Washington, in 1905 and previously had borne the names **EVELYN BERG** and **JOHAN POULSEN**.

Stripped and abandoned, the ancient sidewheeler **ELIZA ANDERSON** is left to die on the rocks at Unalaska, after running aground on parting her lines at Dutch Harbor. The date was March 1, 1898, after she had carried a contingent of goldseekers to Nome. The old river steamer was built at Portland, Oregon in 1859 and was one of the best known steamers in the Pacific Northwest.

Forlorn and forsaken—the passenger liner **MOUNT McKINLEY**. As a unit of the Alaska Steamship Company, she was wrecked March 18, 1942 near Scotch Cap, Alaska, the details being smothered by wartime restrictions. The vessel was in command of Captain Arthur Ryning; he, the passengers and crew were safely removed. Later, the mail and most of the cargo were recovered and plans were laid to salvage the vessel. However, the prevailing heavy seas eventually tore the heart out of the liner and she became a total loss. The **MOUNT McKINLEY** was built in 1918, as the **SANTA LUISA** at Philadelphia. The 4,861 ton ship also had the names **EL SALVADOR** and **SANTA ANA** during her career.

Thirty-nine officers and crew members of the wrecked MS **CROWN REEFER** were rescued after their ship struck a rock at Amchitka Island, Alaska, January 27, 1946. The survivors were taken to San Pedro by the SS **ELK BASIN** after being rescued by a Navy tug. The **CROWN REEFER**, operated by Coastwise Line, was carrying cargo for the Army at Kodiak when she struck off Kirlof Point on the east side of the island. Navy divers found that the ship's hull had been ripped open, and the wreck was ultimately abandoned, later breaking up.

Coated with ice, like a floating ghost ship, is the wreck of the Alaska cargo vessel **FARALLON**, driven ashore in a heavy snowstorm at Iliamna Bay on January 5, 1910. Owned by the Northwestern Steamship Company, the vessel was en route to Dutch Harbor from Valdez when she stranded; the passengers and crew narrowly escaping with their lives, were forced to set up camp on the inhospitable shores to await rescue. The ship was insured for only $70,000, and was under command of Captain J. C. Hunter. The 749 ton steamer was built at San Francisco in 1888.

German tramp steamer MARIECHEN, Captain Rudolph Heldt, ran into a series of troubles. The 2,521 ton vessel departed Puget Sound for Vladivostok January 19, 1906 with a cargo valued at $250,000, and, under charter to Barneson, Hibbard & Co. The ship encountered a series of gales off Cape Flattery, and her engine room flooded after a deadlight was stove. The boilers were doused and the vessel drifted north, stranding at False Bay near Sitka. She is seen above on a severe list with the steamer CORNELIA COOK standing by. In a major salvage job the vessel was patched and pumped out and later towed back to Seattle.

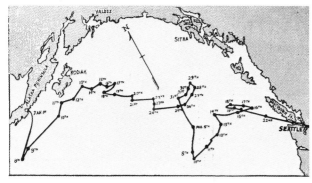

Map showing the course of the steamer DORA during her 63 day drift through the North Pacific in 1905-06.

The steamer DORA, known as the "bull terrier of Alaska," became famous for her drift in 1906 under Captain Zim Moore. For 63 days, while the world mourned the suspected total loss of ship and crew, the rugged vessel, broken down, drifted about the Pacific. She had departed Cold Bay, Alaska for Chignik when a steam pipe broke and rendered her immobile. The vessel broke down on December 30, 1905 and drifted from one side of the Pacific to the other. She was not sighted by another ship, until under an improvised jury sail rig, she was sighted February 23, 1906 off the Strait of Juan de Fuca and brought in to Port Angeles, food and water virtually gone. After several strandings in Alaska, the DORA was finally lost on the shoals of Alert Bay December 23, 1920 after stranding off Noble Island reefs. She was owned by the Northwestern Steamship Co. throughout much of her career.

Hard aground, the passenger-cargo vessel FARALLON with lifeboats just dropped from the davits. She grounded at Iliamna Bay, Alaska January 5, 1910.

Salvage steamer RESCUER wrecked near Seal Cape, Unimak Island, Alaska, while involved in an attempt to salvage the Russian freighter TURKSIB. The RESCUER was driven aground in an 80 mile gale on the night of Dec. 31, 1942 and January 1, 1943. One lifeboat was launched and the crew was taken aboard the Navy minesweeper ORIOLE, which had been standing by. Some volunteers joined Captain W. J. Moloney, salvage master and skipper of the RESCUER, transferring to the Russian vessel to continue salvage efforts. The Russian crew of 31, including four women, had remained aboard the wreck which had grounded in November of 1942. Continued storms and high seas battered the rock-impaled Russian ship. Captain Moloney suffered a broken collar bone; Captain Mashnikov of the TURKSIB, a broken hip, and Klas Smit, an engineer, was lost overboard and drowned. Harry Kirwin, yoeman on the RESCUER had earlier suffered a broken neck but joined the salvage crew on the TURKSIB anyway. After the men and women were rescued from the TURKSIB she and the RESCUER became total losses.

Victims for Davy Jones—The Russian freighter **TURKSIB** being creamed by a wave, the gun on her stern pointing skyward. At the right is the salvage steamer **RESCUER** also aground. This photo was taken early in 1943 (January 12), off Seal Point, Unimak Pass, Alaska. The **TURKSIB** of 3,160 gross tons, was built in 1922 as the **HARDENBERG.** When the above photo was taken, 70 men and five women were reported aboard the Russian ship. All but two got ashore on January 13, 1943.

Confidential official Navy aerial photo made for Captain Moloney of the USS **RESCUER** which tried in vain to salvage the Russian freighter **TURKSIB.** The **TURKSIB** is pictured here from 600 feet elevation after grounding off Seal Cape near Scotch Cap, Nov. 21, 1942. The photo was made three days later.

165

"Ghost ship of the Arctic," was the name applied to the SS **BAYCHIMO** of the Hudson's Bay Company. Under command of Captain S. A. Cornwall, she was abandoned in the Beaufort Sea bound from Point Barrow to Vancouver B. C., September 21, 1931. The ice closed in around the vessel forcing her crew to take to the ice. They set up camp on the ice to stand by their fur-laden ship. Then the vessel disappeared and was believed to have sunk. Instead she moved for several years around with the ice packs appearing and vanishing like the Flying Dutchman. Eventually the cargo of furs was recovered after the ship was first sighted by Leslie Melvin who was going across the ice by dog sled. Many feel the old ship still drifts about with the ice. When last seen she had been badly stove by the icepacks.

Whip-lashed by the surf at Cape Fairweather, Alaska, the MS **PATTERSON,** owned by Alaska Patterson Inc. (former survey vessel), ran aground December 11, 1938. Captain Gustaf F. Swanson and James Moore, the winchman drowned. Eighteen others were eventually rescued after supplies had been dropped to them from the air. The Coast Guard cutters **SPENCER** and **HAIDA** eventually rescued the survivors. The **PATTERSON** was en route from Kodiak to Seattle. The old vessel was built in 1883 at Brooklyn, N. Y. as a survey vessel and was sold commercially in 1924.

Forward half of the freighter **COLDBROOK,** lost off Middleton Island, Alaska during World War II. This photo by O. H. Welch was taken in June of 1962. The **COLDBROOK,** operated by American Mail Line, was a Hog Islander, and was carrying military cargo when she stranded June 28, 1942. Salvage efforts failed and she was abandoned.

Slowly slipping beneath the waters after striking an uncharted reef, west of Kiska Island, Alaska, is seen the U. S. Revenue Cutter **TAHOMA,** September 20, 1914. The freighter **CORDOVA** rushed to the aid of the **TAHOMA'S** crew who abandoned in the boats. The 1,215 ton cutter was valued at $310,000 and was one of the finest of her class.

Somebody pulled the plug. The SS **NORTHWESTERN** is seen high and dry here at Eagle River, Alaska, July 25, 1933. When the tide came in and a salvage vessel arrived, the **NORTHWESTERN** was refloated with little damage.

Burning furiously, the Canadian National passenger liner SS **PRINCE GEORGE** was virtually destroyed September 22, 1945 when a fuel tank exploded following her stranding during a fog at Ketchikan, Alaska. Some crewmen can be seen still aboard on the ship's fantail. She was towed to Ravina Island by the Coast Guard to prevent the fire from spreading to the Ketchikan waterfront. The passengers were evacuated without mishap and the crew fought the fire until ordered to abandon. One seaman was killed when trapped in the engine room. The gutted ship lay on the beach until 1949 when it was refloated and towed to Seattle for scrap.

Acrobatic ship—the MS **DECORAH** wrecked six miles west of Point Augusta, Alaska in Icy Straits, August 24, 1933. The crew managed to salvage most of the cargo while they made camp on the beach. The 103 ton vessel was built at Seattle in 1911 and owned by Shepard Point Packing Company.

Precarious balance—MS **DECORAH,** near Point Augusta, Alaska in 1933. Some months later this vessel was refloated and rebuilt.

Two action shots of the old power schooner **P. J. ABLER** which caught fire September 29, 1915 while at anchor near Juneau, Alaska. The fire lasted 24 hours and Captain E. B. Hoffman and his crew were finally forced to quit the vessel. The charred shell of the schooner was beached, and beachcombers picked it apart. The vessel is seen here burning and exploding, the fire said to have been started by a candle dropped in the bilge. The vessel was en route to the Kuskokwim, and put into Juneau leaking. She was operated by Shields & Knaflich. *From Leslie Melvin collection, courtesy Pete Hurd.*

This photo shows the **ADMIRAL RODMAN** aground. It is believed taken at Naket Inlet, Alaska about 1924. She was later refloated and returned to service.

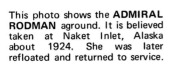

169

On March 9, 1918, the Pacific Steamship Company's SS **AD-MIRAL EVANS**, in command of Captain Charles Glasscock, was beached on the shores of Hawk Inlet, S. E. Alaska after striking a reef while inbound to the P. E. Harris Cannery. The 91 passengers aboard were removed and the salvage steamer **SALVOR** called in to refloat the vessel. A hole in her bottom had to be patched before she could be pumped out. The **EVANS**, built at Toledo, Ohio in 1901 went back to work and was finally scrapped in Japan in the 1930's. *From Joe Williamson collection.*

The ill-fated SS **ISLANDER** which reputedly struck an iceberg in 1901 off Douglas Island and went down with 42 persons, is pictured here a couple of years earlier in a minor stranding, probably in southeastern Alaska waters. The fast, twin screw passenger liner was a unit of the Canadian Pacific Steamship Company.

Driven ashore at Chignik, Alaska April 17, 1911, the Columbia River Packers Association cannery ship **JABEZ HOWES.** En route to Astoria, the ship stranded with 114 cannery hands and crewmen aboard. All reached shore safely but the vessel, of 1,648 tons and dating from 1877, was a total loss. She was beached to save her cargo of canned salmon. Also driven ashore in the same gale that claimed the **HOWES**, was the **STAR OF ALASKA** and the **BENJ. F. PACKARD.** Both were later refloated.

Taking a punishing wave broadside, the steam schooner **DAWSON CITY** is seen aground on the beach, believed to be in the vicinity of Nome, around the turn of the century. *Hammond photo courtesy Ralph Mackay.*

Wreck of the Alaska Packers' steel sailing vessel **STAR OF FALKLAND** which piled up on Akun Head the night of May 22, 1928. The 2,163 ton vessel, built in 1892 as the British square-rigger **DURBRIDGE,** became a total loss. She grounded in adverse weather and all but one of her crew reached safety. The wreck occurred in Unimak Pass near Pinnacle Rocks.

The tugs **RESOLUTE** and **CITY OF ASTORIA** stand by the barge **MERCURY,** sunk in Skagway Harbor, Alaska April 11, 1898, under ownership of the Pacific Clipper Line. The ex sailing vessel was built at New York as a Havre packet. *Webster & Stevens photo.*

172

With her sternwheel disjointed and her hull hogged, the forlorn steamer **DAWSON** dies a slow death at Rink Rapids on the Yukon River in the fall of 1926. The river steamer dated from 1901 when she was built for the British Yukon Navigation Company. She was a 779 ton vessel. *Courtesy Mabel E. Thompson.*

This photo of the **PANOCEANIC FAITH** was taken a short time before her fatal voyage from San Francisco to Yokohama with a 10,200 ton cargo of fertilizer. The vessel foundered in the North Pacific, 870 miles southwest of Kodiak on October 9, 1967, going to Davy Jones Locker with 36 of her crew. Only five survived after a hair-raising ordeal for survival. The Polemus—owned C-2 freighter is pictured here at San Francisco in a photo taken by Mike McGarvey.

The steamer **TOWNSEND** ran aground three miles south of Haines, Alaska at Haines Mission, January 16, 1900. Value of the hull and cargo was set at $40,000. The wreck is seen here heeled over, snow plastering part of her hull. Captain William McKenzie was skipper and A. Gillespie, pilot when the **TOWNSEND** stranded, following an engine breakdown. The vessel was built at Astoria in 1887 as the **ALLIANCE** and had a checkered career of misfortunes, once almost being destroyed by fire. *F. H. Nowell photo.*

On February 17, 1946, the Russian tanker **DONBASS** broke in two in the Gulf of Alaska, 300 miles S. E. of Adak, claiming the lives of her entire Soviet crew. Five days later the tanker **PUENTE HILLS**, sighted the after section and took it in tow, battling stormy seas for 21 days before reaching Port Angeles, Washington and claiming salvage rights. The claim was upheld. WSA paid $110,000 for the return of the lend-lease ship, built orginally in 1944 at the Kaiser yard in Portland, Oregon. The forepart of the **DONBASS** was picked up by the Russian freighter **BELGOROD** and later scrapped. The after section became a power plant at Eureka, California, and several years later was scrapped.

Scene of desolation—States Line freighter **NEVADA** ground up on the outcroppings of jagged Amatignak Island in the Aleutians on the night of September 27, 1932. Only three crewmen survived the tragedy. The **NEVADA'S** SOS was answered by the Japanese steamer **OREGON MARU** which reached the scene, but due to huge seas was unable to perfect a rescue. Next on the scene was the **PRESIDENT MADISON**, in command of Captain J. R. Healey. Third officer E. J. Stull (still living at this writing), was placed in charge of a lifeboat from the **MADISON** which approached shore as closely as possible after which seaman Eddie Blomberg swam through the breakers with a line and lifebelts and was credited with rescuing the only three survivors, from the beach. The **NEVADA** carried a crew of 37 of which 34 perished. The ship was built in 1920 and was of 5,645 gross tons.

The liberty ship **JOHN P. GAINES**, broke in two and later foundered off the Alaska Pensinula, south of Chirikof Island November 25, 1943. Ten crew members were lost. The remaining crewmen on the after half of the ship were rescued. The **GAINES** was built in 1942 and was of 7,167 tons. The after half of the vessel, pictured here, drifted ashore on Big Koniuji Island. In all, the **GAINES** carried 90, most of them being rescued by Naval patrol craft. Structural weakness in heavy seas was believed responsible for the tragedy.

Appearing more like an accordian than a ship, the MS **KINGSTON** of Juneau, 204 tons, is pictured, a total wreck in Whitestone Narrows, Alaska, May 20, 1933. Built at Tacoma in 1901 as the **DEFIANCE**, the vessel carried a crew of 12 on her fatal voyage, all of whom were picked up after the stranding. She was owned by Capt. Charles West & Associates.

174

More than a half century after her mysterious wreck, the schooner, (ex brigantine) **COURTNEY FORD** appeared (at right), land-locked in the sand about a mile from the water. The vessel was originally wrecked in a storm on Glen Island, 35 miles northeast of False Pass, Alaska near Izembek Bay. One crewman was left to watch over the ship while the rest of the ship's company took out in the **COURTNEY'S** boat to find help. The watchman froze to death in the terrible winter that followed. The **FORD** was wrecked September 7, 1902, and the survivors eventually reached civilization, but on return to the wreck scene, hopes of salvage were hastily abandoned. The uninhabited island held the vessel a solitary victim. The build up of sand on the island left the **FORD** far from the water.

Evacuation—The Canadian SS **PRINCESS KATHLEEN** on the rocks at Lena Point, Alaska. A Coast Guard vessel is seen pulling close to remove passengers and crewmen and transport them to Auke Bay shortly before the 6,000 ton queen of Alaskan passenger liners slipped from the reef, September 7, 1952. The **PRINCESS KATHLEEN** (of Canadian Pacific) was 18 miles from Juneau on the final voyage of the season from Vancouver, B.C. to Skagway. It was 3:15 a.m. Most of the 425 passengers and crewmen, including Captain Graham Hughes, were sleeping. A light rain was falling, but the lookout reported fair visibility. Suddenly there was a violent shock and the frightening screech of tearing metal. Dazed men and women thrown out of their bunks, rushed on deck in confusion. Unbelievably, for the **KATHLEEN** was supposed to have been following a well charted and well traveled channel, she had steamed right into the shore onto a high ledge on the Alaska mainland. Over the vessel's loud speaker, the purser told the passengers to prepare to abandon. One by one they went over the ship's side, down ladders and onto the rocky beach. As the **KATHLEEN'S** passengers waited for response to the SOS the captain pondered what to do about his wrecked $4 million ship. A gaping hole had been torn in the ship's bottom from the bow to the midships, as if sliced by a giant can opener. Captain Hughes had two alternatives: to back her off or to let the high tide take her off and hope she would stay afloat long enough to be beached in shallow water. He tried to back her off and failed. Day broke and even the wet disconsolate passengers forgot their plight as they stood about on shore sharing the captain's foreboding and awaiting the tide to come in.

Ens. Richard Lacey, commanding officer of the Coast Guard cutter **CG-83524** confers with Captain Hughes of the **PRINCESS KATHLEEN** as tense final decisions were being made following the stranding of the vessel.

Then came the dramatic moment. No longer was there a need for decision. The great $4 million liner began to slip from the reef as Coast Guardsmen, the ship's master, her crew and passengers stood in silent awe watching the three-stacker grind to her final resting place. The **PRINCESS KATHLEEN** was doomed. Chief Officer C. W. Savage was on the bridge when a miscalculation in course change first put the ship aground. *Coast Guard photo.*

September 7, 1952, the day the SS **PRINCESS KATHLEEN** ran aground will long linger as a black day in the records of Canadian Pacific. In her death throes, she is seen here slipping to her grave. The ship went down in 120 feet of water, salvage efforts being abandoned as impracticable. She slipped to her doom at 11:45 a.m. The Scottish-built liner which established an enviable record as a troop transport during World War II, was re-converted after the war as a passenger ship at a cost of $1.5 million. The vessel was built on the Clyde in 1925. As the writer pens this account he is looking at the 100 pound ship's bell of the SS **PRINCESS KATHLEEN,** one of the few items recovered by divers from her watery grave 120 feet down. *Coast Guard photo.*

Wreck of the large fishing barge **SKOOKUM** on the beach at Nome, Alaska after the vessel parted her moorings in a gale and crashed ashore September 10, 1900. Nearby, also swept ashore, was the little schooner **JESSIE.** *Webster & Stevens photo.*

Under Captain Thomas Moore, the SS **CORDOVA** steamed 2,000 miles to the rescue of the crew of the ill-fated revenue cutter **TAHOMA** in the Gulf of Alaska in October 1914. She brought the survivors back to Seattle making a total voyage of 7,902 miles in just 59 days. *Maude Dempsey photo.*

Taken several months before her fatal voyage, the **ISLANDER** is pictured pulling into Vancouver B. C. from Southeastern Alaska loaded to the hilt with passengers and miners. The fast, twin-screw vessel was the ultimate in luxury. The Canadian Pacific ship foundered in 1901 off Douglas Island, Alaska with the loss of 42 persons and a large amount of gold. *Photo courtesy Pete Hurd.*

In better days, the SS **YUKON** of Alaska Steamship Company is pictured in Alaskan waters. The staunch steel liner after many strandings and escapes, finally ended her days when she broke in two on the jagged teeth of black sea-washed rock off isolated Johnstone Bay, Alaska on February 3, 1946. Eleven persons lost their lives. The ship carried 371 passengers and 124 crew members. Captain Christian Trondsen was in command and Captain Amego Soriano was the pilot, when the ship piled up in a storm and broke in two after 47 years of service. *Schallerer's photo.*

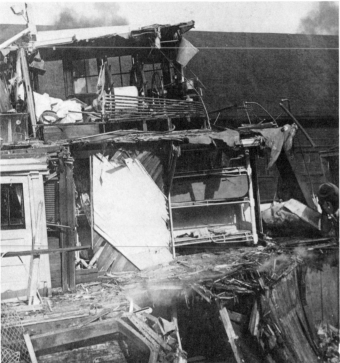

Ripped open like an envelope, the bow section of the SS **COTTAGE CITY** following a collision, just after the turn of the century.

Virtually no tears shed, no publicity. That was the way the units of the sealing fleet often passed into oblivion. As the apostle James stated, "For what is your life? It is even a vapor that appeareth for a little time, and then vanisheth away." How true that was with the nomads of the sealing fleet. Dirty little craft manned by rugged individual challenged the sea roaming over many parts of the North Pacific, most often in the chilling waters off the Alaskan and Siberian shores, risking life and limb for a hopeful catch of seal and otter. Each season required an astounding toll in the lives of the hunters, and a large part of the fleet was wrecked on the bleak shores of the northland. Even more distressing, however, were the large number of

vessels that vanished with all hands, for a time a blot on a vast sea, and in a moment, snuffed out forever, the ocean covering over the traces.

Following is a list of some of the sealing ships that mysteriously vanished from the face of the sea: Schooner *Sanborn* and the sloop *Dolphin* in 1875; schooner *Cygnet* in 1876; schooner *Felix* in 1885; schooner *Sarah Louise* in the 1880's; schooner *Otter* in 1888; schooner *Caroline II* in the 1890's; Canadian schooner *Maggie Mac* in 1892 with 23 persons aboard, bits of wreckage found at the north end of Vancouver Island; schooners *Helen Blum* and *Mary Brown* in 1893; schooners *Mary H. Thomas*, *Mascot* and *Rose Sparks* in 1894. (Jack London turned down the position of boat puller on the *Mary H. Thomas*). Schooner *Walter A. Earle* lost off Cape St. Elias with the loss of six white men and 26 Indians in 1895; Canadian schooner *May Belle* in 1896 and the *Matinee* in 1897.

In addition, the Canadian schooner *Active* foundered off Cape Flattery in 1887 with the loss of 28 lives, and the schooner *Lottie*, capsized off Tillamook Rock, losing her entire crew plus 28 contraband Chinese in 1892. The ex sealer, *Allie I. Algar* was lost with all hands in 1916, and the list goes on and on.

Outside of the goldrush days in Alaska marine transportation, perhaps the second most rip-roarin' era was that of the sealing industry. Before the U.S. Coast Guard, formerly the U.S. Revenue Cutter Service, took over the duty of protecting the breeding rookeries, the herds were hunted to near oblivion. Nobody quite immortalized those days as did Jack London in his renowned book, *The Sea Wolf*. It was a vivid portrayal of how the skipper, Wolf Larsen pillaged the breeding grounds with wanton abandon, mistreated his crew with outright cruelty and was finally done in by his hateful brother who commanded the only steam powered vessel in the sealing fleet. The novel was based on truth. Indeed in those years it was almost open warfare between the sealing fleets of Canada, Japan, Russia and America, all anxious to get a lion's share of the booty outside the areas under surveillance.

When the bloody occupation was outlawed the killing continued, the pirating of pelts became a game of cat and mouse as the schooners crept about in the irascible Alaskan seas trying to escape the arm of the law. Though the American and Canadians agreed to outlaw the pelagic sealing trade in 1895 which tied up a large segment of the fleet, there were those that defied their governments. Some went over to the Siberian side and risked capture by Russian gunboats. During that era, numerous sealing schooners were involved in rivalry, at times pitched battles being fought between crews of vessels, and on frequent occasion shipwreck in

179

Precarious position, but she lived again. SS **CURACAO** sitting on bottom of the sea at Warm Chuck, Prince of Wales Island. She stranded June 21, 1913 and was initially thought to be a total loss, but a major salvage effort proved successful and the vessel operated for many years thereafter.

frigid surroundings that demanded the lives of the castaways.

Sometimes the shipwreck involved government patrol vessels, such as the U.S. Revenue Cutter *Perry*. In 1910 she was cruising among the sealing fleet, at that time mostly Japanese, hovering about just outside the three mile limit off the protected Pribilofs, haunt of the seals. The foreign vessels were sometimes boarded, and positions constantly checked by the *Perry*. One fog-filled morning the close check proved an ill-omen when the cutter crunched up on the outcrops of the Pribilofs and was unable to back off. The captain and crew made a determined effort to get their charge afloat again, but the jagged rock teeth dug deeper into the ship's hull and she had to be abandoned to die in agony. Even the sending down of her yards, the striking of the topmasts and the jettisoning of heavy gear failed to afford sufficient buoyancy to lift the *Perry* from the wedge of rock that impaled her. A distress message brought the cutters *Tahoma* and *Manning* to the rescue but all they could do was to pick up the survivors of the wreck. Within a decade only the rusted boilers remained visible with the ebbing tide. And as earlier told, the USRC *Tahoma* was also to become a victim of the elements four years later while involved in a mercy mission.

In the early days of the sealing fleet the two-masted schooners carried from ten to fifteen men, working three to a boat, two hunters and a boat steerer. Many Northwest American Indians were among the crews and were extremely adept in their work, their talents handed down from one generation to the next in catching seals and whales from their dugouts. Most of the Indians used spears while the whites used rifles to kill the seals.

When a schooner came up on a herd, the boats were lowered and fanned out, often getting out of sight of the mother ship. Sometimes they were lost for days only to be picked up by another unit of the fleet. If the mother ship was wrecked, as was often the case, the men in the boats joined the company of another vessel, the skins being added to the rescue vessel's haul.

As previously mentioned several units of the sealing fleet were lost with all hands and with the loss often went a valuable cargo of pelts. Little mercy was shown in the northern seas where the schooners battled gale, sleet, snow, fog, ice and some of the most frightening sea conditions to be found anywhere on the globe.

In modern times the whole routine has changed. Seals are killed only under strict government control and the Probilofs are one of the most valued protected areas. Only well planned slaughter is permitted each year to keep the herds at propagating levels, and much to the chagrin of commercial fishermen up and down the Pacific Coast the seal is protected, despite the fact that they gulp down a large portion of the cherished

Like the proverbial cat with nine lives, so it was with the tug **DANIEL KERN** pictured here aground on Boulder Reef in February 1923. Built in 1879 at Baltimore as the Lighthouse tender **MANZANITA**, the vessel had a string of mishaps during her years but always seemed to pop back. Twice she was declared a total loss. Still she lived to an old age, finally burned for her scrap on Puget Sound in 1939.

180

SS **ADMIRAL ROGERS**, formerly the SS **SPOKANE**, is pictured here in one of the many strandings along the Inside Passage during her years of service. She was freed from her imprisonment and was still afloat in the 1940's.

End of the line for the forlorn barge **COLORADO** in Wrangell Narrows Alaska in 1900. She was formerly a proud bark, built on the east coast in 1864, and cut down to a barge in 1898. Breaking loose from a tug she went hard aground and was unsalvageable.

salmon. Some would like to join the Aleuts who roam among the herds with clubs in hand killing the selected bachelors for commercial purposes.

From the monetary standpoint, no whaling ship disaster ever came near to eclipsing the one that occurred in the crushing ice of Alaska in 1871. In one sense, one might blame greed for the great whale catch sought by the whaleship skippers. They were warned by the Eskimos to remain clear of the target area, that the ice would soon solidify with its crushing, awesome destructive powers. The advise was not heeded and as a result 31 whaling vessels were to be crushed like eggshells forcing the survivors to scramble for their lives, over solid and broken ice.

It all started in May of 1871 when the whaleships began arriving from the Japan Sea hugging the Siberian shore following after the leviathans as they

Up a creek without a paddle. The venerable old sternwheeler **NORTHWESTERN** veteran river vessel, sits on the bottom of the Kuskokwim near Bethel, Alaska, in the 1950's. She was built as the **GRAHAMONA** at Portland, Oregon in 1912 and operated for many years on the Willamette and Columbia Rivers.

moved toward the Arctic Ocean. The shipmasters had been warned by the Eskimos not to hug the American shores too closely. Charts were of little use in that part of the world and an iceberg could pop up anywhere. Though the stars were helpful, fog sometimes lay over the Arctic wastes blanking out the heavens. A word to the wise should be sufficient, but of the 40 whaleship masters who got advise from the natives only seven weighed the odds and decided the gamble was not worth the risk. They sailed southward in a waiting tactic.

Then tragedy struck. On June 14, the barkentine *Oreole* was stove in by the ice. Though her people were picked up, the incident did not deter the rest of the fleet, for every year it was a common occurrence that one or more of the vessels became victims of the Arctic ice. By the end of the month all of the vessels save the seven had entered the Arctic from Bering Strait and passed into the whale rich grounds, skippers anxious for a profitable haul.

At East Cape, the survivors of the whaleship *Japan*, wrecked the year previous, anxiously awaited rescue after spending the better part of a year facing the perils of the northland. After their ship was crushed in the ice in October 1870, the crew of 31 set out to reach the Siberian shore, but en route eight of their number perished forcing the others to remain among the Eskimos and a diet of walrus blubber for their very survival.

The castaways were picked up and distributed among the whaling fleet and the hunt got underway with positive results. The Arctic seas ran red with the blood of the sperms and grays and the slaughter continued throughout the summer despite persistent fogs. In late July, the winds increased clearing the American shore of ice, prompting the fleet to head for Icy Cape. The pursuit continued and the next big haul was off Wainwright. Within a week the wind hauled around to the westward, the ice began to reappear and solidify. In an ice-choked sea canvas is useless, and with no other form of propulsion, a whaleship was at the mercy of the elements. Some of the vessels were already solidly trapped forcing the others to seek open waters. Whaleboats were spread out in a wide arc and in order to get back to their respective vessels, their occupants were forced to drag the craft up on the ice and over the hummocks in a desperate effort to regain home base. Still the whale seekers would not give up and the hunt went on in the waters not yet in the icy grip. It was like a game of Russian roulette, pitting the creeping ice pack against the dwindling brine. The bonanza was such that each skipper was trusting that the ice would sweep out to sea. Ah, but one never fools Mother Nature, at least not immediately.

It appeared that things might work their way when a sudden northeast gale swept the area on August 25 breaking up the ice and driving it seaward. In fact, two

Frozen in solid—the wrecked SS **CROWN CITY**, operated for the military by American Mail Line struck an uncharted rock off Sledge Island, Alaska September 1, 1942 with a full load of military cargo. Though some of the cargo was salvaged the vessel was a total loss. A. Polet photo.

Two popular passenger liners in the Seattle-Alaska run became victims of the rigors of the Far North. The SS **STATE OF CALIFORNIA**(upper) was wrecked at Gambier Bay in August 1913 with the loss of 35 lives, and the **OREGON** became a total loss off Cape Hinchinbrook in September 1906, but Captain Horace Soule and his passengers and crew evacuated without a casualty.

days later even the imprisoned whaleships were able to break free and head out to deeper water. The devil icepack, like the devil himself lured the fleet by a spell of sunny weather, and then sprung the trap. The wind swung around to the southwest shoving the ice back to the American side and locking the victims between the shore and the ice. Some of the ships were anchored in shallow water as the frigid squalls erupted.

By September 2, the brigantine *Comet* was solidly in the trap, its timbers splitting in the crunch. Within five days the barkentine *Ramon* fell victim and in an hour was reduced to kindling. A day later the barkentine *Awashonka* sent her crew scurrying as the icy fingers squeezed her in a frozen fist. Finally there was general alarm among the remaining units of the fleet, only one narrow ice-free path remaining, and the worst was yet to come with fall and winter promising to menace its prey. The shipmasters got their heads together and all agreed that they were fast losing the battle, a gamble that had failed to pay off. Holds were filled with whale oil, a gold mine of fluid, but it was as worthless as putrid water if it could not be delivered. It was decided to send a party to the vicinity of the seven ice-free vessels that had not taken the big gamble. Volunteers took a single whaleboat and sailed southward in search of assistance. Fortunately that small portion of the fleet were still in open waters and agreed to stand by. On receiving the news, the imprisoned shipmasters conferred once again and though crestfallen, had to reckon that to stay with their respective commands meant they might all perish. Survival was better than wealth. Maybe, just maybe some of the whaleships could stand the rigors of the ice till the next season. But that was wishful thinking.

On September 14, the 29 vessels were abandoned and all hands, men, women and children took out in the open boats all of which had been provisioned for the rigorous voyage. Hundreds of souls were involved, the overcrowded craft offering only misery for their occupants. The first night they camped on the frigid shores and awakened to a bitter wind. It was misery with a capital M but they were a tough breed of people used to the demanding life of seafarers, and despite much suffering few complained. The days were long and the nights an eternity, but ironically they reached Icy Cape and were gratefully divided among the remaining seven whaleships which upped anchor for Plover Bay packed to the gunwhales. Later the ships set sail for the Sandwich Islands (Hawaii) and the popular wintering anchorages at Honolulu and Lahaina.

The amazing finale to this epic was not the fact that it was one of the greatest peacetime tragedies among American merchant ships, let alone the whaling fleet, but not a single life was lost on any of the 31 whaling vessels swallowed up by the Arctic ice in the fateful 1871 season.

Built at Portland, Oregon in 1859, the sidewheeler **ELIZA ANDERSON** became a household word on Puget Sound for her long service and musical calliope. Old and tender, she was drafted into the fleet sailing north for the Alaska goldrush and there came to an ignominious end.

SS **FARALLON** ran aground near Wrangell, Alaska July 23, 1899, one of many mishaps she suffered in the Puget Sound-Alaska service. She was totally wrecked 11 years later at Iliamna Bay, Alaska, January 5, 1910.

Wrong turn—One of the big news stories of 1970 was the stranding of the Alaska state ferry **TAKU** near Prince Rupert, B.C. at West Kinahan Island. Only four persons of the 342 aboard were injured, none seriously. The mishap occurred July 29 and knocked the 352 foot ship out of service during the peak of the tourist season. Captain Jim Sande was master of the vessel which piled up just as the midnight watch was being changed. The vessel was steaming at 17 knots, eight miles from Prince Rupert when she struck the island, pushing her snout right up in the trees. The ferry was southbound when she struck. After evacuation, the vessel was temporarily patched, pulled off and escorted to Seattle for costly bottom repairs.

Joe Williamson, marine photographer took these photos of the wreck of the SS **OHIO** in 1947, almost four decades after her demise. The decking on the forecastle had sprouted small seedling trees and weeds; the iron plates, though rusted, still were well in tact.

Pathetic scene. The Canadian National steamship **PRINCE GEORGE** gutted by fire, left in agony in September 1945. The steamer caught fire at Ketchikan and was towed to Gravina Island until the fire burned out. Three years later the wreck was towed to Seattle and scrapped. All passengers were safely evacuated after the fire broke out. One crewman died in the engine room following a fuel tank explosion which started the fire.

Hard aground on Mary Island, Alaska in the 1920's, the **BANGOR** struggles for life. She was built as a four-masted schooner at Eureka, California in 1891 and ended her career as a barge at Vallejo, California.

SS **NORTHWESTERN** pushes her bow up on the beach in Wrangell Narrows, Alaska, June 1, 1919 as a result of fog. Salvaged and repaired, the accident prone ship began her career at Chester, Pennsylvania in 1889 as the **ORIZABA**.

Tombstone for the wreck of the SS **PRINCESS SOPHIA**, the most tragic wreck ever recorded on the Alaska waterways. The vessel slipped off Vanderbilt Reef in Southeastern Alaska during a blizzard in October 1918 and every passenger and crewman went to a watery grave—343 in all. After the storm, the above is all that was visible, a lone mast surveyed by a disconsolate viewer. Winter and Pond photo.

The narrow view. The Pacific Coast Steamship Company's SS **ADMIRAL ROGERS**, pokes her nose in unfriendly territory in one of the minor strandings during her service in the Alaska trade.

185

CHAPTER SEVEN

British Columbia Shipwrecks

Canada's fabulous western province skirting the Pacific is composed of numerous irregular miles of seafront, with topographical characteristics likened onto the Scandinavian Peninsula. These waterways, intricate, tricky and dangerous to the novice are beautiful to the eye, marked with some excellent harbors and necessarily polka-dotted with more than 500 aids to navigation. Included in the British Columbia province is 200 mile long Vancouver Island, a western barrier between the Pacific Ocean and the great inland waterways. There is also the elaborate chain of Queen Charlotte Islands extending southward from Southeastern Alaska. Further, there are hundreds of other salty islands and islets, many uninhabited, spread all along the lengthy coastline that runs from the eastern end of the Strait of Juan de Fuca northward to Alaska.

British Columbia ports have long been among the most important in the world and a huge volume of shipping from yesteryear to the present day has been handled at Vancouver, New Westminster, Victoria, Nanaimo, Prince Rupert and numerous smaller lumber, log and pulp ports. It is the England of the Pacific and it has often been said if one could wring out British Columbia it would still be covered with salt from the sea.

There are many parts of British Columbia's unending waterway system that are seldom visited, creating a virtual yachtman's paradise during the good weather season, but it only stands to reason that a salt water-oriented province, the likes of British Columbia, would also be the scene of many unfortunate shipping mishaps, in adverse weather. Thousands of craft, large and small have fallen victim to the reefs, rocks and obstructions of its often inhospitable coastline.

The Clarksdale Victory Disaster

Grim was the word for the *Clarksdale Victory* disaster. With a toll of 49 lives, it was one of the worst wrecks in North Pacific waters in recent times.

The *Clarksdale Victory* was serving in the capacity of a U.S. Army cargo transport when she came to a sudden and tragic ending November 24, 1947. Now, only a regretable memory, the twisted, mangled wreck lies at the bottom of the Pacific off Hippa Island Reef, British Columbia, a rusting steel tomb.

Seattle-bound, on her fatal voyage, the *Clarksdale Victory* dropped her lines at the military port of Whittier, Alaska on a bleak Fall day. Fifty-three persons were aboard, most of whom comprised the crew of the 7,600 ton vessel. She carried only a small parcel of cargo.

In command, was a youthful 29 year old skipper, Captain Gerald Laugeson. Several hours out of Whittier a biting, cold wind born in the frigid Arctic released its lungs upon the waters of the Gulf of Alaska. It caught up with the *Clarksdale Victory* off the British Columbia coast. Massive seas were formed and the vessel pitched and rolled at dangerous angles. A mightly deluge of rain poured down from voluminous black clouds.

To this day nobody knows quite how, but the course being followed indicated the transport should have been 25 miles offshore when she slammed into Hippa Island reef with a shocking impact. Perhaps it was an erroneous compass, the set of the tidal currents, strong winds or a navigational error-who can say? What difference now. . .none can bring back the dead.

The *Clarksdale Victory* rammed head on into a devil's caldron, steep jagged ridges of rock surrounded by an isolated, uninhabited island.

It all happened so suddenly that it was as if the men aboard had been struck by a bolt of lightning. Within minutes after plowing into the reef the vessel split in two at No. 3 hold, and the after section settled beneath the turbulence as fifty foot-high breakers roared over its grave. The men were denied even a try at saving their lives. It was destruction in its most hideous form as frigid seas twisted the steel plates like clay in the hands of a potter.

Only the battered forepart of the ship remained cradled on the reef. On it were a few pitiful men living out a nightmare. Great seas barreled in from every direction working the forward section like a toy. It seemed that any moment it too would be lifted free of its rocky cradle and dropped into the depths along with the after part of the ship.

Hippa Island, located just south of Graham Island in the Queen Charlotte group is only 2.8 miles in length and a maritime trap for any ship unfortunate enough to fall within its grasp.

Just one distress message eminated from the *Clarksdale Victory* before she broke up. It read: "Pounded by huge swells—immediate aid needed."

But the message was too late. The first ship to reach the scene of the disaster was the Alaska passenger ship *Denali;* but she was helpless to render aid against the insurmountable seas that lashed the shore though an heroic attempt by a lifeboat crew of eight was made, the men narrowly escaping with their lives.

Coast Guard planes and cutters combed the area for survivors without success. It was with great difficulty that small parties were finally landed on the island to continue the search by foot. Coastguardsmen from the cutters *Wachusett* and *Citrus,* fanned out over the virgin terrain. They searched the precipitous cliffs, combed the rock-laden beaches and the interior of the island. After an exhaustive search, four survivors, suffering severely from exposure were removed from the bow of the vessel. They were ship's officers, Henry H. Wolf, William Rasmussen, Clair E. Driscoll and seaman, Carlos Sanabria. All were given food and medical treatment while a plane was dispatched from Ketchikan to take them to a hospital. One was suffering from a fractured hip.

The search was finally terminated with the four survivors and the bodies of three others who had drowned in a desperate struggle for survival after the ship had crashed ashore. The others were evidently trapped hopelessly in the steel confines of the submerged ship's after section, drowned like rats.

The sea had won a deadly victory—49 lives and a ship only two years-old, valued in excess of $2 million.

The four survivors spoke in hushed tones of their frightful experiences. They told how the stranded ship was lifted bodily by seas and pounded violently against the rocky reef.

All hands had been called immediately to the boat deck, to abandon ship, but because of the mountainous breakers it was decided it was safer to stay aboard rather than risk an escape in the lifeboats.

For ten minutes this seemed the right decision.

Then the vessel broke in two at No. 3 hatch. The aft section with all the lifeboats and most of the crew started to settle and tremendous seas crashed over the deck.

The awful howling of wind and sea drowned out the frantic cries of the doomed men—and it was all over.

But for the will of God there would have been no survivors—but the forward section remained temporarily cradled and permitted four men to escape the awful chill of death in all its hideousness.

The Tale of Ripple Rock, The Ship Killer

At exactly 9:31 a.m. April 7, 1958 the largest non-nuclear explosion to that date, some 2.75 million pounds of high-potency nitramex-2-H rocked Seymour Narrows, British Columbia, where lay dreaded Ripple Rock. Like a giant mushroom, the explosion shot skyward in a brilliant display of rock and spume.

So great was the shock that nearly 400,000 tons of rock were shot sky high. The double-peaked rock was lowered from ten feet below low water to more than 47 feet.

After countless human failings to obliterate this long-feared hazard to navigation which had claimed 114 lives and destroyed or damaged some 120 vessels of all descriptions, the battle was at last won.

In its final and most concerted effort to eradicate the rock, the Canadian government had ex-

SS **PRINCE ALBERT** wrecked on Butterworth Rocks off South Dundas Island, B. C. August 18, 1914. Although she appears beyond salvage, the vessel was eventually refloated and repaired. Formerly the **BRUNO**, built at Hull, England in 1892, she became the first vessel of the Grand Trunk Pacific "Prince" fleet, and some time later was sold by Canadian National Railway and operated as a rum runner, after which she was converted to the steam tug **J. R. MORGAN**. As the **MORGAN**, she was broken up at Vancouver, B.C. in 1949.

pended well in excess of $3 million. This amount and the great sums expended earlier in unsuccessful attempts was small indeed in comparison to the loss of property and lives incurred there.

Today, mariners no longer need fear this cantankerous obstacle. For the first time in history they can pilot their ships over the spot where the devil-like tentacles so long reached toward the surface awaiting their prey as the tides swirled through this narrow waterway on the inside passage to Alaska.

Those who go down to the sea in ships had recognized Ripple Rock as a killer since 1875. It was in this year that the first recorded shipwreck occurred there. The rock's sinister reputation grew with the years.

Centuries back, geologists and historians believe that the controlling depth of water over the summits of Ripple Rock (prior to explosion), was considerably less than in its latter days.

Indian legends tell of braves showing their courage by standing on the north pinnacle at low tide with water up to their waists. The rock vibrated so much that it allegedly shook their cheeks. It is further told that faithless squaws were forced to stand on the rock at low tide, and left there to be carried away by the swift-rising tides.

The first official information concerning Ripple Rock was recorded in the journal of Captain George Vancouver, British Royal Navy commander, who, in the year 1792, sailed his command, the HMS *Discovery,* through Seymour Narrows.

The amazing part of his endeavor was that he took his cumbersome ship through under sail, skirting Ripple Rock without incident. With a

Salvage work is underway on the steamship **NORTHWESTERN** after she stranded near Cape Mudge, B.C. on December 11, 1927. The Alaska Line passenger ship was refloated by the Pacific Salvage Company in February, 1928 following a long and costly effort.

skill known only to those ancient mariners he piloted his vessel around the west side of the rock, instead of taking the east passage frequently used today.

Vancouver named the narrows, Yuculta, for the savage natives which lined the shores waiting to plunder the vessel should it have the misfortune of being wrecked. It is said that the savages caused the explorer more concern than did the treacherous barrier and the swift currents in the narrows.

Indians in this Campbell River area claimed their forefathers once paddled out to help rescue Captain Vancouver after his ship ran afoul of Ripple Rock. This claim has never been substantiated except in legend. The Indians, however, claimed this was so and that the British explorer deleted it from his journals because of embarrassment.

It would have seemed, however, that any man who would attempt to take a sailing vessel around Ripple Rock would have to be a most daring individual.

If any embarrassment was to be attached to the rock it would seem as if it would have to fall to the later ships with motive power, other than sail. There was the U.S.S. *Saranac* which foundered in those unpredictable waters on June 15, 1875. The vessel was a paddle-wheel steamer of 1,484 tons, mounting 13 cannon. She was out of San Francisco bound for the seal islands in the Bering Sea to collect exhibits for the centennial exhibition in Philadelphia. Fortunately none of those aboard the *Saranac,* including the representatives of the Smithsonian Institution were lost, but they had an uncomfortable wait on the isolated shore while their captain and their pilot made the long voyage to Victoria by canoe to secure help from the Royal Navy.

And then there was the H.M.S. *Satellite,* an account of the wreck having been handed down by the late Admiral B. M. Chambers. The vessel struck "Ol Rip" in 1884.

"I saw our ship steaming at a speed of 13 knots caught in the swirling torrents of Seymour Narrows like a chip in a gutter," Admiral Chambers reported. "We were swept into the very center of the pass. I saw the great upright waves above Ripple Rock seemingly rush toward us. I felt the ship heel over as her keel struck the top of one of the rocks. For a moment she hung there, then we were free with the loss of 40 feet of our false keel."

The vessel then slowly settled to the bottom.

On October 8, 1915, the Alaska steamer **MARIPOSA** struck a rock ledge at the upper end of Fitzhugh Sound, B.C. and stranded at Llama Pass, tearing a hole in her bottom, forward. She had departed Seattle in command of Captain C. J. O'Brien with 95 passengers and cargo for S. E. Alaska and Cook Inlet when she got in trouble. The coaster **DESPATCH,** came to the rescue and picked up the passengers from the beach, transporting them to Ketchikan. The Canadian salvage steamer **SALVOR,** several weeks later, was able to refloat the **MARIPOSA** and she and the **WILLIAM JOLLIFFE** towed her to a Seattle drydock, arriving November 15. *Thwaites photo.*

Steamer **VALENCIA,** built of iron, at the Cramp yard in Philadelphia in 1882 and which later came to the Pacific Coast as a passenger liner, was to become involved in the most tragic of all shipwrecks on the British Columbia coast. Purchased from the Pacific Packing & Navigation Company by the Pacific Coast Company in 1902, the vessel came to a tragic end four years later. *Joe Williamson collection.*

One of the only known photos of the actual wreck of the SS **VALENCIA** aground on the rocks ten miles east of Cape Beale off the west coast of Vancouver Island. In command of Captain O. M. Johnson, the vessel grounded at midnight, January 23-24, 1906. She carried 154 passengers and crew. Over-running the entrance into the Strait of Juan de Fuca, en route from San Francisco to Puget Sound, she crashed on the rocks and became hopelessly entrapped. Escape was virtually impossible and rescue ships were unable to get near the disintegrating wreck due to the perilous waters. Before it was all over, only 37 had survived, 117 perished. *Provincial Archives Photo, Victoria, B. C.*

This re-copied photo shows the grim remains of the **VALENCIA** amid a cluster of sharp rocks, off the precipitous west coast of Vancouver Island. After the sea had completed its devastating assault on that dreadful night in 1906, 117 perished.

Wreck of the U.S. Army tug (LT-62), **MAJOR RICHARD M. STRONG,** which ran aground on a rocky reef off Camp Point, Vancouver Island, B.C. September 23, 1949. Built at Tampa, Florida in 1944, at a cost of $577,000, the tug was feared to be a total loss. But bids were put out for salvaging the steel vessel. Straits Towing, Island Tug & Barge and Pacific Salvage Company pooled their efforts and performed a remarkable salvage job in just 14 days. The 123 foot tug was later acquired by Island Tug & Barge Ltd. of Victoria, B.C., rebuilt and renamed **ISLAND SOVEREIGN.**

Earlier the U.S.S. *Wachusett,* was corkscrewed around in a vast whirlpool and destroyed, followed down through the years by a long list of liners and freighters.

The following description of Ripple Rock and Seymour Narrows appeared in the *British Columbia Coast Pilot* for 1885, published by the Hydrographic Branch of the Admiralty, London, England.

At 10.5 miles N.W. of Cape Mudge, is a narrow strait about one and a half miles long, and only from three to five cables wide, the shores of both sides being high, rugged and steep. The southern entrance to the narrows lies between Maude Inlet to the east and Wilfred Point on the west.

Ripple Rock, a dangerous rock about one and a half cables in extent in a N.N.E. and S.S.W. direction with only a depth of two and a half fathoms, lies nearly in the center of Seymour Narrows, but rather on the western side between Maude Inlet and Wilfred Point. The shoalest part lies three cables S.S.W. from the nearest land of Wilfred Point.

Geologists labeled Ripple Rock as a submarine outcropping in the shape of a hog's back, surmounted by two pinnacles, or humps, reaching to nine and 20 feet below low water.

The outcrop was really part of an underwater mountain on the east side of the rock, the channel being 325 feet deep, and on the west side, 400 feet deep.

The massive obstruction rising as it did in the center of the channel caused great turbulence with the changing swift flowing tides. Whirlpools were known to have capsized small craft and to have carried liners onto dangerous pinnacles, with surprising suddenness.

Spring tides rose 13 feet, moving at a speed of ten to twelve knots and neaps six to eight knots. The greatest velocity occurred off Maude Island, and at full strength of spring tide, the speed of a ship had to be seventeen knots to take her through. The average duration of slack water was and is ten minutes.

Agitation in earnest, for the removal of the rock was begun in 1905. From that year on, committees of the Canadian government sat, proposals were submitted and acted upon, and attempts involving considerable amounts of money were passed in a vain attempt to do away with the obstruction.

The United States made a serious bid to influence removal of the rock after the stranding of the U. S. cable ship *Burnside* in the early part of this century. The vessel received serious damage and a memorandum was forthcoming from the office of the Chief of Engineers, U. S. Army sent to Hon. William H. Taft, then secretary of war. It was recommended to Taft that the existence of Ripple Rock should be brought to the attention of the Dominion Government of Canada, with a view to such action as the government might see fit to take.

The Canadian aircraft carrier HMCS **NABOB** ran aground five miles east of Point Roberts, Washington in March 1944 at a speed of 18 knots. Salvage master Loring Hyde was in charge of refloating the vessel. The job was accomplished, the vessel receiving only minor damage, and was returned to service shortly afterward.

Death scene—the U.S. Army Transport **CLARKSDALE VIC-TORY**, only her forward section showing, crashed onto the rocks off Hippa Island, B. C. near Graham Island November 24, 1947, with a death toll of 49 lives. The 7,600 ton vessel was southbound from Whittier in command of 29 year old Captain Gerald Laugeson. She broke in two shortly after striking the rocks in very heavy seas. The after half sank immediately, claiming 45 lives. Only four, including the second and third mates remained alive on the bridge. The steamer **DENALI** launched a boat in an effort to save the men but it swamped, its eight man crew narrowly escaping with their lives. The Coast Guard cutters **CITRUS** and **WACHUSETT** finally managed to miraculously save the four survivors from the wreck and picked up three bodies as well. The survivors claimed that the ship was 25 miles off course when she struck. The Victory type ship was built at Los Angeles in 1945.

The recommendation was kept alive although it had to make more than one detour, being channeled through the secretary of state, and the British Embassy in Washington. It was dispatched to Lord Grey, the governor general of Canada, at Ottawa on January 17, only eight days after Taft made the recommendation.

Following were years of red tape, requests for funds and unsuccessful attempts to polish off the navigational hazard. Meanwhile the rock continued to plague ships, large and small, when they were unfortunate enough to get trapped in the swift tides of Seymour Narrows.

Perhaps no other single maritime project in Canada was bantered about government offices as much as Ripple Rock.

Among the local disputes concerning the rock, was a serious difference between Vancouver and Victoria, principal British Columbia cities. Shipowners of Vancouver were strongly in favor of removal of the rock, while industrialists of Victoria advocated a "hands off" policy, one of the reasons being that the rock could serve as the foundation for a proposed pier to support a railway bridge which could put Vancouver Island into direct communication with the mainland.

Studies, surveys and investigations were made and a roster was posted in 1928 as to the best means to eradicate the menace.

Placing large explosive charges on the surface of the rock was considered impracticable; underground tunneling, the source used in the final 1958 blast, was dismissed as too expensive; drilling and blasting from a structure built on the rock was dismissed as being too dangerous from the standpoint of loss of lives. Drilling and blasting from suspended platforms was considered impracticable. Drilling and blasting from a floating plant was given consideration inasmuch as it was reasoned to be less expensive and gave promise of success.

Still differences between Vancouver and Victoria raged over the question of a railroad bridge. The obvious menace overruled the Victoria dissenters when informed engineers claimed that a bridge might constitute an even greater hazard to navigation.

The commission recommended removal of the rock, and submitted the following statistics to support their findings:

Passages by large passenger, freight and tramp vessels—1500 to 2000 per year.

Passages by other vessels—4000 to 5000 per year.

Number of passengers carried—175,000, plus crews.

Value of Vessels—$25 million

Cargo tonnage—in excess of 150,000 tons per year.

Value of cargoes—$107 million per year.

Another view of the ill-fated SS **CLARKSDALE VICTORY** (serving as an Army transport), hopelessly aground in a perilous port of no return off Hippa Island, the grave of 49 of her company.

Definitely not a joy ride—a crew member comes ashore in a bosn's chair rigged between the wreck of the MS **KENNECOTT** and the shore near Hunter's Point, Graham Island, B. C., October 8, 1923. The freighter, under Captain John Johnson got off course and stranded en route from Cordova to Tacoma. The Canadian salvage steamer **ALGERINE**, rushing to the aid of the **KENNECOTT** also got ashore on the rocks a few miles south of the scene but escaped with serious bottom damage. The 30 man crew of the **KENNECOTT** came ashore mostly by breeches buoy, and the ship soon broke in two, drifting away and sinking. Note distress signal, (burning drum of oil) on the fantail of the **KENNECOTT**. The ship was owned by the Alaska Steamship Co. Captain Johnson committed suicide after being rescued.

These figures varied with the years but gave a fair picture of the large amount of shipping using Seymour Narrows, and the need for removing the obstruction.

Another decade passed and World War II broke out. The rock remained.

When the United States got involved in the war in 1941, it became more than ever concerned because of the Alaska-bound ammunition ships using Seymour Narrows. The War Committee of the Canadian Cabinet instructed the department to take necessary steps to remove the rock.

The following year public tenders were invited for the removal of the obstruction to a depth of 30 feet below low water. No offers were received on the terms specified but two firms did agree to tackle the job on a cost plus basis.

The British Columbia Bridge and Dredging Company secured a contract in 1942 to drill and blast from a floating plant. A study of a suitable barge securely anchored was made on a hydraulic model of the narrows at the University of Washington.

A specially equipped drill barge, 150 feet long was built and two concrete anchors, each weighing 250 tons, and four of 150 tons each were also contrived. By heavy steel cable made fast to these anchors, the position of the barge could be shifted at a given notice.

The undertaking at rock-side began in the summer of 1943, but vibration of the steel cables not only caused the cables to part, but also disrupted the drilling and blasting. Not yet ready to give up, attempts were made to anchor the cables to heavy bolts set in rock on the mainland, but this method was no more successful than the initial attempt, for, on an average, a bolt would last no more than 48 hours.

Overhead cables were then tried, with a minimum clearance of 135 feet above high water, from which anchor cables would reach to the deck of the barge. This scheme was tried in the

Wooden motor vessel **CHALLAMBA**, 2,401 tons, wrecked on White Cliff Island, B. C. June 17, 1927. She was abandoned as a total loss. The **CHALLAMBA** was built as a World War I emergency freighter. Owned by the Pacific Motorship Company, the 262 foot, twin-screw vessel was built at Olympia, Washington in 1918.

summer of 1945. Two steel cables, one and three quarter inches in diameter, 3,500 feet long and weighing ten tons each, had their ends attached to Douglas fir masts 100 feet high, on each shore, and supplementary cables from these overhead cables to the deck of the barge, permitted the barge to be maneuvered as desired.

On the drawing tables it was estimated that 1,500 blast holes would be required to blow the so-called "L" out of Ripple Rock.

By the end of the summer season scarcely 120 holes had been blasted. At this pace well over 12 years would be required to decapitate the twin peaks. This would never do, especially with the incalculable cost involved. Canada's Federal Government slapped an immediate padlock on the project and the whole problem reverted to the place it had been when the first known ship tangled with the rock in 1875.

The menace continued. Man had again failed in his efforts to conquer this undersea mountain. But the wheels of genius were forever spinning. Modern engineering knowhow and innovations were coming to the fore. In the drawing rooms, the plot for an all-out offensive was gradually gaining momentum.

In 1953, almost a decade after the previous failure, the National Research Council made further studies relative to removal of the rock. And, with this end in view, a diamond drill hole was bored for a distance of 2,500 feet from Maude Island on the east side of the narrows, curving down to a depth of 325 feet, so as to pass under the channel with ample clearance, terminating at a point under Ripple Rock.

The conclusion drawn was that the rock was mostly basalt with a sprinkling of andesite and some strips of volcanic breccia. Some faulting was discovered, but there was no evidence of water intrusion through the fault zones, and the tunnelling which would be necessary, was an ordinary mining problem.

Things were looking up.

The committee of the National Research Council therefore recommended tunnelling downwards on Maude Island, under the Narrows, and upwards into the two pinnacles known as Ripple Rock. This was joyful news when the powers concerned received approval of the recommendation, and the Department of Public Works was instructed to proceed.

To Dr. Victor Dolmage and E. E. Mason, geological and mining engineers of Vancouver, was given the task of preparing detailed plans and elaborate specifications. The entire undertaking was placed under the direction of the Chief Engineer, Harbours and Rivers Branch.

Under the watchful eyes of skilled engineers, Canada's best, the final designs were provided for: (a) a shaft on Maude Island seven feet by 18 feet in cross section, 500 to 580 feet in depth.

(b) a tunnel six feet by seven feet in cross section at a minimum depth of 100 feet under the lowest part of the east channel.

(c) two main access raises, each 15 feet by seven feet in cross section, leading upward into the two pinnacles for a height of 300 feet.

(d) tunnels six feet by seven feet in cross section, to be driven off each raise under each of the pinnacles, lengthwise for approximately 370 feet.

Government motor vessel **BOXER** aground on White Cliff Island Reef, B. C. in the 1920's in the service of the U. S. Bureau of Indian Affairs. The vessel was aground for several days but eventually refloated and repaired. She was originally built at Portsmouth, N. H. in 1905 as a training brigantine for the Annapolis Naval Academy.

(e) small tunnels, approximately six feet by six feet on a 45 degree slope, and coyote drifts on various grades to be driven from the sublevels, (tunnels described in (d) to various points and levels under each pinnacle. These are the chambers into which the explosives for the final blast were carefully placed.

Contract for the undertaking was awarded in the fall of 1955, and throughout the entire course of operations every precaution was practiced. This was a game where the slightest mistake could be a costly one, and one that immediately separated the men from the boys.

All tunnelling was proceeded by diamond drilling, all cores being carefully recovered. Test hole drilling and grouting was carried out whenever required.

Pains were taken with timbering and concreting of the work being done, and the provision made for flood control gates and emergency doors. At all times forced ventilation was maintained and explosives for the final blast were encased in watertight containers, all metal and vapor proof. Scores of men and expensive equipment were employed in the undertaking. With all efforts bent toward the largest non-nuclear explosion then known to man, every detail was carefully mapped out in advance.

After many difficult months of concerted hard labor, the job drew to a climax and all went according to schedule. When April of 1958 arrived, the job was finished except for making a last minute check to see that the explosives were all correctly placed and wired for the big blast. Then the working crews retreated and the government engineers and overseers were given assignments for viewing the explosive fruit of their fantastic project.

Prior to the Ripple Rock explosion the largest non-nuclear explosion on record had been touched off on July 21, 1957, at Promontory Point, Utah, when a total of 1.79 million pounds of explosives were used to break up an estimated three million tons of rock for the Great Salt Lake crossing for the Southern Pacific Railroad.

Now all was ready to blast Ripple Rock, the explosives placed at the end of a tunnel that passed from an island entirely under a channel of water and up into the inside of the obstruction. The powerful Nitramex 2-H dynamite was far more powerful than the older agent used at Great Salt Lake.

As the long awaited day approached, the press informed millions the world over. The government meanwhile summed up its efforts on the project like this:

Number of men employed—between 40 and 80.

Amount and type of underground work completed to Dec. 31, 1957—shaft from Maude Island to main tunnel level—572 feet.

Total length of main tunnel—from shaft to pinnacles—2,941 feet.

Total length of the two raises driven from main tunnel up into pinnacle—644 feet.

Total length of sub-level driven at 120 foot level under each pinnacle—120 feet.

Level under each pinnacle—570 feet.

Total length of box holes, six feet by six feet, tunnels on a 45-degree slope, driven from sub-level at 120 feet elevation to coyote tunnels—355 feet.

Total length of coyote tunnel driven in both pinnacles—2,750 feet.

Total footage of test drilling underground including diamond drilling and percussion drilling—31,000 feet.

* * *

Among the yellowed records of Ripple Rock history in the Victoria, B. C. archives is found a list of ships that have locked horns with Ripple Rock.

Since 1875, two dozen ocean going vessels and barges were lost or damaged as a result of striking the rock. More than 100 smaller vessels, fishing boats, tugs, yachts etc., were also damaged or totally lost through striking the rock or falling victim to the treacherous waters in the immediate vicinity. As was mentioned earlier, 114 lives were claimed.

A pinnacle rock piercing her hull, the SS **NORTH SEA** of the Northland Transportation Company rests abandoned on Porter Reef, near Bella Bella, B. C. where she ran aground February 13, 1947. Southbound for Seattle, the passenger liner, in command of Captain Charles Graham, with 150 passengers and crew aboard, also had a cargo of general freight and canned salmon. The passengers, 85 in all, were evacuated by small boats and later picked up by the steamer **PRINCE RUPERT**. A skeleton crew remained aboard for awhile and then gave up. The Pacific Salvage Company of Vancouver gave up on attempts to refloat the vessel and later a storm arose and broke the liner's back. The **NORTH SEA** was built at Elizabeth, N.J. in 1918 as the **PLAINFIELD**. She was later named **MARY WEEMS** and then **ADMIRAL PEOPLES**, sister to the ill-fated **ADMIRAL BENSON**, lost at the entrance to the Columbia River in 1930. *Joe Williamson photo.*

Following is the list of the larger ships, liners, freighters and warships that suffered in an encounter with Ripple Rock.

Year	Name	Type	Nature
1875	Saranac	U.S. Navy Ship	Total Loss
1875	Wachusett	U.S. Navy Ship	Total Loss
1884	Satellite	British Warship	Total Loss
1902	Bonita	Steamer	Serious Damage
1904	Danube	Steamer	Stranded on Rock
1904	Burnside	U.S. Cable Ship	Serious Damage
1906	Themis	Steamer	Stranded on Rock
1911	Spokane	Steamer	Struck Rock, Nearly Foundered ($115,000 salvage job)
1914	Gerard C. Tobey	Barge	Total Loss
1916	Henry Villard	Barge	Near Total Loss
1916	Princess Maquinna	Steamer	Stranded on Rock
1918	Palmyra	Barge	Partial Loss
1918	Queen	Steamer	Struck Rock
1919	Princess Ena	Steamer	Stranded on Rock
1920	Prince George	Steamer	Stranded on Rock
1926	Kaikyu Maru	Steamer	Struck Rock, Total Loss
1927	Prince Rupert	Steamer	Stranded on Rock
1929	Aleutian	Steamer	Stranded on Rock
1929	Princess Mary	Steamer	Grazed Rock
1930	Koprino	Steamer	Broke Rudder on Rock
1931	Camosun	Steamer	Damaged Propeller on Rock
1934	V.T. No. 2	Barge	Collided with Scow
1936	Prince Rupert	Steamer	Collided with Anna J.
1941	S.O.C. No. 95	Oil Barge	Stranded on Rock
1946	Wm. J. Stewart	U.S. Survey Ship	Struck Rock, Nearly Foundered (salvage and damages $500,000)

A cresting breaker combs the deck of the U. S. Army transport **KVICHAK** which grounded on rocky shoreline in Finlayson Channel, Sisters Rock, B. C. January 26, 1941. Twenty-three passengers and 35 crew members were rescued. The **KVICHAK** was en route to Seward from Seattle in command of Captain W. W. Williamson when she struck. The survivors were picked up by the gunboat **CHARLE-STON**, a skeleton crew remaining. The Pacific Salvage Company attempted to salvage the vessel, but on March 5, she slipped from the rocks and sank in 80 feet of water. Later, salvage work continued and with the use of four scows and cables, the wreck was moved under water and beached at Prince Rupert in July. The **KVICHAK** was built at Portland, Oregon in 1900 and later, being converted from steam to diesel, operated for the Alaska Packers Association.

As scheduled, on April 7, 1958 a titanic explosion, rocked Seymour Narrows as the world watched on their television screens and listened over their radios. It was an epic day in history as modern genius produced the formula to pulverize the deadly peaks of Ripple Rock. The end result far exceeded the expectations of the engineers and overseers. It was planned to take the rocks to a depth of approximately 40 feet below low water, but an additional seven feet was realized and even more in some spots.

Photos of the blast were seen in every newspaper around the world as well as in all leading news periodicals. Ripple Rock once known only to one sector of the world became known the world over.

At last man's long battle to conquer this natural barrier was over and for the first time he could sail over the spot where danger once lurked, with peace of mind.

After the government re-opened Seymour Narrows to commercial traffic, Captain Henry Hall, skipper of the small freighter *Samish Queen,* had the distinction of commanding his ship over the place where the rock had once been. He was the first to do so. In sailing over "Ol Rip," as the seafarers commonly called the rock, Captain Hall smiled broadly as his echo sounder showed 52 feet under his ship at slack tide directly over the spot where the dreaded twin peaks had for so long been a destroyer of men and ships.

Broken in two on the rocks of Zayas Island off the northern British Columbia coast, is seen the freighter **DENALI**, which ran aground on May 19, 1935 at 3 a.m. Captain Thomas E. Healy, skipper of the **DENALI**, his officers and crew, seven passengers and four stowaways, 42 in all, were removed by the Coast Guard cutter **CYANE**, (Lt. Cmdr. L.E. Richards), which had sped from her Ketchikan base in answer to the **DENALI'S** SOS. The cargo vessel, belonging to the Alaska Steamship Company, was en route from Seattle to S. E. Alaska with a full cargo including 30 tons of dynamite. The vessel and cargo were valued at $650,000. A short while after the ship stranded, fire broke out in her hull. As the seas battered her, she worked on the rocks and broke in two. The **DENALI** was built for the USSB in 1920 as the **JEPTHA**.

Wreck of the S.S. Denali.

Ghost of the Valencia.

Of all of the shipwrecks on the outlying tentacles of British Columbia's graveyard of ships off Vancouver Island's West Coast, none is more recalled than that of the SS *Valencia*. It was this wreck that prompted in 1907, the year after the mishap, the construction of a lighthouse at Pachena Point. The government was forced to act by an agitated public, many of whom had loved ones among the 117 souls that perished in that regrettable tragedy.

The ship went on the rocks not far from where the lighthouse was built. She overran her course and struck a reef around midnight January 11, 1906. What had begun as a joyful voyage north from San Francisco ended up in a virtual night of horror for the 154 persons aboard the vessel. Only 37 were to escape, not a single woman or child among them. Captain O. M. Johnson, the *Valencia's* master, perished with his ship.

Some of the eerie remains of the *Valencia* are still scattered over the ocean floor and skin divers have explored them in recent years. The rusted, twisted and broken hull has been robbed of all its wares by the elements of the sea.

Still in her wartime colors, the Northland Transportation Company's SS **NORTH SEA** awaits the end, on Porter Reef, near Bella Bella in 1947. People boarding the wreck, a few years later, said it had been taken over by rats, which flourished in droves until all semblance of food was gone. *Joe Williamson photo.*

Coated in snow, the wounded SS **COTTAGE CITY** lies hard aground at Willow Point, near Cape Mudge, after being wrecked on January 26, 1911. Built at Bath, Maine in 1890, the 1,885 ton vessel was en route from Puget Sound to Skagway in charge of Captain A. C. Jansen when she encountered a snowstorm. Losing her course, the vessel hit the rocks and a distress signal went out over the wireless. The 38 passengers and most of the crew abandoned safely in the boats and went to Campbell River. Baggage and mail was recovered by the revenue cutter (tug) **SNOHOMISH.** Hopes for salvaging the liner failed and she became a total loss. The ship was owned by the Pacific Steamship Company.

Like a wounded whale, the fishing steamer **WEIDING BROS.**, Captain Otto Holmstrom, lies stranded on Graham Island in the Queen Charlottes, July 29, 1913. Owned by the Weiding Bros. and Independent Fishing Company, the vessel was written off the books as a total loss shortly after the stranding. The previous year she had grounded on a shoal on Hackney Island, near Holmes Harbor, Puget Sound while running at top speed. They got her off 12 hours later.

En route to Victoria, B. C. from Port Townsend, under charter to O. R. & N., in command of Captain L. E. Angerstein, the steamer **IDAHO** was listening for the fog signal on Race Rocks, which was inaudible. The skipper ordered full astern when suddenly the vessel struck the rocks off Rosedale Reef, November 29, 1889. Laden with 800 barrels of lime, 150 barrels of fish oil, 370 barrels of salmon, 65 bales of hemp and 200 tons of coal, the **IDAHO** commenced leaking badly. The sea water set fire to the lime, and big holes were cut in the hull to squelch the fires. She was on the rocks till Dec. 20 when she drifted free and floated about the Strait of Juan de Fuca. Three tugs at various times put lines on the **IDAHO** without success. The tug **MOGUL** finally towed the derelict into Port Angeles where she sank in deep water. Her crew of 42 had earlier been removed at Rosedale Reef.

British freighter **TUSCAN PRINCE** aground on Village Island outcroppings in Barkley Sound, B. C. She was impaled on the reef as a result of a blinding snowstorm while en route to Vancouver, B. C. from London. The crew was removed and the 5,275 ton vessel was declared a total constructive loss. Salvage crews later broke up part of the wreck for scrap. The wreck occurred on February 15, 1923.

Another view of the SS **TUSCAN PRINCE** after running aground off Village Island in February, 1923. Pacific Salvage Company retrieved most of her cargo and a Bellingham junk firm removed upper steel plating before the wreck slipped off the reef and went down in deep water. She was owned by Prince Line of London.

Half a vessel—all that was left of the Seattle halibut schooner **ORIENT** cut in half on August 31, 1930 by the SS **ADMIRAL NULTON**, 30 miles south of Seymour Narrows near White Island, B. C. The steamer overhauled the fishboat at night in clear weather and struck her so hard that she broke in two, part of her sinking. Captain S. H. Rudd, master, and nine other men were drowned. Three others of the **ORIENT'S** company were rescued.

Victim of Ripple Rock, the Japanese freighter **KAIKYU MARU** ripped her hull open on the dreaded menace to navigation, August 29, 1926. The vessel was en route to Port Alice from Vancouver, B. C. when she struck. The engine room filled and the boiler exploded. She was beached and abandoned as a total loss. The 8,134 ton vessel was built in 1919. The twin-screw steamer was owned by Katsuda Kisen Kabushiki Kaisha, and measured 445 feet in length.

After performing many salvage jobs in British Columbia waters, the old Canadian salvage tug **SALVAGE CHIEF**, was wrecked early in March 1925, within direct view of the Merry Island Light, B. C. (in background). The crew of the vessel was rescued by Will Franklin, keeper at the light, but the vessel became a total loss. She was the former **WILLIAM JOLLIFFE** and **NITINAT**, a unit of the Pacific Salvage Company.

High and dry—the steamer **FAMOUS**, owned by Captain Albert Berquist, beached after striking Louise Rock in British Columbia, April 4, 1926. Patched and refloated, the veteran 907 ton vessel was the former **AMUR** of Griffiths Steamship Company, and was built at Sunderland, England in 1890.

A Canadian tug stands by the stranded Union Oil tanker **SANTA MARIA** which stranded on the approaches to Vancouver, B. C. Harbor. The incident occurred in 1938, but the tanker was refloated and repaired. She was built at Glasgow, Scotland in 1922.

Wreck of the steam collier **SAN PEDRO** astride Brotchie Ledge, after stranding November 23, 1891, outbound from Comox, B. C. to San Francisco. In command of Captain Charles Hewett and Pilot James Christiansen, the vessel hit the ledge in full view of the people of Victoria. She could not be backed off. During the night, about 300 tons of her cargo was removed and the next morning she slipped off the reef and went down in 8½ fathoms. T. H. P. Whitelaw spent nearly $100,000 in a vain attempt to raise her. Others also tried in vain, the last attempt being made in 1894 by Moran Bros. of Seattle; but a storm ruined most of their equipment and the stern of the wreck broke off. The bow and foremast were visible till 1895, and dismantlers gradually tore away the metal. The original cargo of the ship was 4,000 tons of coal. At 3,119 gross tons, the steamer was one of the largest on the West Coast at the time of her loss.

Awkward position—the coastal passenger steamer **CATALA** of Union Steamships, stranded November 12, 1927 on Sparrow Hawk Reef, B. C. near Port Simpson. The crew got off safely and the Pacific Salvage Company's **SALVAGE KING** moved in to go to work on the wounded vessel. The **CATALA** was refloated on December 5, of the same year and ushered off for bottom repairs.

Another view of the **CATALA** hard aground on Sparrow Hawk Reef in B. C. waters in 1927. This was one of several strandings she suffered, but her Scotch-built hull was rugged. The **CATALA** ended her days on January 1, 1965, a victim of a storm at Ocean Shores, Washington, while serving as a fisherman's hotel. She was built in 1925 in Scotland.

Salvage operations underway on the SS **OTSEGO** aground at Napier Point, B. C., March 13, 1943. The vessel stranded while operating under the War Shipping Administration, after long service with Libby McNeil & Libby interests out of Seattle. All-out efforts were rewarded when the vessel was refloated a few days later. The 4,638 gross ton vessel was originally the German SS **PRINZ EITEL FRIEDRICH**, built at Hamburg in 1902, and serving as a raider under the German flag in World War I. The **OTSEGO** was sold foreign after World War II.

Appearing more like a submarine than a ship, the SS **ELNA**, is being catered to after grounding on Fiddle Reef, near Trial Island, B.C. September 20, 1943. The vessel, operating as a government transport for Uncle Sam, was eventually refloated and repaired.

The ship **JOHN ROSENFELD** aground on East Point, Saturna Island, B.C. The vessel was in tow of the tug **TACOMA,** with a 4,000 ton cargo of coal when she hit the spit February 19, 1886. The ship's master James G. Baker was accused of abandoning and removing fittings before the ship was claimed a loss. The vessel later slipped off the reef and sank in deep water. A suit involving 2,200 pages of testimony brought the owners $12,500 in damages from the towing company and $2,500 other damages, plus insurance. The ship bequeathed her name to Rosenfeld Reef.

After a long search, the missing Canadian motor vessel **JESSIE ISLAND NO. 4.** was found by the Bamfield lifeboat January 5, 1927, near Pachena Bay, B.C., her entire crew of four missing. Their bodies were never found. The **JESSIE ISLAND** departed Chemainus for Port Alberni December 24, 1926 and was subject of a wide search. The craft was totally wrecked.

Pinnacles of rock had to be blasted away before the Grand Trunk Pacific passenger liner **PRINCE RUPERT** could be refloated after running ashore on Genn Island in a 70 mile gale, March 23, 1917 en route from Seattle to Anyox, B. C. Her bow rested only 30 feet from Genn Island forest. Captain Duncan McKenzie was in command. The cutter **McCULLOUGH** and the fishboat **FISBA** picked up the passengers. The liner was later refloated.

The SS **PRINCE RUPERT** suffered many strandings during her career; she is seen here in a precarious position, partially sunk in Swanson's Bay, en route to S. E. Alaska from Vancouver, B. C., September 28, 1920. She was later refloated and repaired.

Grim sight—last remembrance of the States Steamship Company freighter **PENNSYLVANIA**, lost with her master, Captain George Plover and his entire crew of 45, 450 miles off the northern tip of Vancouver Island, outbound from Seattle to the Far East, January 9, 1952. The last radio message from the ship stated that she was sinking and that the crew was abandoning. A huge sea-air search was started, but the lone lifeboat seen capsized in the photo here, was the only sign of the ship or crew. Before the lifeboat could be recovered, it too sank, 600 miles off the Washington coast, 125 miles from the reported position of the **PENNSYLVANIA** sinking. (It was sighted Jan. 15). The **PENNSYLVANIA**, built at Portland, Oregon in 1944, was a 7,608 ton Victory ship, formerly the **LUXEMBOURG VICTORY**. *Official Coast Guard aerial photo.*

Limping to a shipyard at Esquimalt, B.C. in charge of the Canadian tugs **SUDBURY II** and **ISLAND MARINER** is the fire-gutted, collision-damaged 700 foot long Liberian oil tanker **MANDOIL II.** She was in a costly collision with the Japanese freighter **SUWAHARU MARU** on February 28, 1968, the impact and subsequent raging fires in her naptha-rich fuel cargo accounting for the death of 11 of her crew, 340 miles west of the Columbia River. Both vessels caught on fire, were abandoned and towed in. The **SUWAHARU MARU** was taken to Burrard Dry Dock in North Vancouver, where repairs came to $275,000. The **MANDOIL**, partially sunk, was very difficult to tow and almost sank before they got her to Nootka, B.C., where she lay for months. Declared a total constructive loss, the **MANDOIL** wreck was eventually towed to Esquimalt, temporarily patched and towed to Taiwan for scrapping. When she was reboarded and inspected after the fire and explosion, the ship's parrot mascot near starvation, was found, still very much alive and talking. *Edward Goodall drawing, courtesy Island Tug & Barge Ltd.*

Shades of the past are seen in this wreck of the steam tug **BEAVER**, hard aground at Prospect Point at the entrance to Vancouver, B.C. harbor. The tug stranded July 15, 1888. The **BEAVER** was famous as the old Hudson's Bay Company steamer that was built on the Thames in 1835 and sailed out to the West Coast, having her paddle wheels connected at Fort Vancouver, on the Columbia River in 1836. After stellar service in waters of Puget Sound and British Columbia throughout most of her long career, she ended her days as a grubby tugboat. Several parts of the vessel have been recovered by divers in recent years.

The Chilean ship **CARELMAPU** near Gowland Rocks off Portland Point, November 25, 1915, distress flags flying. The ship, inbound to Puget Sound from Caleta Buena, Chile, via Honolulu, in command of Captain Fernando Desolmes, was unable to locate a tug off Cape Flattery and in a rising S. E. gale was swept toward the West Coast of Vancouver Island, her sails being torn away. Anchors were dropped in 240 feet of water and the SS **PRINCESS MAQUINNA** came to her aid and got within 200 yards of her. Two boats from the **CARELMAPU** were launched and both swamped in 50 foot seas. Both ships lost their anchors and the **CARELMAPU** drifted ashore. Nineteen members of the **CARELMAPU** drowned, but Captain Desolmes, three members of the crew and one passenger crawled from the wreckage and survived. The **CARELMAPU** was the former British ship **KINROSS**.

Abandon ship! The SS **MARIPOSA**, aground near Pointer Island, B. C. in October, 1915. She was one of the fast passenger liners in the Puget Sound-Alaska trade. From this position the **MARIPOSA** was freed and repaired, being lost for good two years later. *Thwaites photo from Joe Williamson files.*

Wrong turn. Wrecked in a gale on Barkley Sound, February 27, 1924. The Norwegian SS **TATJANA** is seen on the Village Island shore in bad shape while en route to Vancouver, B. C. from the Far East, under charter to Yamashita Kisen Kaisha. After 27 hours of peril, the crew of 27 was rescued by the Bamfield lifeboat; the ship was abandoned as a total loss. Later, however, the Pacific Salvage Company managed to refloat the ship in an uncanny piece of salvage work. The vessel had to have 110 plates replaced and 200 frames straightened after being towed in to Esquimalt drydock by the tugs **SALVAGE CHIEF** and **BURRARD CHIEF**.

Salvage efforts underway to raise the SS **UMATILLA** in Esquimalt Harbor in 1884. In one of the remarkable sea sagas in West Coast history, Captain Johnny "Dynamite" O'Brien, then first mate of the **UMATILLA**, defied the order of Captain Frank Worth, master of the **UMATILLA** and later reboarded the abandoned ship after it ran on uncharted Umatilla Reef. The badly bashed ship did not sink and eventually got a tow to Esquimalt by the steamer **WELLINGTON.** After weathering severe seas with a badly crumpled bow, the vessel sank at Esquimalt. The Whitelaw Salvage Company was called in to raise her from 40 feet of water. The **WELLINGTON** demanded $50,000 for tow fees; Lloyd's of London countering with a $100,000 suit against the salvagers for not leaving the vessel in a shallow water area at the request of O'Brien. Several months were required to refloat the vessel, using a cradle and a cofferdam. Later refitted in San Francisco, she sailed till 1918 when lost off the Japanese coast.

British freighter **SIBERIAN PRINCE** of Newcastle, aground on Bentinck Island, B. C. July 30, 1923. The Prince Line vessel was refloated three weeks later after most of her cargo was removed. The **SIBERIAN PRINCE** was of 5,604 gross tons.

At Todd Shipyards Corp. in Seattle, the SS **SEATTLE** is seen after colliding with the tanker **EAGLE COURIER** off Estavan Point, B. C. in the fog, August 7, 1968. Her entire bow section was missing, imbedded in the tanker. The slashed container ship reveals her ballast, compartments and containers. She was a unit of the Sea-Land Service fleet on the Seattle-Alaska run.

Rare photo of the 627 foot tanker **EAGLE COURIER** with the SS **SEATTLE'S** bow broken off in her starboard side forward. The name Seattle can be made out. The **SEATTLE'S** bow was snapped off after the two ships collided off Estavan Point, B. C. August 7, 1968 in a terrible rending of steel. Both ships limped into port for costly repairs. Fortunately nobody was killed by the impact. *Photo by George B. Robinson Jr., U. S. Coast Guard.*

One of the many strandings suffered by the SS **ALASKA** during her service between Seattle and Alaska is seen here. The vessel is aground in British Columbia waters just before World War II, with a Canadian tug standing by. The 1925-built liner was re-floated without serious damage.

Russian freighter **UZBEKISTAN** hopelessly aground at Darling Creek, B.C., not far from Pachena Point Light. The vessel, a war victim, was wrecked in April, 1943 while bound to Seattle from Portland to top off on loading lend-lease cargo for Vladivostok. Her course was overrun and the vessel could not be refloated. She gradually went to pieces, after her crew, including some women, were escorted overland and through the thicket to Bamfield. *U.S. Coast Guard photo.*

Coast Guard aerial view of the Russian freighter **UZBEKISTAN**, as Pacific breakers slam into her, two miles east of Pachena Point April 30, 1943. The vessel is aground here, due in part to being off course and partly because B.C. coastal lights had been blacked out. First on the scene was the Canadian lighthouse tender **ESTAVAN**, but on seeing the freighter was armed, the incident was turned over to the Canadian Navy. The **UZBEKISTAN** was built at a French shipyard in 1937 and after being wrecked and abandoned was the target of many looters.

208

The world's greatest non-nuclear explosion erupted when the top of Ripple Rock was blasted to bits, ending a long and costly rash of shipwreck and damage, where the tide flows through like a river. Once Indians were punished by their tribes by having to stand on the inundated rock at low tide and let the sweeping waters rise around them. The explosion took place in April, 1958.

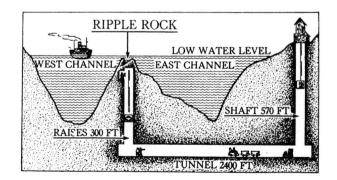

Sketch shows shaft sunk from British Columbia's Maud Island, 570 feet across a 2,400 foot tunnel and up 300 feet underneath the peak of dreaded Ripple Rock. There, explosives were set off to eradicate one of the most dreaded menaces to navigation on the Pacific rim.

Salvage operations underway on the **BEULAH**, a Panamanian freighter, at Victoria, B. C. The deck is awash. She was finally refloated March 12, 1938.

Sleek appearing SS **UMATILLA** of 3,069 tons, bequeathed her name to Umatilla Reef off the Washington Coast after ramming the reef, February 8, 1884. Miraculously, the vessel refloated herself and was reboarded, despite her badly smashed bow. She was later towed to Esquimalt, B. C. harbor where she sank. *Joe Williamson photo.*

One of the most famous of salvage ships—the tug **SUDBURY** of Island Tug & Barge Ltd., Victoria, B. C. saved many distressed ships in the North Pacific and from along the ragged B. C. coast. The 204 foot vessel, of 892 tons was built at Kingston, Ontario in 1941 and had a triple expansion four cylinder engine. Retired a few years back, her running mate the **SUDBURY II** carried on a proud tradition of aiding distressed ships. *Photo by George N. Y. Simpson.*

It couldn't happen, but it did—the Gulf Lines Ltd. motor vessel **GULF STREAM**, in local freight and passenger service, grounded on Dinner Rock, eight miles north of Powell River, B.C. on October 11, 1947 while steaming at 14 knots. She ended up in this position. The 147 foot vessel virtually climbed the rock at a precarious angle, going over on her port side and drowning two women and three children inside their cabins. Captain Jack Craddock, the remaining 15 passengers and 22 crewmen got out alive and were picked up by the fish packer **BETTY L.**, Captain Bob West. The **GULF STREAM** proved beyond salvage. The vessel was originally built on the East Coast in 1915 as the steam yacht **STRANGER** and was owned for many years by Captain F. E. Lewis. *Photo courtesy Fred Rogers, taken by a fisherman from Lund, B.C.*

Canadian salvage tug **SUDBURY II** at work in freeing the million dollar log barge **FOREST PRINCE** at Wickannish Bay, Vancouver Island, B.C. in recent years. Despite the fact that the huge barge was beached over 700 feet above the normal high water mark, the powerful Island Tug & Barge Ltd. vessel of 3,800 hp, with the aid of a helicopter and miles of rope, managed to get her off in just 72 hours working time.

No Dutch treat! The big Dutch cargoliner **SCHIEDYK** hopelessly aground on Bligh Island, B.C., partially laden with cargo, in January, 1968. A course error caused the vessel to run hard aground. She was eventually abandoned to the underwriters, when surveyors learned her bottom plates had been badly ripped. She later slipped off the rocks on which she was hung, and sank. The 9,472 ton Holland-America Line vessel, measuring 493 feet in length, was on the Pacific Coast-northern European run at the time of her loss. The vessel was built in 1949, and was diesel powered.

That's a ship's bow section? It was in May of 1968 that the big Japanese bulk carrier **YOHO MARU** locked horns with the concrete caissons of the Second Narrows Railway Bridge at Vancouver, B. C. After she backed away it was realized she had picked the wrong opponent. The **YOHO MARU** was ushered off to the dockyard at Esquimalt for badly needed repairs. When this photo was taken, the vessel had 20,000 tons of coal in her holds, destined for Japan. *Bill Cunningham photo.*

Jigsaw puzzle? No! This was the result on October 30, 1962 when the Norwegian MS **GRANVILLE** rammed into LaPointe Pier at Vancouver, B.C. while being shifted from another pier, during a thick fog. The 10,000 ton freighter smashed the dock and grain gallery to the tune of some $500,000. The ship sustained more than $50,000 in damages including a six foot hole in her bow. It took nearly six months to completely repair the pier and it required the services of eight tugs 12 hours to pull the **GRANVILLE** away from the wreck strewn scene at No. 1 jetty. The **GRANVILLE** was owned by A. F. Klaveness interests of Oslo. *Photo by Gordon Sedawie.*

Slightly over one week was all the time required for the hammering Pacific surf to completely obliterate the 16,000 ton Greek bulk carrier **TREIS IERARCHAI,** after she crashed onto the rocks near Ferrer Point on the West Coast of Vancouver Island, December 7, 1969. The ship's 28 man crew was immediately removed from the $3.5 million vessel after a structural crack in the hull appeared. Ruptured fuel tanks leaked out oil into the sea but it did little to calm the tempest, which rose with each wind-whipped day. The 630 foot, seven-hatch vessel, was only four years old and was inbound to B. C. ports to load cargo. She was in ballast when she got off course and stranded. *Vancouver Sun photo, courtesy Marine Digest.*

Like a porpoise out of water, the wounded Panamanian motor vessel **BEULAH** on her side after sinking at Victoria, B. C. December 27, 1937, refused to be salvaged. The vessel had weathered a terrific gale and high seas off the West Coast of Vancouver Island and had arrived at the harbor on a 31 degree list. The vessel, owned by Flood Brothers and built in Norway in 1923, resisted eight attempts at being refloated and finally on the ninth, after a cofferdam had been built around her, she was righted and pumped out. Before arriving at Victoria, the vessel's first mate Trygve Bragdo had been washed overboard and drowned and the boatswain injured. The steering apparatus became inoperative and the vessel almost went on the rocks.

Epilogue

As we come to the end of our shipwreck venture, it is hoped that this effort has accomplished one thing—to make us realize the power of the elements through the hand of God, and the weakness of man. To stand in wonder at the mind-boggling power of the giant acclivities and the thundering surf as it pounds against the shore; to see a footprint in the sand disappear so quickly in the ebb and flow, and to realize that this present life is of temporary substance.

Mans' frail craft have tested the oceans of the world for thousands of years and his adventures upon its surface must well antedate the wheel. The vast ocean system—a continuous interlocking sea floods seven-tenths of the globe, shelters an undersea kingdom of billions of creatures and is the resting place of a million fleets and the souls that went down with them. From the sunny climes of the South Seas to the frigid waters that bathe the Polar shores, from the crest of a mighty wave to the dark domain of the ocean depths, a great mystery abounds and the thrilling chapters of mans' continual battle against the sea and the benefits he has attained from the ocean system are in marvelous contrast. Without the oceans of the world life could not be sustained on our planet. We have the only water planet that is presently known.

If we had yet hundreds of other oceans on our continent to be probed, man would undoubtedly have conquered them all, for there is a determined effort on behalf of the human soul to discover all that is feasibly within his ability to gain. From the teeming shallows of mangrove swamps and salt marshes to the bottom of the deepest trench in the sea every challenge has been met. The sandy beaches and the rocky headlands, the river bars, bays, inlets, straits, coves, spits, shoals, outcrops and islands of the sea have all been discovered and man's knowledge of the sea and its ramparts grows by leaps

Poking her nose into the wrong hole, the Japanese trawler **KAISHIN MARU NO. 32** is snagged by Waihee Reef, two miles outside Kahului Harbor on the island of Maui. Going aground January 6, 1975 with 52 tons of tuna aboard and a crew of 17 headed by Captain Harutaka Kume, she was initially abandoned, but eventually refloated. Photo by Randy Miller.

At noon on August 21, 1970, a mariner's nightmare became reality for the crew of the Philippine MS **DON JOSE FIGUERAS.** Flames of an unknown origin raged out of control in the number three and four holds and an urgent SOS was flashed which was to launch an eight day search and rescue effort involving the Coast Guard, Air Force and Navy units as well as merchant marine vessels. Position of the **FIGUERAS** was 900 miles off the Pacific Coast 43 degrees 58 N. 144 degrees 27 W. Despite fire fighting equipment air dropped to the ship she continued to burn and took a 30 degree list. In the interim the crew of 42 and a mascot dog were evacuated and the Coast Guard tug **YOCONA** stood by, her crew going on board to further fight the fire. Later the salvage tug **SALVAGE CHIEF** took over and towed the stricken vessel into Port Angeles and put her aground outside the harbor still smoldering. After considerable salvage work the vessel was finally towed to the Todd yard in Seattle to await decision by the owners. Value of the vessel was reported at $3.5 million. It would cost $2 million to repair the 466 foot ship. She went to the scrapyard.

215

Driven onto Shira Hami Reef, 40 miles south of Yokohama, the giant Great Northern liner **DAKOTA** in her death throes. Wrecked March 3, 1907, in command of Captain Emil Francke, the mishap occurred in clear weather. All hands were safely evacuated but only a third part of the cargo was salvaged. The vessel broke up three weeks later.

and bounds. Yet man has never, and will never in this present age find a way to stop the storm, the waves, the fog and the other deterrents to navigation from being a reality and a source of concern to those who go down to the sea in ships.

As asserted in Ecclesiastes, isn't it amazing that, "all the rivers run into the sea; yet the sea is not full."

Despite the fact that every ocean has claimed its share of victims, its good far outweighs the bad. The mighty ocean currents are the freeways of the seas carrying warm and cold water around the globe. Churning up and mixing cold water on the ocean floor with the warmer water at the surface, they maintain an overall deepwater temperature of around 40 degrees, the stabilizing influence of the earth's atmospheric temperature.

The ebb and flow of the ocean tides do not actually come in and go out but rather the globe is dipped down into the ocean and lifted out by magnetically controlled powers of the heavens. The salt content is a permanent preservative force. Refuse is handled in the world's greatest laundramat. Every 12 hours the seacoasts are systematically washed by the tides. Debris and contamination brought from the interior by the rivers is carried out to the depths of the sea and much of the matter consumed by sea creatures. There is a revolving movement of the waters and a unique filtering system. Clouds pull sea water upward and when the winds blow the clouds over the earth, the lightning causes the clouds to release their contents of water upon the earth in life-giving rain.

The Almighty placed a great belt of sand around the flat seacoasts and barriers of rock in between as a permanent barrier against a world He promised never to flood again.

So all and all it is a grand mysterious wonder, our ocean system, and the greatest of all the oceans is the Pacific. It is not only almost twice the size of the Atlantic but also is the deepest. It covers 64,186,300 square miles with an average depth of 13,739 feet. The greatest depth is the Mariana Trench at a whopping 36,198 feet.

In our present age the Pacific has taken on new importance as the greatest highway of commerce in the world, especially with the rising industrial revolution in the Orient. Larger and larger cargo ships cross its waters at speeds twice those of the World War II era, and American and Russian submarines with enough nuclear firepower to destroy a large part of the earth frequent its depths slithering about in silence, waiting, waiting, waiting.

God created a fabulous ocean system, but man must realize that his frail craft, including the largest ships afloat, despite every precaution, can be destroyed under the right combinations of inclement seas, nasty weather and hostile shores. What man fails to realize is that more often than not it isn't the elements but human error that causes tragedy at sea. Erroneous navigation instruments, and over indulgence in alcohol, even barratry have played a big part in the loss of ships about the Pacific. Excessive speed in fog, failure to yield the right-of-way or error in plotting a course, etc., have all played a part in wrecks that litter our shores.

The computer world of commerce now uses instruments that do the thinking for many mariners, but sometimes human error can occur there too, when the watchman, or woman, is not fully trained at his or her occupation.

Deepsea vessels no longer have to hug the shoreline as they once did, due to innovative navigation aids, and thus the basic calls for assistance today handled by the Coast Guard come from commercial fishing and sports fishing craft as well as tugs, barges and pleasure vessels. But nothing that sails the sea is guaranteed safety. The average age of a deepsea ship is about 20 years and that is not guaranteed either. The disaster books at Lloyds of London are full and never a year passes but what several new entries are inserted. Improved aids to navigation, qualified pilots at bar ports and deepwater ports are required just about everywhere and some brilliant records of safety have been established, but still the vigilance can never be relaxed. Danger lurks at every turn.

Oh pilot, 't is a fearful night!
There's danger on the deep
......Bayly

Let Go The Anchor

Battered by the breakers, the steam schooner **FORT BRAGG** is torn to pieces after stranding on Coos Bay bar September 7, 1932. The vessel missed the Coos bar in the fog and first struck near the south jetty. The crew of the **FORT BRAGG** was safely removed, but the little 705 ton coastal lumber vessel was short for this world. She was built by J. H. Price at the Bendixsen Shipyard at Fairhaven, Calif. in 1910.

Would you believe it? This fully-laden lumber barge was eventually salvaged. While in tow of the tug **RESTLESS** the barge and the tug both went aground on the South Jetty at the entrance to Coquille River on the Oregon coast. The barge, named the **CEDAR**, carried four million board feet of lumber and was outbound for California when the mishap occurred on March 19, 1964. The tug **THOR** managed to pull the **RESTLESS** (of the Oregon Coast Towing Company) free of the rocks and the salvage vessel **SALVAGE CHIEF** was called in to refloat the barge and salvage the lumber, much of which was carried overboard by the ceaseless breakers. The **CEDAR** finally floated free and drifted across the channel to the North Jetty where it stranded again. The **SALVAGE CHIEF** pulled her free and towed her away for bottom repairs.

The death of a ship and her captain, the German passenger-cargo liner **MONTE CERVANTES**, 13,913 tons, under Captain Theodor Dreyer in early 1930, en route to Ushuaia, Tierra del Fuego, due north of Cape Horn, with a cargo of maize struck a rock and capsized in Beagle Lanne off Ushuaia, Argentina January 23. The passengers were safely evacuated as was the crew, except Captain Dreyer and steward August Jager. The shipmaster insisted in going down with his ship, but Jager finally talked him into jumping overboard at the last minute. Only the former made it to one of the boats. Captain Dreyer (seen above) drowned in the rough seas. Courtesy W. Wilfried Schuhmacher Gadstrup, Denmark.

Tragic loss of the replica bark **CARTHAGINIAN** of Lahaina, Maui in 1972. The Danish built vessel was later replaced by a smaller sailing vessel replica. Note diver in the water at left.

She never made it out of the Pacific. Wrecked in 1903, the photos show all that remained of the big sidewheel steamer **OLYMPIAN** (at Possosion Bay) in the Straits of Magellan in March 1979. Built at Wilmington, Delaware in 1883, she came to the Pacific Northwest for service between Portland and Ilwaco and to southeast Alaska from Puget Sound. Costly to operate she was sold back to east coast buyers and was wrecked on the return trip, a grim reminder of the past.

Favored competitor in several transpacific yacht races, the graceful **KAILOA** was swept from her anchorage near Kaanapali Beach in a gale January 1, l974 and slammed down on the sands directly in front of Maui's Royal Lahaina resort hotel. She had recently arrived from the South Seas. Her owner carried no insurance and the vessel was a total loss.

Another of several small craft that met her demise in the raging storm that swept the Hawaiian Islands for ten days starting December 31, 1973, was the ketch **WINDAGE**. She called for Coast Guard help and was towed to what was believed temporary protective anchorage while the Coast Guard attended to a host of other distress calls. In the interim she was swept on a reef north of Lahaina and totally wrecked—no insurance. A threatened suit against the Coast Guard never came to fruition.

Scenes at Shipwreck Bay on Lanai where old ships that have outlived their usefulness have been cast away in years past to a fate of ignomy. Above is an old deck winch, probably from the Inter-Island steamer **KINAU**. At center are the remains of an abandoned pineapple barge and lower, large deck bitt from an Inter-Island steamer protrudes from the sands.

In a graveyard of ships at Lanai's Shipwreck Beach atop a reef sits an abandoned oil barge purposely grounded in 1967. This photo taken in 1973 shows the hull still intact.

Salvage efforts underway on the transpacific liner **MANCHURIA** off Waimanalo on the island of Oahu September 13, 1906 after the big vessel ran hard aground. Passengers and cargo were all offloaded and for awhile it was feared the ship would be a total loss. A concerted salvage effort freed the holed liner eventually. Courtesy San Francisco Maritime Museum.

Burning furiously, the passenger liner **CITY OF HONOLULU**, caught on fire at sea between California and the Hawaiian Islands October 12, 1922. The 10,688 ton vessel was towed to port still smoking and red hot, her interior totally gutted. Courtesy San Francisco Maritime Museum.

Illfated steamship **GRAPPLER** burned with a loss of 88 lives in 1883.

Steamship **BROTHER JONATHAN** went down with about 200 souls in 1865 off St. George Reef.

Appendix

The worst marine disasters from the standpoint of loss of life, other than military action, on the North American Pacific rim from the Mexican border to the North Pole.

Princess Sophia passenger steamship, Canadian (British), stranded on Vanderbilt Reef in southeastern Alaska, October 24, 1918. A blizzard lifted her off the reef and she went down with her entire complement of 343 passengers and crew. No survivors.

Quinault Victory and *E.A. Bryan,* cargo steamers American flag, exploded at the Port Chicago Ammunition facility in California, July 17, 1944 taking the lives of 325 persons.

Fishing fleet disaster, May 4, 1880. A flash hurricane caught a fleet of 240 boats between the entrance to the Columbia River and Willapa Bay destroying most of the fleet and claiming somewhere between 200 and 325 lives.

Pacific, sidewheel passenger steamer, American flag, collided with the sailing vessel *Orpheus* off Cape Flattery November 4, 1875, and foundered immediately afterwards, taking an estimated 275 souls to a watery grave. Only two survived the ordeal.

Brother Jonathan, sidewheel passenger steamer, American flag, struck the outcrops of St. George Reef, northern California, July 30, 1865 and foundered with an estimated 190 to 210 souls.

City of Rio de Janeiro, passenger steamship, American flag, struck foul ground at the entrance to the Golden Gate February 22, 1901, and went to the bottom claiming an estimated 129 lives of passengers and crew.

Valencia, passenger steamer, American, stranded in thick weather near Pachena Point, Vancouver Island, January 22, 1906. Somewhere between 117 and 126 lives were lost in the harrowing hours that followed.

Tonquin ship, American, exploded after the powder magazine was set off in June 1811 when numerous savages were aboard the John Jacob Astor trading ship following the massacre of the ship's crew. The disaster occurred in the vicinity of Village Island and Tofino in Clayoquot Sound B.C. The entire ship's crew of 25 plus, were earlier massacred and more than 100 natives were blown to oblivion. The remains of the ship have yet to be found.

Condor, British war ship (sloop of war) vanished off Cape Flattery, December 2, 1901 enroute to Honolulu from Esquimalt claiming every man aboard, the death toll ranging from 104 to 140, the Admiralty setting it at 110.

Star of Bengal, bark, American, broke loose from the towline of the tug taking her to open water, and in a gale crashed on Coronation Island, Alaska, outbound from Wrangell for San Francisco, claiming the lives of 110, mostly Chinese cannery workers, September 20, 1908.

Clara Nevada, passenger steamer, American, went missing after departing Dyea, Alaska. Her battered hull several days later ground up on the outcrops of Eldred Rock, showing traces of a fire, the entire ship's company having drowned, numbering more than 100 passengers and crew. The tragedy occurred off Berners Bay on the night of February 5, 1898, in the throes of a gale.

Grappler, passenger steamer, Canadian (British) flag, caught on fire near Duncan Bay B.C., April 28, 1883 and burned furiously claiming the lives of an estimated 88 persons, 68 of whom were Chinese, many cannery workers.

San Juan, passenger steamer, American, foundered off Pigeon Point, California after colliding with the tanker *S.C.T. Dodd.* The vessel went down in three minutes taking at least 77 souls with her, perhaps more. The tragedy occurred September 29, 1929.

Columbia, passenger steamer, American, collided with the steam schooner *San Pedro,* 16 miles south of Punta (Point) Gorda, California July 21, 1907 with a loss of life generally set at 88.

Francis H. Leggett, passenger-cargo steamer, American, foundered in a gale 60 miles southwest of the

Columbia River September 18, 1914 with the loss of 65 lives, only two survivors. The vessel laden with railroad ties was en route to San Francisco from Grays Harbor.

Bennington, USS gunboat, suffered a boiler explosion at San Diego July 12, 1906, claiming 65 lives.

Clallam, passenger steamer, American, foundered in a storm in the Strait of Juan de Fuca after departing Port Townsend January 8, 1904. She went to the bottom claiming 54 lives.

Sagamore, river steamer, American, exploded at Central Wharf, San Francisco October 29, 1850, with an estimated loss of 50 lives.

Clarksdale Victory, U.S. Army transport, crashed ashore on Hippa Island, B.C. November 24, 1947. All aboard, 49, perished.

Pennsylvania, cargo steamship, American, founded 450 miles off Cape Flattery, January 9, 1952 with the loss of 45 lives. No survivors.

General Warren, sidewheel passenger steamer, American, grounded on Clatsop Spit at the mouth of the Columbia River, January 28, 1852 with the loss of 42 lives.

Islander, passenger steamer, Canadian (British), struck an iceberg off Douglas Island, southeastern Alaska August 15, 1901 and foundered with the loss of 42 lives.

Alaska, passenger steamer, American, stranded off Blunts Reef, California, August 6, 1921 with the loss of 42 lives.

Northerner, sidewheel passenger steamer, American, struck Blunts Reef near Cape Mendocino, January 5, 1860 and went down with the loss of 40 souls.

Discovery, passenger steamer, American, foundered with all hands, in the Gulf of Alaska after departing Kodiak in November 1903. Though the number aboard was not known, it was estimated at about 50 passengers and crew, some wreckage coming ashore at Middleton Island. No bodies were found.

J.A. Chanslor, tanker steamship, American, wrecked near Cape Blanco, Oregon, December 18, 1919 with the loss of 36 lives.

Dix, inland steamer, American, foundered between Alki Point and Port Blakely on Puget Sound November 18, 1906 after colliding with the SS *Jeanie.* Of the 77 persons aboard, 39 died or were missing.

State of California, passenger steamer, American, struck rocks at Gambier Bay, Alaska August 17, 1913 and went down in 240 feet of water carrying 35 of the 146 aboard to a watery grave.

Iowa, cargo steamer, stranded on Peacock Spit at the Columbia River entrance and went down with her entire crew of 34, January 12, 1936, last raked by 76 mile-an-hour winds and giant seas.

Alaskan, sidewheel passenger steamer, American foundered off Cape Blanco, Oregon May 12, 1889 with the loss of well over 30 souls. She broke up in heavy seas 18 miles offshore.

Rosecrans, tanker, steamship, American, wrecked on Peacock Spit at the Columbia River entrance January 7, 1913 claiming 33 lives, only three surviving the ordeal.

Jane Gray, schooner, passenger-cargo, American, foundered off Cape Flattery May 22, 1898, en route from Seattle to Kotzebue. She went down with 37 souls. Twenty-seven others survived.

Panoceanic Faith, cargo steamer, American, foundered in Gulf of Alaska September 29, 1967, bound for Yokohama from Oakland. Thirty-six lives were lost. Only five survivors.

Lottie, schooner, Canadian, found bottom up off Tillamook Rock May 1892. Her crew of four plus, 28 contraband Chinese were missing.

Author's note: The above are only a few of the better known marine tragedies along the Pacific rim of North America. There are countless others that could be listed, many vessels being lost with all hands, the death toll being less only because of the limited number of souls aboard. There have been many costly wrecks where the death toll has been minimal but the loss of hull and cargo have been extremely high.

Photo Index